COMMUNITY ORGANIZATION

COMMUNITY ORGANIZATION

THEORY, PRINCIPLES, AND PRACTICE

MURRAY G. ROSS
with B. W. LAPPIN

SECOND EDITION

HARPER & ROW, PUBLISHERS
NEW YORK · EVANSTON · LONDON

COMMUNITY ORGANIZATION:
Theory, Principles, and Practice, 2nd ed.

Library of Congress Catalog Card Number: 67-10801

TO

Jan, Susan, and Rob

CONTENTS

PART THREE
Principles of Community Organization

PART FOUR
Principles and Practice

INTRODUCTION

TEN YEARS HAVE PASSED since I was asked to write an introduction to the first edition of this volume. The fact that sales have exceeded 30,000 copies and that the book has been translated into five languages (Dutch, German, Italian, Japanese, and Portuguese) demonstrates how great the need was in the field for a comprehensive, systematic, and creative theoretical formulation.

The decision to produce a new and enlarged edition is based on a realistic assessment of a continuing need, itself radically extended, not alone by community development efforts in developing countries, but by the introduction and acceleration of massive programs of planned change directed at poverty and renewal in urban, rural, and remote areas of underdevelopment in the more highly developed countries, such as in the United States and Canada.

Since the first edition of this book was published in 1955 many influences have combined to bring community organization, community development, and community planning into more meaningful alignment. The concept of development planning as used by the United Nations in its approach to a *Decade of Development* has proven to be of critical revelance. Two U.N. documents, in particular, illustrate this point: the *Report of the Ad Hoc Group of*

Experts on Community Development (1963), undertaken at the request of the Economic and Social Council, and the *Reappraisal of the United Nations Social Service Programme* (1965) by Dr. Eugen Pusić, consultant to the Secretary-General. The *Encyclopedia of Social Work* (1965) contains three substantive contributions, which, taken together, provide an invaluable overview: "Community Development" (Hendry), "Community Organization" (Schwartz), and "Community Planning and Development" (Stumpf). Special note also should be taken of the creation of the International Society for Community Development, at Rio de Janeiro in 1962, which by 1966 had already published two issues of a *Journal* concerned with community development.

It is within this context of conceptual refinement and operational expansion that one must view this revised and enlarged edition of *Community Organization: Theory and Principles.* It is as relevant today as on the day of its initial publication. Dr. Ross wrote his original manuscript when he joined the teaching staff of the University of Toronto School of Social Work and took over responsibility from the present writer for teaching, research, and consultation in community organization. In 1956 Dr. Ross became Executive Assistant to the President of the University, then Vice-President (1957), and in 1960 was appointed President of York University, a new university also located in Toronto. It is eminently fitting that Dr. Lappin, who has been a student and a colleague for over twenty years, and who now has succeeded Dr. Ross on the teaching staff of the School, should have been invited by Dr. Ross to collaborate with him in this new edition of his important and highly useful book.

I am both proud and grateful to share in this continuity of collaboration and I again take satisfaction in commending this new volume to the thoughtful study of all who channel their concern, competence, and commitment in the direction of helping communities to realize their fullest possible development.

CHARLES E. HENDRY

Toronto, Canada

PREFACE

THIS REVISED EDITION was prepared at the request of many teachers and leaders who have used the original text in university classes and training programs for peace corps and other overseas personnel. Material in the body of the book has been brought up to date where necessary, new references added, the bibliography expanded, and a new section (Part Four) added. The latter, mainly the work of Dr. B. W. Lappin, my collaborator, is the result of testing the use of case material in the context of the principles set out in the early chapters. It seeks to show how some of the principles apply or do not apply in specific situations. Principles are general statements and do not readily lend themselves to narrow interpretation and application. Therefore, some liberties have been taken in Part Four as we seek to show how certain community organization principles are evident in the case material. For the beginning student some such clear and simple interpretation is apparently necessary as he begins to explore the immensely complicated field of community organization.

There has been a tendency in community work to group, under some convenient heading, methods of work which are quite different in nature, and a disposition to differentiate among methods which resemble one another to a remarkable degree.

Thus there has been a tendency to assume or claim that all welfare councils use a "community organization" process, even though more careful study indicates that different councils use radically different methods, and any one welfare council uses a wide variety of methods depending upon a number of factors in the situation with which it is dealing. On the other hand, somewhat artificial distinctions have been made between essentially similar methods. For example, the term "community development" has been used to describe efforts to help communities in developing countries; the term "community organization," to label attempts to plan welfare services in North American communities; and some such term as "community relations," to identify efforts of an organization, agency, or industry, to participate in the life of the community in which it is located. But careful analysis suggests that a similar, if not identical, approach is frequently found in these three rather different settings.

Such a tendency is not only confusing, but may actually go some way to prevent development of a consistent and meaningful theory of community organization. It is surely not the setting (India or America) or the content (agriculture or welfare) that determines the nature of the community organization process; this process exists as a distinctive pattern of work which can be utilized in a wide variety of settings to deal with any one of a number of problems.

I therefore attempted in this book to set forth a conception of the community organization process, to describe its nature, and to outline principles which facilitate its development. I am not suggesting that this is the *only* approach to dealing with problems in a village, a welfare federation, or a national association of agencies. Obviously, there are many different approaches. Nor do I wish to imply that this particular conception of community work is the most useful in all situations. There will be problems which, in light of a number of variables, will require a different approach or method of attack than that outlined here. But these approaches should be studied as separate and distinct operations, so that the particular uses, values, and results of each can be clearly identified and appraised. I merely aim here at identifying one process, which I call the community organization process, in the hope that its place in any community program may be adequately evaluated.

Blummer makes an interesting distinction between "sensitizing concepts"—ideas which, while not validated in a given field, yet provide clues for its work—and "definitive concepts"—ideas which, because they have been carefully tested, provide clear direction for work in a particular situation. Most of what is suggested in this book with respect to principles and methods of work must be referred to as "sensitizing concepts." We have some useful clues for community organization work, but our principles are little more than that. Extensive and intensive research in this area has still to be undertaken, and we are forced to depend upon such clues as are provided by research in other areas, experience, and common sense. The methods suggested here must therefore be considered highly tentative, to be tested and tried, and to be modified as experience and research proceed. They result from my yielding to the persuasion of colleagues who argue that since we are seeking to develop disciplined understanding in this field, we desperately need any contribution which will encourage debate and discussion, if not ferment, in respect to methods of work in the community.

I am deeply indebted to many organizations and individuals for encouragement and help in the preparation of the first edition of this work. I wish to thank the United Nations Educational, Scientific, and Cultural Organization for a Fellowship which permitted study in England, Israel, and the United States; the Harry M. Cassidy Memorial Research Fund for sustained interest and support; and the University of Toronto for providing the opportunity to pursue the study represented by this book. I am appreciative of many helpful suggestions of my colleagues in the School of Social Work, of the many questions and comments of my students at the University, and of the studied reaction of Mrs. Mildred Barry, Professors Gordon Hamilton, Charles E. Hendry, and Nicolaas Pansegrouw, who read some, or all, of the chapters in draft form. I am particularly grateful to John R. Seely, whose detailed and penetrating analysis of my first draft made the task of rewriting an extremely difficult but a challenging and rewarding one.

Mrs. Florence Strakhovsky, research secretary of the Harry M. Cassidy Memorial Research Fund, supervised the preparation of the original manuscript and this revised edition, and Dr. Lappin and I are appreciative of her superior and devoted work.

MURRAY G. ROSS

Toronto, Canada

Part One

The Nature of Community Organization

1

Some Conceptions of
Community Work

INTRODUCTION

The expanding role of the community organization worker constitutes a marked change from the limited position he once held as deliverer of social, educational, or health services[1] in the community. Not only has community organization made remarkable strides within social work and education but it has also moved beyond these fields to become the substance of an ideology taken up by newly emerged youth movements battling the powers of what they perceive as the staid "establishment." Moreover, many groups see community organization and community development as the primary means by which they may be effective in North American society.[2] Indeed, the community organization worker has gained new prominence in programs to combat poverty recently mounted in the United States and Canada. However, the helping professions have been largely concerned with what Galbraith has called case poverty rather than with insular or community poverty. Community organization, as originally perceived by the leaders

[1] A view espoused by Mary Ellen Richmond in *The Long View,* papers and addresses by Mary E. Richmond, Russell Sage Foundation, 1930, pp. 214–221.

[2] Thomas D. Sherrard and Richard C. Murray, "The Church and Neighborhood Community Organization," *Social Work,* X (July 1965).

of the Charity Organization Society movement, called essentially for the involvement of the affluent, leaving the friendly visitor to deal with the pauper. As these pioneer caseworkers gained professional status the responsibility for direct service to the poor shifted from the laymen to them. Thus the impoverished became increasingly invisible to the upper classes and to the community organization practitioner working with the privileged members of society. By his very proximity to prestige and power the community worker has been traditionally related to that element which has controlled the purse strings of the community social agencies. With this leadership he has coördinated and planned the orderly development and maintenance of the various social services. It is only within the past few years, and especially since the anti-poverty programs have come into being, that the community organization worker has again been brought face to face with the poor as a group, and thus acquired a "clientele" of his own, which is becoming the primary target of his professional skill.

Quite apart from these professional developments there has been in recent years a fresh concern with life at the local community level, which has arisen as a result of the expression of social forces in the lives of groups of people throughout the world. But because of the rather different stages of development, or diverse ways of life, in many countries, these social forces manifest themselves in various ways and create what appear to be quite different sets of problems.

In countries in which industrialization and urbanization are relatively well advanced, the focus of concern is the loss of community as a meaningful form of social and moral association. In fact, as Nisbet points out, the current popularity of such words as *disorganization, disintegration, decline, insecurity, breakdown, instability,* and the like has relevance to trends in community life in industrialized countries.[3] The urban center is impersonal, lacking in cohesion, an ineffective political or social unit which pro-

[3] R. A. Nisbet, *The Quest for Community,* Oxford University Press, 1953, p. 7.

vides inadequate soil for full personality development. In metropolitan centers, there is little sense of belonging, or feeling of
identification, or intimate association with others because these

. . . are not communities in any real sense of the word, but unplanned
monstrosities in which as men and women we are segregated into nar-
rowed routines and milieux. We do not meet one another as persons in
the several aspects of our total life, but know one another only fraction-
ally; as the man who fixes the car, or as that girl who serves our lunch,
or as the woman who takes care of our child at school. Pre-judgment—
prejudice—flourishes when people meet people only in this segmental
manner. The humanist reality of others does not, cannot, come through.
In this metropolitan society, we develop, in our defence, a blasé manner that reaches deeper than a manner. We do not, accordingly, experience genuine clash of viewpoint. And when we do, we tend to consider
it merely rude. We are sunk in our routines, we do not transcend them,
even in discussion, much less by action. We do not gain a view of the
structure of our society as a whole and of our role within it. Our cities
are composed of narrow slots, and we, as the people in these slots, are
more and more confined to our own rather narrow ranges. As we reach
for each other, we do so only by stereotype. Each is trapped by his confining circle; each is split from easily identifiable groups . . .[4]

Some appraisal of the effect of urban life on the individual is seen
in Lawrence K. Frank's *Society as the Patient,* and in the writings
of Karen Horney, Erich Fromm, and Harry Stack Sullivan, all of
whom see the impersonality and remoteness of relationships in the
city as contributing factors to man's inability to find security in the
western world. Loneliness, anxiety, depression, neurosis are prevalent, negating man's attempts at dignity, stability, and happiness.

For these reasons, therefore, there has been, as indicated, fresh
concern with the community in industrialized societies. This concern has manifested itself in a great variety of ways. Withdrawal,
restructuring or decentralization of the city, creation of meaningful
forms of primary association to replace old forms of group life, and

[4] C. Wright Mills, "Are We Losing Our Sense of Belonging?" paper delivered at Couchiching Conference, August 10, 1954, pp. 8–9. See also Geoffrey Vickers, *The Undirected Society,* University of Toronto Press, 1959.

other programs all have their advocates. In the field of community organization, the main foci of attention have been attempts to develop (1) meaningful functional communities as members of which individual citizens may have some sense of belonging and control over their environment, and (2) a new sense of neighborhood in the large metropolitan area through creation of citizens' councils and other forms of neighborhood organization.

In the developing countries, the problem has had a rather different focus. In these countries one finds, on the whole, relatively cohesive communities, closely knit kinship systems, and intimate interpersonal relations. But powerful political, economic, and humanitarian forces are at work, stimulating these countries to change, to "develop," to adopt modern techniques of work and living. While these forces have been at work over the last century or longer, they have been accelerated by substantial aid programs of some of the major industrialized countries and by the United Nations Technical Assistance program. Some of these assistance programs have been developed with more good will than skill, but it has been increasingly recognized that imposition of modern techniques on ancient cultures may destroy old values, create disruption, and lead to the problems which exist in all large urban centers. Ralph Linton emphasized this when he said:

Modernization of the unmechanized cultures, with their unexampled opportunities for individuals with intelligence and initiative, cannot fail to weaken or even destroy joint family patterns. This in turn will entail a whole series of problems for the societies in question. They must develop new mechanisms to provide for the economic and psychological needs now taken care of by family organization.[5]

There is, therefore, a growing concern as to how whole communities in the developing countries may be stimulated or helped to adapt new techniques that will lead to greater economic productivity and will provide them with better food, shelter, health, education,

[5] Ralph Linton, "Cultural and Personality Factors Affecting Economic Growth," in B. F. Hoselitz (ed.), *The Progress of Underdeveloped Areas*, University of Chicago Press, 1952, p. 84.

etc. without disrupting or destroying the more valuable of their traditional ways of life. If such movement is to take place, it is recognized, the community as a whole must make the adaptation.

Throughout the world there is, then, new interest in the development of "community." The community unit is, in some instances, a geographical area; in other cases it is a community of interests or association of interests. In either case, the problem of concern is how the members of these communities may come to be identified with, and share responsibility for, development of a community life which is alert and active in solving some of the problems which prevent it, and the larger society of which it is a part, from utilizing the riches which the humanities and sciences have made available to modern man.

There is a variety of ways in which experts and professional people work in the community. In this chapter we wish to identify three major divisions of community work, namely, community development, community organization, and community relations. While these areas represent different situations or "settings" for work, it will be readily seen that there are fundamental similarities in what is being attempted. Within each of the three areas various approaches are described. Again, it will be seen that in spite of the sharp differentiation we make in these approaches, they differ in degree rather than in absolute terms. While each approach described has distinctive characteristics, some elements of a particular approach may be similar, if not identical, to some other approach we describe.

COMMUNITY DEVELOPMENT

In the developing countries, or in "backward" parts of developed countries, the phrase used most frequently to designate efforts to provide for the advancement of communities is "community development." Perhaps the definition that is most widely accepted is set forth in a United Nations document as follows:

The term "community development" designates the utilization under one single programme of approaches and techniques which rely upon local communities as units of action and which attempt to combine outside assistance with organized local self-determination and effort, and which correspondingly seek to stimulate local initiative and leadership as the primary instrument of change. . . . In agricultural countries in the economically under-developed areas, major emphasis is placed upon those activities which aim at promoting the improvement of the basic living conditions of the community, including the satisfaction of some of its non-material needs.[6]

Such a definition as this, concise and useful as it is, leaves some issues unresolved. What is the primary goal of community development? Is it, as may be implied, "promoting the improvement of the basic living conditions"? Or is the primary goal coöperative work of local leaders and outside experts? Or is it the development of self-determination and effort in the local communities? Are all these objectives of equal importance? What is to be done if "self-determination" conflicts with "improving basic living conditions"?

When one views the work going on in the developing countries or in backward parts of developed countries, it is obvious that different persons answer these questions in quite different ways. There is, in fact, a wide variety of objectives and of methods in use, of which we will identify but three.

PROGRAMS IMPLANTED BY EXTERNAL AGENTS

The first approach represents the disposition of external agents to implant a specific technique or program in a community. The program or technique may relate to a new method of farming, an industry of some kind, a new school, a medical program, or a housing project, which the external agent (or the organization he represents) thinks will benefit this community. The external agent may appear at the request of the national government in which the community is located, but seldom at the request of the people most

---

[6] United Nations Document E/CN 5/291, *Programme of Concerted Action in the Social Field of the United Nations and Specialized Agencies.* See also Charles E. Hendry, "Community Development," in *Encyclopedia of Social Work,* 15th issue, N.A.S.W., 1965, p. 171; and "Community Organization: Theories and Values," *International Review of Community Development,* No. 5 (1960), p. 34.

directly affected, namely, the people of the community. But, regardless of the source of the external agent's directive, he enters a community as an expert in some area (e.g., agriculture, education, medicine, etc.) and his task is to implant a project or develop a program associated with his special area of competence, in the community to which he is assigned.[7]

The methods by which he implants and secures acceptance for his project or program vary with the agent and the situation. Among the prevailing methods evidenced in some of the experiences in the developing countries are: (1) the agent diagnoses the community's need for his services, prescribes a program, and seeks to establish this program, which he leaves for the community to use as it sees fit; (2) the agent seeks not only to prescribe but to persuade, and by a variety of "sales methods" he convinces the people of the community to use the facility or service provided; (3) the agent discusses with the people the need for such a project or program as he has in mind, he passes out literature, shows movies, organizes committees, and seeks to win the coöperation of the people of the community in establishing the new project or program. In general, it may be said that the trend is away from crude methods of imposition of a project, which neglect the attitudes of residents to the innovation, and toward winning the support of the community for the project. However, the element of time and the nature of the need are influential here: a medical team sent to a community in which a contagious disease rages does not pause to discuss treatment with the local residents. But, regardless of the methods used, the basic objective of this approach is to introduce and implant a particular project or plan, the general nature of which is determined by the external agent. The criterion for the success of the work of the latter is the degree to which he can establish this project in the life of the community. He is concerned about the feelings of the people in the community in respect to the innovation only to the degree that they support, and do not oppose, introduction and use of the technique or service.

One of the more sophisticated (yet in the long run unsuccessful)

[7] See also Wm. Biddle and Loureide J. Biddle, *The Community Development Process: The Rediscovery of Local Initiative,* Holt, Rinehart & Winston, 1965, pp. 81–83.

projects in this area is illustrated in the following account of an agriculture agent's attempt to introduce hybrid seed corn in a small farm community:

The county agent's relations with the farmers were good. He spoke Spanish in the same manner, was familiar with their background and agricultural practices, and had served as agent for several years immediately preceding this venture. The seed corn, he felt, had degenerated and he suspected that this was an important factor in keeping production low. He decided to introduce a hybrid seed that was known for high yield, and proceeded carefully, consulting with the college agronomist, who selected a variety . . . that had been tested in the immediate area. It was considered disease-resistant and capable of producing a good growth. . . .

Then the agent discussed the problem of low corn yields with the leaders of the village, having chosen this particular community as a likely place for a good response. The men readily recognized the need for better production and were willing to think that, perhaps, their seed strain was weakening after long continuous propagation.

The soils of the fields used by this village were tested and found to be of good fertility. . . . After discussion with the leaders of the various problems involved, a meeting was called in order to present the county agent's plan.

Everyone in the village was invited to the meeting. The agent showed movies of the hybrid corn, and cartoons to enliven the demonstration. Then the leaders took over the meeting and explained in their own words the plan for introducing hybrid corn. All those present seemed to agree that the new seed was the answer to many of their problems and that they would be well able to afford the price of the seed, once it was available locally.

By special arrangement with a grower of seed, the new hybrid was furnished in exchange for the old seed. A demonstration plot which clearly showed a tripled crop was set up near the village, with the result that 40 farmers planted hybrid and each doubled his production the first year.[8]

[8] Edward H. Spicer (ed.), *Human Problems in Technological Change,* Russell Sage Foundation, 1952, pp. 36–37.

"MULTIPLE" APPROACH

The second approach to be discussed here is distinguished by its concern with the effect of the introduction of a new technique on many aspects of community life. Thus Hoselitz says:

Industrialization . . . and the accompanying process of urbanization, may mean an increase in physical and mental ill-health, an increase in crime and other forms of conflict, the development of ethnic discrimination, and often the growth of those aspects of personal and group disorganization resulting from an increase in *anomie*. It calls for the establishment of new social services, new public utilities, and the vast enlargement of an administrative apparatus. Not all these social costs can be foreseen or estimated correctly, but the very recognition of these problems and their inclusion in some form in developmental plans means that such planning ceases to have a purely economic dimension.[9]

There is recognition here, then, of the indivisibility of community life and the need to provide for "the social consequences of technical change" in the whole community. This leads to what is often called the "multiple" approach in which a team of experts seeks to provide a variety of services, such as education, recreation, medical, to deal with some of the problems which emerge, or may emerge, as alterations are made in the economic system of the community. Thus, in introducing a new industry in a community, the economists or industrialists may be accompanied by a group of experts in other areas, who seek to help people use constructively their increased earnings, to learn to read and write, to take advantage of modern medical knowledge and skill, to build better houses, etc. In other words, an effort is made to move the whole community in a direction which will permit the use of modern tools, techniques, and methods of living. "To move a century in a decade" is a slogan frequently heard among such planners. The pressure "to adapt or die" is, of course, prevalent, and without evidence to the contrary,

[9] B. F. Hoselitz (ed.), *The Progress of Underdeveloped Areas*, University of Chicago Press, 1952, p. vii.

one cannot readily suggest that such radical readjustment is not necessary at many points in the world today.

It is of interest to note, however, that while the "multiple" approach considers the impact of certain changes on the culture as a whole, it deals with the whole through quite distinctive parts (such as education, industry, health) as if the sum of these parts represented the whole. There are, of course, many aspects of life in the community which relate to customs, beliefs, ceremonies, and rituals, which may be affected in a fundamental way by technical changes. The units of services provided in the multiple approach seldom provide a program to facilitate adaptation or adjustment in these areas.

But a second interesting idea is apparent in this approach. Frequently it is said that it seeks to take account of the "social consequences of technical change." It is not concerned merely with technical change, but seeks to provide for the impact of these changes—usually by education, health, and welfare programs. A profound difference exists, as will be shown later, between those who are concerned with the "social consequences of technical change" and those who are concerned with "technical change as a consequence of social action." The former assumes that a technical change can be imposed or induced, and that plans can be made to care for the community's reaction to this change. The latter assumes that the community must make its own adaptation, and that this can be done only if the community itself initiates, works through, and makes its own changes. These are obviously quite different points of view in respect to the ways a community may adjust and develop.

Often in developing a "multiple" approach program, social scientists are used "to identify the particular traits of the particular groups of people who would be affected by these proposed changes; to advise about the resistances to, or support for, these changes likely to be found in the local culture and society; and to recommend modifications in the proposed program of development or in the proposed methods of introducing changes." [10] It is interesting that social scientists, most of whom have been reluctant to become part of "value-laden undertakings," become involved in these community development projects and lend their knowledge and insight to these programs, without serious questioning of the ends for which they are being used. But many seem ready to be so used, and to advise on how the program may be adapted to the culture, or, vice versa, how the culture must be changed if the program is to be implemented. An anthropologist will see, for example, that introduction of a public health clinic may sever old relationships with midwife and medicine man and priest, will predict resistances, and may recommend ways in which these latter may be cared for. The usefulness of social scientists has been amply demonstrated in this way, for they see the underlying and fundamental web of a culture not apparent to the untrained observer.

For example, the illustration provided of the county agent's work in the preceding section might suggest marked success in introducing hybrid corn. Actually the project was a dismal failure, for three years after the hybrid corn was first planted, all but three farmers had given up raising it and had gone back to raising the old corn. The reason was relatively simple, although not one the agriculture expert might have anticipated.

As one farmer said, "My wife doesn't like that hybrid, that's all." He and others explained that the new corn had not been popular from the first harvest. All the wives had complained. Some did not like its texture; it did not hang together well for tortillas; the tortillas were not the color of nixtamal (the corn flour dough to which they were accustomed).[11]

In commenting on this experience the social scientist is able to point out the limits of the average technical expert and the special role of the social scientist:

It cannot be said that he (the agent) ignored any of the well-tried, and

[10] Samuel B. Hayes, Jr., "Personality and Culture Problems of Point IV," in B. F. Hoselitz (ed.), *The Progress of Underdeveloped Areas,* University of Chicago Press, 1952, p. 209.

[11] Spicer, *op. cit.,* pp. 38–39.

often reiterated, rules of extension procedure. Nevertheless the agent's exploration of the context of the change sought did not go quite far enough. He had paid attention to the relations between the agriculture technology and the environmental conditions, and to those between farming practices and the social organization of the community. He failed, however, to inquire into the food habits and their influence on the selection of crops. . . . He learned that the interests and wishes of the village women had to be taken into account as an important factor in the agricultural economy. Finally, he found that in the system of values of the community, corn quality was more important than corn quantity.[12]

While it may be questioned whether the agent took adequate account of the social organization of the community when he neglected the involvement of women in his plans, certainly this illustration demonstrates that which the social scientist is skilled in identifying and analyzing, namely, the systems of values of a community and the behavior patterns which stem from these values. His knowledge at such points makes the introduction of changed techniques more palatable and realistic.

But it must be noted that in this approach, as in the first mentioned, the primary source of direction for change comes from a small group of experts, planners, or leaders. The people of the community may be involved, may have a share in shaping the nature of the change, and may participate in the actual operations of change, but the initial impetus for change, the general area marked out for change, and to a considerable degree the character of the change, are external to the majority of the people in the community. The area of concern is wider, the introduction of change more "scientific," but the direction and nature of the change is externally, rather than internally, imposed.

"INNER RESOURCES" APPROACH

In contrast, out of the third position stems what is sometimes designated as "the inner resources" approach. Here stress is laid on

[12] *Ibid.*, p. 39.

the need to encourage communities of people to identify their own wants and needs and to work coöperatively at satisfying them. Projects are not predetermined but develop as discussion in communities is encouraged, proceeds, and focuses the real concerns of the people. As wants and needs are defined and solutions sought, aid may be provided by national governments or international organizations. But the emphasis is on communities of people working at their own problems. In such an approach, technical change follows social movement and not vice versa. Change comes as a community sees the need for change and as it develops the will and capacity to make changes it feels desirable. Direction is established internally, rather than externally. Development of a specific project (such as an industry or school) is less important than development of the capacity of a people to establish that project.

Such an approach has, in the minds of many technicians, a number of disadvantages: action is slow; the action taken is not subject to control by the technician; the program that develops may not be the action which the government or the expert feels is really required; and even the action taken may move in unsophisticated fashion, oblivious to many more effective ways of carrying on the program. On the other hand, those who advocate such an approach emphasize the importance of the people's learning to work together at the problems they conceive to be important, and the probability that such projects as the community does undertake in this fashion will have a meaning and a permanence which imposed projects, no matter how subtly introduced, will not have.

The classic example of this approach, which in its simplicity is both revealing and instructive, is that of one of the first community developmental projects in Egypt:

Mohamed S—— was different from any other government official the fellaheen had ever known. He didn't collect taxes. He was not interested in catching criminals. He just walked around the village, talking to people and helping them with whatever task they happened to be doing.

At first, the fellaheen were suspicious, but as time went on, they began to take him for granted and no longer fell silent when he joined a group of them.

One day, he came upon three fellaheen angrily discussing their school fines. It was bad enough that the children must go to school in another village three miles away, but it was worse that the fathers must pay when the children failed to arrive. The fines were large. It would take three days' work to pay them off.

"Why don't you build a school here?" asked Mohamed. "Then you could see that the children arrived."

The fellaheen shook their heads. They had thought of that, but every inch of ground was under cultivation and could not be spared.

"Build it over there," said Mohamed, pointing to a strip of useless swampland.

Everyone laughed, but Mohamed persisted. The land could be filled with rubbish and dirt from the streets. Level off the hills and the bumps in the roads and there would be plenty of earth to add to it. The government might loan them a truck.

The men shook their heads, but they began talking about it and soon everyone in the village was talking. Some old men, no longer able to go to the fields, began collecting the rubbish into heaps. Soon almost everyone was picking up rubbish as he walked along and the rubbish heaps grew bigger and bigger, the streets cleaner and cleaner. The truck came. The swamp disappeared.

By the time the school was built, the village was almost convinced that the government really had sent Mohamed there for no other reason than to help them. They talked to him about many other problems.

"Is the rich water of the Nile unhealthy as some have tried to claim?"

When Mohamed showed them what the water looked like under a microscope, the fellaheen began to talk about a well. But, again, there was the problem of finding land on which to place the central tank, and again, it was the old swampland that held the answer. Deep underground water, entirely suitable for drinking, was found beneath the filled-in land.[13]

Here it can be seen that the worker was not seeking a specific reform such as change in agriculture methods or housing arrangements. Rather he was seeking a means of initiating a process. This latter could be achieved only by finding an issue about which there

[13] U.S. Federal Security Agency, International Unit, Social Security Administration, *An Approach to Community Development*, Washington, D.C. 1952.

was a good deal of feeling. The problem happened to be the matter of schools—and later of water supply. But the issue which provided the opportunity to initiate the process might have been the price of figs, the spread of a contagious disease, or the lack of radios. The worker was less concerned about the precise nature of the problem than he was of using it as an opportunity to get the villagers working together to solve the problem. The conviction of the worker, which was later validated in this case, was that if he could get the villagers actively engaged in dealing with one problem about which they were concerned, they could continue to work coöperatively as they identified other community problems.

COMMUNITY ORGANIZATION

In North America the phrase most commonly used to designate community planning and action is "community organization." The major effort in this respect has been in the welfare field, and usually community organization is considered to be a social work responsibility. While there are many definitions of community organization, one which has considerable acceptance is the following:

Community organization . . . has been defined as the process of bringing about and maintaining a progressively more effective adjustment between social welfare resources and social welfare needs within a geographic area or functional field. Its goals are consistent with all social work goals in that its primary focus is upon needs of people and provision of means of meeting these needs in a manner consistent with the precepts of democratic living.[14]

The tendency to restrict community organization to welfare needs is objected to by many who see the potential needs of a community as being far broader than the current concept of welfare. One finds on this continent an increase in both the quantity and quality of efforts, outside the welfare field, by persons in adult education,

[14] C. F. McNeil, "Community Organization for Social Welfare," *Social Work Year Book*, American Association of Social Workers, 1951, p. 123. See also Ernest B. Harper and Arthur Dunham (eds.), *Community Organization in Action*, Association Press, 1959, pp. 54–59.

agriculture, and religion, to initiate and carry on community organization projects.

Here, as in community development, however, one finds the same differences in practice which suggest fundamental differences both in objectives and method. There are, again, many fine shades of difference and we indicate below what seem to us to be the major ones.

"SPECIFIC CONTENT" OBJECTIVE

The first of these approaches we term the "specific content" approach. Here an individual, an agency, or an organization becomes concerned about some needed reform in the community and launches a program to secure this reform. A comparable situation is a Community Chest or agency financial campaign whose concern is to secure its goal of X dollars. The primary, if not exclusive, focus of the group is a specific reform or objective. Usually time is an important element, for the group seeks to secure this goal as quickly and simply as possible. The methods used to secure the objective will depend to a considerable degree, however, upon the situation. In some instances, a straight line to the goal is possible: the need or objective is placed before the proper authorities or the public, and a satisfactory response follows. In other situations, consultation and conferences are necessary, and selected individuals and groups are involved in exploration of the problem before action is taken. In still other circumstances, publicity in respect to the problem or need is undertaken; pressure is put on parties resisting the reform or goal; and open or "behind the scenes" lobbying and manipulation of ideas and people are attempted. One or some combination of these methods may be used. But whatever the method or group of methods, it is directed at the single goal of securing the reform or objective which the original individual, agency, or organization had in mind. Because this approach has a single and specific objective, the methods used are conditioned only by the conscience and morality of the promoting group.

The success of this process tends to be measured, primarily, in terms of the degree to which the reform, goal, or objective is secured. This is the principal criterion for the initiators of the process. If the objective was reached, the process was a useful and profitable one; if not, the experience was hardly successful. There are, of course, likely to be concomitant results of any process such as this. The group initiating the project may develop cohesion or may disintegrate, the community may develop great pride in the result of the project or be chagrined by failure, community identification may increase or decrease, attitudes of mutual trust or of suspicion and hostility may ensue. But since the objective is focused exclusively on securing a specific reform or goal, these concomitant results are incidental, and whether they are good or bad, positive or negative, is often a matter of chance. Consideration of these by-products of the process is placed far behind the content objective and is usually, in this approach, given little (if any) conscious attention.

A brief example of this approach is evident in the following report of a worker in a small Canadian city:

We (four social workers) decided that P____ was in need of a mental health clinic. But it was not an easy idea to sell, for laymen in this city knew little of what such a clinic does or how it would help us in our work. We did a careful study of the influential people in town and selected sixteen without whose support it would be difficult to move. We each canvassed four of these people personally and received a warm, if not enthusiastic, reception. They agreed to come to one meeting. Twelve came to the meeting to which we had invited Dr. S. T. of T____ Mental Health Clinic. He did a wonderful job and the community leaders were clearly impressed. They agreed to call a larger meeting inviting leaders from all the service clubs, the mayor, the librarian, and several church leaders. This meeting also went well and Dr. S. T. again did a fine job of interpretation. At this meeting an *ad hoc* committee was set up, and we were well on our way.

Preliminary to a mass meeting, each of us (the four originals) spoke at a service club meeting, announcements were made in several pulpits, notices were posted throughout the city and interest spread rapidly. Prior to the meeting the committee worked out a plan, talked with city officials, and were ready with a concrete proposal when the public meeting was held. Over five hundred people came. The need was interpreted, the way the clinic would operate described, and the plan for getting the project started outlined. There were many questions from the floor but the plan was approved, a permanent committee set up, and canvass for money begun. Twelve months after we four began, the money for the clinic was in the bank and the committee were looking for a staff.

Here it can be seen that the primary goal of securing a mental health clinic was reached. The other results in terms of community involvement, effort, and sense of achievement are also probably positive. But that these latter are so is purely by chance, for the effort of the group of four was exclusively on securing the mental health clinic as quickly and effectively as possible.

There are some who are critical of such an approach as has been described here. But surely this is fundamental method in a democracy—in which the minority seeks to win the support of the majority for its program, or, to put it another way, in which the minority seeks to become the majority. It may not be, for some, consistent with the best social work or educational practices, yet it must be considered valid procedure in a social system in which ideas compete for existence and support.

"GENERAL CONTENT" OBJECTIVE

The second general approach we call the "general content" objective. Here, there is a group, association, or council, such as an Adult Education Council or a Welfare Council, whose objective is the coördinated and orderly development of services in a particular area of interest. Thus the welfare council may seek to coördinate existing services (i.e., relate present services and prevent overlapping), to extend present services, and to initiate new services to meet welfare needs in the community. The objective is not a single reform but a more general objective of effective planning and operation of a special group of services in the community.

The methods used in this approach are related to the objective. Coördination of the services of autonomous agencies or associations cannot be forced. Therefore these groups (by representation) must be involved, to some degree, in the planning and decision-making process in respect to coördination. Further, since extension of services and initiation of new services are matters of prime interest to groups operating in this field, involvement of these groups is again a necessity. And since action in the community may require the support of influential citizens, it is often considered desirable to secure the participation of "power figures" in the planning process. Thus the objective here requires (at least in practice) involvement of a considerable group of interested and influential people in planning ways and means of coördinating and expanding services in a particular area.[15]

This process therefore requires a relatively large group—usually an elite—participating in consultations and conferences to secure agreement on plans and to exert consistent pressure to secure action on these plans. The ways that action in the community is secured are similar to the methods suggested in the "specific content" objective described above. In the "general content" objective, of course, formulation of the plan for action is the work of a considerable group. Time cannot be permitted to be dominant in this approach, since consultation and planning in a group representative of numerous interests can hardly be rapid. Nonetheless, there tends to be an expectation for action and the need to "get things done" is likely to be consistently felt.

The result of this approach is steady pressure for reform and development in a particular area of community life, such as the welfare field. This is the primary goal. A secondary goal is development of an interested and informed group of citizens with conviction of the need for community movement in the welfare field. There may be concomitant results here as well, but the primary and

15 One welfare leader in the field told the writer, "Of course you have to realize that planning is a sophisticated process and is one in which we can engage only the better people in the community." While there is a large group involved, in most cases it is an elite who are engaged in such planning. See also Robert Morris, "Social Work Preparation for Effectiveness in Planned Change," in *Education for Social Work, 1963,* Council on Social Work Education, 1963.

secondary objectives are as stated. But in the particular approach described here, movement in respect to content (actual services) is primary and the development of a cohesive group of interested planners is secondary and, indeed, included only because the primary goal could not readily be secured without such participation.

One professional worker, in an interview with the author, described this approach thus:

> We recognize that if we are going to get the new services we need, and the money required for these services, we have to have a strong council. And if you are at all sensitive to the structure of our society, you will recognize that businessmen are the group that can provide that strength. We try, therefore, to enlist the outstanding business executives in our council. Many of them have proven to be excellent committeemen who understand, support, and secure our objectives in this community. Take the matter of increasing allowances for the aged. It is not something that one would expect conservative businessmen to support, yet it passed with unanimous support in our council.

It will be seen that this approach is concerned both with *planning* in respect to a general interest or field (such as welfare) and with development of *power* to implement the plans made. Thus this approach differs from the first mentioned under the heading of community organization by the more general nature of the field in which it desires change and reform; by its consistent involvement of agency, group, and "elite" representatives; and by its conscious effort to develop a continuing power group or association that can exert constant pressure on individuals, agencies, and the public to accept its recommendations.

"PROCESS" OBJECTIVE

The third approach here we term "process" objective. Here the objective is not content, i.e., facilities or services of some kind, but initiation and nourishment of a process in which all the people of a community are involved, through their representatives, in identifying and taking action in respect to their own problems. The emphasis is on coöperative and collaborative work among the various groups in the community (be it functional or geographic) to the end that they may develop capacity to work together in dealing with problems which arise in their community. What is sought is increased motivation, responsibility, and skill in recognizing and securing reforms the community considers desirable. The objective is less that of some specific reform than it is development of community integration and capacity to function as a unit in respect to common problems.

Thus the methods utilized in this approach place great stress on involvement of the major subgroups of the community through the accepted leaders of these groups, careful exploration of the common problems which the community faces, and development of a program in which all share. Time cannot be allowed to become a factor of first importance, for development of working relations among diverse groups is not, it is felt, a matter that can be hurried, but is one that must proceed at a pace which the group leaders find acceptable and comfortable.

The result sought in this process is primarily greater capacity on the part of the community to function coöperatively in respect to common problems. A secondary aim is action on certain common problems and gradual elimination of these problems. But this latter is clearly a secondary goal, the primary goal resting on the assumption that if this collaborative and coöperative process is active, the community itself will gradually find the strength and resources to deal with needed reforms in the community.

Such a process as described here could be illustrated only by lengthy documentation, but the following, from a private document, may suggest some aspects of the process:

The _____ neighborhood council began because the people in this neighborhood were up-in-arms about the lack of police protection in this area. There had been several acts of violence, the saloons were breaking the law right and left, kids were getting liquor and dope, and the situation was pretty bad. Some folks got together and called a public meeting, at which block captains were appointed. A petition from each block was prepared, a delegation was sent to city hall, and the group put forward its views in no uncertain terms. They did fairly well, several saloons were closed and they got regular police patrols.

The neighborhood was so enthusiastic about their success that they wanted to continue. At this point they asked for our help and we assigned a professional worker to serve as their consultant. They carried on with a club in every block in the neighborhood, each club sending two representatives to the council. Over the years they've worked on rat elimination, clean-up campaigns, T.B. detection campaigns, housing and redevelopment, expansion of play areas and recreational programs, and many other matters. They worked on things that were important to everyone in the neighborhood. They've learned to work together and they've gained recognition everywhere in the city. In spite of a lot of moving in and out of the neighborhood, it has developed a real spirit of unity and the feeling that there aren't many problems that it can't handle itself.

Advocates of this "process" objective do not feel that this approach need be confined to small towns or villages or to urban neighborhoods, but that it is equally applicable in functional communities. They suggest, with some conviction, that if adult education or welfare councils would be less concerned initially with action in the geographic community and more concerned with involving all parts of the adult education or welfare community in the identification of their common aspirations and problems and in developing a program to meet them, these functional communities would gradually develop cohesion, strength, and a program which would be far more vital than that found in most such (functional) communities today.

COMMUNITY RELATIONS

"Community relations" implies the methods or ways by which an agency, association, or council relates itself to the geographic community. Such approaches are relevant here, because they are often referred to as the "community organization component" in the operation of a club, welfare agency, or educational institution. They are important, too, because many functional communities (such as the welfare council, the recreation council, the adult education council) must relate their activities to those in the wider geographic community, and are in such circumstances involved in a program of community relations, a procedure which they often fail to distinguish (as we will later show) from the procedure within the functional community. Again there are a variety of approaches in the field of community relations. We will identify three such approaches.

PUBLIC RELATIONS

The first approach, public relations, is simply the attempt of an organization or agency to enhance its prestige, position, or product in the community at large. As the public relations field has grown in sophistication, this no longer means simply advertising and news reports, nor even highly polished receptionists and telephone-answering service, but careful study (again often using social scientists) of employees, consumers, and the community at large, so that there is awareness within the organization of the strengths and weaknesses of its own position in the community. For example, a businessman told the writer recently: "One of the surveys we did showed some resentment that our top executives were from the head office (in another country). We hadn't worried, or even thought about this before, but now we have six young (native-born) men at the head office for training. In three years we think all our executives here will be home-bred."

COMMUNITY SERVICES

A second method of improving the position of an organization in the community and/or helping the community to develop is the provision of services to (or for) groups in the community, or to the community as a whole. This trend has become quite general as business subsidizes and sponsors playgrounds, research, scholarships, conferences on national affairs, and welfare agencies extend the scope of their services to provide special projects, such as free learn-to-swim classes, coöperate with labor unions in providing counseling services, loan professional workers to special projects, open free clinics, prepare special educational publications. Some of these activities are offered purely as "public relations" in the sense that they are provided as a means of enhancing the status of the agency or institution in the community. But many, obviously, are motivated by a desire to render what is considered to be a much needed service in the community. The nature and extent of such service, of course, is invariably determined by the organization or agency, and is not often a project which the people of the community themselves decide is required.

COMMUNITY PARTICIPATION

Another approach is that of participation on the part of the group, agency, or council in the life of the community. Thus industries and agencies of all kinds may send representatives to the city planning commission or to a special meeting to study delinquency, or to a meeting to discuss the need for a new hospital. Or functional communities like the welfare council or the adult education council may send representatives to sit on a civic committee studying transportation, or city planning, or housing. Such participation may stem from a variety of motives, such as (1) keeping the agency or association or council related to other important groups in the community, (2) maintaining contact with new developments, (3) keeping some control over plans for future developments in the community, (4) coördinating services with those of other agencies, (5) supporting coöperative planning and development of new services in the community. For whatever reason, or combination of reasons, there appears increasingly to be a consciousness on the part of formal organizations of the importance of community participation, and a disposition among these organizations to play an active and responsible role in the life of the community. Almost any community project likely to be considered "respectable" can, in North American society, count on support (of varying degrees) from the multiplicity of formal organizations (i.e., the leading industries, the welfare agencies, the educational associations, the churches, etc.) in the community. So pronounced has this trend become that one finds frequently at community meetings, which may be held under a variety of auspices, representatives from precisely the same organizations, and often exactly the same people.

FACTORS IN COMMUNITY WORK

It is obvious from the above descriptions that these approaches to the community vary greatly in a number of respects. Among these variables one may readily distinguish the factors of time, objective, and method. These three items, in fact, constitute appropriate concepts in respect to each of which a scale may be drawn, on which may be plotted the approaches described, and many others as well.

The *time scale* extends from one polar position, at which emergency action is necessary and time is, in consequence, of the essence. The task must be completed in the shortest time possible. This would be the case in a flood or disaster situation

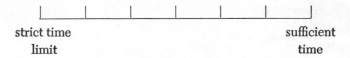

| strict time | sufficient |
| limit | time |

TIME SCALE

in a community in which rapid action to alleviate suffering is required. At the other end of the scale there is adequate time to do the job that has to be done. As with Abraham Lincoln's dictum that a man's legs should be long enough to reach the ground, so here there is enough time (no more, no less) to complete the required task. The process may not be extended unnaturally or artificially, but moves at a pace which is indigenously comfortable and is not subject to time pressures. This is the situation at, for example, the Quaker Meeting where the group is prepared to delay action indefinitely if consensus is not forthcoming on the issue under discussion. Full agreement, not time or action, is the important consideration. Between these extremes are many positions at which time is of more or less importance, in which time limits of various proportions exist in the operation. Often, of course, restrictions of time are self-imposed (and frequently are imposed subconsciously) but this makes them no less real and no less subject to plotting (probably) on the left side of the time scale.

A second factor about which there are a variety of views is that of the objective of the approach or operation in the community. Thus we have an *objective scale* at one end of which is a quite specific plan or reform. The goal may be a home for retarded children, a correctional institution for girls, a new sewage system, a junior college, a housing project, election of the liberal candidate for mayor. This is a "content" goal, is quite specific in nature, and is not subject to modification. The content—a specific project or program—is the goal, and consideration of method is limited to ways by which this specific goal can be achieved. At the other end of the

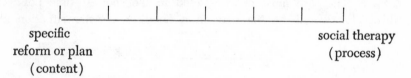

specific   social therapy
reform or plan   (process)
(content)

OBJECTIVE SCALE

scale is social therapy, the objective of which is initiation of that process through which the community strives for greater self-understanding and achieves greater cohesion and capacity to act in respect to its problems.[16] The goal here is not related directly to achievement of any specific content objective, such as a junior

[16] For a full description of this process see pp. 225–232; also, Elliott Jaques, *The Changing Culture of a Factory*, Tavistock Publications, 1951.

college or a correctional institution; it is focused, as in individual therapy, on a process by which self-understanding and integration can be achieved. Again, there are many points on the scale between these polar positions. There is the point at which the specific reform is less rigidly conceived than at the left end of the scale, at which a content goal is modified by concern with process, at which a process goal is modified with some concern for content, etc. But that many of the approaches described in the earlier part of this chapter fall at various points on this scale is quite evident.

A third factor is that of method. On the *method scale* one extreme position is that of imposition. Here an individual or group by propaganda, sales methods, political pressure, etc. persuades, coerces, or cajoles a community to adopt a given idea, plan, service or technique.[17] Thus a technical expert persuades a community in

imposition   self-determination

METHOD SCALE

a developing country to use a new seed about which the residents are suspicious, or a welfare council worker lobbies to have his idea adopted at an approaching meeting. At the other end of the scale, the method is one by which the people of a given community are encouraged to decide for themselves what they consider to be important and what action is appropriate. Here a worker encourages the villagers in a developing country to identify and act on their own conception of their needs, or a welfare council worker seeks to involve all members of the welfare community in a process of seeking out the common areas of concern on which they wish to act together. Obviously, again, there are many positions between these two extreme points. An individual or group may be quite flexible about the nature of the reform he (or it) wishes to initiate, and will modify it in consultation with members of the community; the

---

[17] A plan may be imposed by force, of course, but this is an extreme that we do not include in our analysis.

plan or reform may be quite general in nature, and its precise character may be determined by the community; or the general proposal developed by a small group for action may be quite tentative in nature and may be submitted with some expectation that it will be rejected by the community, which in turn may propose an entirely different project which is approved by all.

When these three scales are considered, it is apparent that current practices in the community vary greatly in philosophy, objective, method, and the results they obtain. No logical design is achieved by grouping all these approaches under one title or phrase, such as community organization. To do so merely confuses the distinctive nature of many approaches to work in the community. Each of these approaches, as already implied, has its justification in particular situations and may be introduced with merit in circumstances appropriate to its use. But if community organization is to be a meaningful discipline, it must be clearly defined and differentiated from other approaches in community work.

TRENDS

Before attempting such a definition, however, it may be useful to identify some trends which seem to support the particular process we will define as community organization.

SELF-DETERMINATION

The policy of imposed projects, even in emergency situations, is coming into sharp question. While it is true that it may appear to outsiders that emergency action is required and that administration of that action by external agents is completely justified, it is increasingly recognized that people in a local community may not always recognize "the emergency" or the nature of the problem seen by the expert or "outsider," and may deeply resent action taken in respect to it. As Professor Margaret Read suggests on this point:

The trained scientist, whether his branch of study and work is medicine, agriculture, forestry or similar fields, is at an initial disadvantage when he tries to put over to the local people new methods of cultivating, new precautions against the spread of disease, new ways of preserving forests on hillsides or of breeding better animals. This disadvantage is based on the fact that he does not know how the local people regard their traditional practices, nor what they think of his new ones. He is sure that he is right in what he is advocating, and he cannot see why, in view of their sickness, or hunger, or lack of water, they do not see his point of view and at least give it a trial. We who in our modern age have been brought up with an almost blind faith in anything labelled scientific do not easily realize that the peasant has a sense of security in his very insecurity. We think he must want to know how to avoid the hungry months, how to reduce the death rate among his children. But that insecurity is the thing he knows, and he understands it in so far as he has always lived with it and adjusted his practices and his ideas in relation to it.[18]

Whether it is adjustment to insecurity or simply adjustment to certain ways of life which seem proper and inevitable, most communities of people, be they in African villages or New York slums, will change their ways only if forced to change or if highly motivated to do so. As to being forced, the experience is that while acceptance of the change may ensue, reactions of suspicion, hostility, or increased insecurity and apathy may also be expected. Thus many of those who are looking toward meaningful change and more capable communities are resisting trying to press or "sell" people techniques, services, or projects which are conceived and developed by experts or small planning groups.

A striking demonstration of this is the procedure of a medical team working under the direction of a South African, Dr. Sidney Kark, in a small village in Israel:

Two elements combine to make this work of special interest: (1) The composition of the population of the village. This community has about 800 inhabitants. They come from many parts of the world, have a great

[18] Margaret Read, "Common Ground in Community Development Experiments," *Community Development Bulletin*, II (June 1951), 45.

variety of ideas about health and physical care, and have a multitude of diet and health practices, many of them unknown in the Western world. Their attitude to modern medicine and its practitioners also varies greatly, many groups being quite superstitious and regarding doctors and nurses with a good deal of suspicion. Some groups have deep-rooted traditions which make no provision for modern medicine and its directives. (2) Kark's philosophy of work is similar to Rene Sand's dictum, "Health cannot be given to people, it demands their participation." Thus the purpose is not to impose a health scheme on the community but to attempt to have the community participate in developing its own health program.

The interesting problem which Kark faces is how to implement such a philosophy in a setting as unfavorable as this appears to be.

To begin with, an attempt is made to clarify philosophy so that all the staff are agreed on fundamental objectives and methods. For those on the staff who had no more than orthodox medical training, this is often a difficult learning process. Kark does not direct, impose, or lead his staff in the traditional sense. There are frequent staff meetings in which village practices are discussed and in which Kark questions many of the assumptions and value-judgments of staff members. This, as suggested, is difficult for some staff persons—all their lives they have been taught what was "right" and what was "wrong." They see many "wrong" practices in the village and feel that their duty is to correct them. This is their job as they conceive it. To have a director who not only does not support their efforts at reform but questions their authority for judging "right" and "wrong" makes for a difficult period of adjustment. But Kark's philosophy with staff is approximately the same as with the villagers. Roughly it might be summarized thus: "As a rule of thumb, one should never attack the fundamental types of belief directly. If erroneous and incompatible with reality, the fundamental beliefs will themselves dissolve in the course of time, but nothing gives them life like a direct attack upon them. Their untruth has to be discovered slowly by the people, and at the same rate at which the people are finding new sources of security. A belief upon which a person's security depends cannot simply be wiped out. Disillusion from the belief has to be accompanied by a shift to dependence upon a new kind of support."

Kark's work begins, then, not with lectures, moving pictures or distribution of literature on how to be healthy (the Western way) but with an attempt to understand the health practices of various national groups in the community and how these practices fit in with their whole culture. This is done with considerable objectivity, with a recognition that these practices have meaning for these people, and may in fact have absolute value which has not hitherto been recognized in Western society.

Secondly, there is no attempt to impose new standards on these people —to challenge existing beliefs and practices. Rather an attempt is made to create a situation (or a social climate) in which free interaction of medical staff and villagers will take place. This interaction will lead to exchange of ideas and it is hoped to a feeling of need on the part of the villagers for change in some practices. Here again it is recognized that people will change only when they feel ready for change. The objective, therefore, is to create readiness for movement.[19]

While such approaches as this are far from prevalent, experience is suggesting the validity of the expert working with the people, learning their culture, sharing his own ideas with humility, and encouraging experimentation rather than pressing for acceptance of his program.

While this may seem obvious in developing countries, it is probably equally true for developed countries. The consistent use of highly specialized planning bodies to deal with problems of the community moves the citizen farther and farther away from the point where he can have anything effective to say about the conditions under which he is to live and work. The result of this process is, of course, disintegration of the community as an association to which one belongs in a meaningful way and for which one feels responsible. While planning by experts is essential in a complex civilization, and while all people cannot be consulted on all details of new developments, it is being suggested that ways and means must be found to provide the average citizen with some sense of participation in, and control over, his changing environment.

The same argument may apply to a functional community. A welfare council worker may be concerned with the "emergency" situation which exists in respect to recording, or personnel practices, or in-take procedures in the welfare agencies in the community and may be able to win the support of influential citizens in pressing for reform and action in one or all of these areas. But the

[19] Murray G. Ross, "The Theory and Principles of Community Development," Report of a UNESCO Fellowship experience, January 1954, pp. 22–24.

result of such procedure is probably to encourage resistance, negative attitudes to the council, withdrawal or overt hostility. The
capacity of the agencies to work effectively at identifying and
coping with their own problems is not increased, but probably
diminished, by such an approach.

COMMUNITY PACE

There is growing recognition that most communities of people
have their own techniques and pace for carrying on the business of
life, and while these may be altered, they cannot be changed
radically without disrupting the life of the people. Professor S.
Herbert Frankel of Oxford University makes this point with clarity
when he says:

. . . to suggest that *rapid* structural changes are what is most required
overlooks the fundamental question whether the real problem is not to
avoid, as far as possible, all types of "catastrophic" action so as to give
time for slower—more organic—and less unstable changes. . . . In my
view a whole people can no more be given rapid economic development
by investment in mass education, than it can be given "democracy" by
"investment" in mass political training. For, quite apart from the time all
this takes, what is involved is neither just another ready-to-hand goal of
action, nor the transfer of a new set of techniques, but the necessarily
slow growth of new aptitudes, and of new ways of doing, living, and
thinking. We should do everything possible to make the life-giving waters
of international culture flow to the uttermost ends of the earth . . . but
let us beware lest pride in *our* ways of life blind us to the social heritage
of others. The problem is not to wipe the slate clean in the underdeveloped countries, and to write our economic and technical equations on
it, but to recognize that different peoples have a different language of
social action, and possess, and, indeed, have long exercised, peculiar
aptitudes for solving the problems of their own time and place; aptitudes
which must be further developed in the historic setting of their own past
to meet the exigencies of the present and the future.[20]

The pace developed by any community of people may seem

[20] S. Herbert Frankel, *The Economic Impact on Under-Developed Societies,*
Harvard University Press, 1953, pp. 94, 96.

extremely slow to the outsider, yet this deliberate pace permits adaptation both to the change introduced and to the many-sided effects arising from the change.

One of the serious difficulties experienced by human beings who attempt to change the culture within which they live is that the very fact of planning itself makes it possible to force through a single line change in disregard of the hundreds of side effects which are taken care of in unplanned change, which occurs within a society unsupported by disproportionate governmental or industrial pressure. Where a system of piped-on water is gradually spread through a country, with each village taking responsibility for its own water supply, the changes may be very slow, but problems of land ownership, of where the clothes are to be washed, of combining watering cattle and arranging business transactions, etc., will be thrashed out slowly, and the disruption of old ways of life will be less serious. When a new impulse towards better water, or better roads, or better land use sweeps the country, implemented by funds and personnel from outside the community, its effective progress is rapid, but fewer such adjustments can take place. . . . It is possible to say that in all old and habitual enterprises, with slow and traditional introduction of small changes, the side effects of a change can be felt and responded to by the members of that society. When change is introduced by external forces, however beneficent in intent, these protective behaviours cannot operate, and changes may go much too far in some given direction before compensatory measures can be taken.[21]

Some will maintain, of course, that while pace is an observable aspect of village or town life, there is no consistent and all-pervading sense of pace in the large urban center. Here all is sporadic and uneven. But this is not to suggest that groups of people in neighborhoods or in functional communities cannot and do not develop traditional ways of carrying on their activities in the city. And what is being implied here is that planning and activity which persistently disregard traditional methods, or which do not permit these communities to grapple at first hand with the possibilities and realities of change, will encourage apathy or disruption that is unhealthy and dangerous.

[21] Margaret Mead (ed.), *Cultural Patterns and Technical Change*, UNESCO, Paris, 1953, pp. 315–316.

INDIGENOUS PLANS

There is increased appreciation of the value of indigenous plans as opposed to externally imposed ideas. As Alexander Leighton has suggested, "No matter how good a plan is, if the people for whom it is made fail to feel it belongs to them, it will not work successfully." [22] The validity of this has been amply demonstrated in assistance programs in developing countries, where vast amounts of money have been spent to launch projects, some of which have been little appreciated, a few of which have been thoroughly disliked, and many of which have not enjoyed coöperation from the local people. There are many stories similar to that of the erection of a factory in which natives will work only a few days a week because this much work will provide sufficient pay to maintain the standard of living to which they are accustomed. But this is equally true in North American cities where, for example, the settlement house is placed in a slum area, or an industry builds a huge recreation plant for its employees. In either of these latter situations one will find counterattractions (less pretentious it is true) organized by the people themselves. They may use the settlement house and the recreation hall, but it is quite clear that these "are not theirs" and that it is in their own setting, where they "feel at home," that spontaneous fun and enjoyment and meaningful experiences are found. These "outside" resources (like the settlement house or industrial recreation hall) are often not quite accepted, and certainly lack the effectiveness of projects developed by the people themselves. Increasingly, it is being assumed that a project or change to be meaningful, and fully used and valued, must be an object of identification for the people who are to use and value it. The methods by which this may be achieved are many and varied, and as we have implied, secure varying degrees of identification, use, and value.

[22] Alexander H. Leighton, *The Governing of Men*, Princeton University Press, 1945.

GROWTH IN COMMUNITY CAPACITY

There is recognition that successfully working through one problem will increase a community's capacity to deal with other problems with which it may later have to cope. This implies that a community may develop problem-solving techniques and capacities in dealing with one problem which may stand it in good stead when it confronts new problems in the community. This has been found true for the individual, who achieves greater self-understanding and integration as he works through his problem with the aid of a therapist. It has been reported that families who have successfully worked through problems of family life develop greater cohesion and increased resistance to forces disruptive to family life than do families that have not dealt with such problems.[23] It has been shown, also, that a whole industry develops greater flexibility and capacity by dealing in a comprehensive way with a few problems than if it were to ignore these problems or attempt to deal with all the problems of the industry at the one time.[24] Similarly, we are coming to recognize that the community that can be involved in a process by which it deals with one of its common problems may be involved in a process of self-understanding and integration that will make it possible to extend the range and scope of the problems with which it can deal successfully. This hypothesis has not been documented for the community as yet, but it is a firm conviction of many workers who have watched individuals and groups grow in their capacity to function in community projects.

THE WILL TO CHANGE[25]

There is recognition that the will and desire of people for a given change should precede initiation of any program leading to such a

23 Lawrence K. Frank, in a lecture delivered at the University of Toronto, March, 1954.

24 Jaques, *op. cit.*, p. 306.

25 See Harriet R. Lynton and P. R. Lynton, "Social Change and Learning," in R. P. Lynton (ed.), *Asican Cases: Teaching Cases from the Aloka Experience,* Aloka Center for Advanced Study and Training, World Assembly of Youth, 1960, pp. 133–136.

change. There has long been recognition, of course, that if will and desire were present, change would be greatly facilitated. But what does one do when no such will or desire exists? The tendency in many community situations has been to push ahead with change without such support. The results have not always been so pleasant or fruitful as one might wish.

One often finds the novelist catching the spirit and nature of a technical point far more effectively than the experts who seek to expound the theory. Thus one finds Robert Lund's hero reflecting on his failure to bring progress to a small island of people whom he has served as governor. His friend raises a fundamental question when he says:

"Petro," Manuel said thoughtfully, "here is the way it seems to me. People do not like change. They live in a certain way, and they are used to that way. Sometimes they are hungry, they are abused, they are poor where there is plenty, and yet they do not like to be disturbed. Look at those five families at Umitac which you punished. They were sick and poor. You gave them ten hectares of land each. You gave them ten chickens and a cock each. You gave them a sow and a carabao each, and they refused it all. Remember what the one man said? 'We did not ask for these things. They belong to our Church and we have no right to them. Why can you not leave us alone? Why do you force trouble and worry on us?' That man and the others were bewildered by these things. It gave them responsibility. They had property to worry about. They were forced to think where they had never thought before. Petro, you want to bring freedom to Guam, and I would like to see it as much as you, but there must be a desire for it. Freedom is a spirit inside of a man. When he has it you can show him the road and he will follow close behind you, but you cannot carry him. Freedom is a hard thing to win whether it is a man who wins his freedom from a nagging wife, and says, 'I am going to the cafe to drink and talk,' and goes, or whether it is freedom from religion, or a bad government, a man must have the desire for it. Do not blame these people, Petro. They have lived in the same way for three hundred years. They were free before that, but you cannot bring back their freedom in a day or a year. You can force it, but then it is not freedom. Perhaps in twenty years, when these children grow up." He stopped and looked at Peter. "But you do not have twenty years."

"No," Peter said, "but my government has, that and longer, and they will bring freedom to the Chamorros." [26]

To seek to impose ideas or techniques or projects in the community when there is no desire for these may not always lead to failure as in the above illustration. The idea, technique, or service may be accepted. But a community does not grow under such circumstances. It grows and develops capacity only as it develops will and desire to grow, only as it struggles and strives to overcome its difficulties, only as it achieves strength in the conquest of its own problems.

We have seen in this chapter the variety of approaches to work in the community and their differences in terms of objective, method, and pace. The question of which is better is largely irrelevant, since this depends on what goals are being sought in a particular and unique situation. However, the trends we had identified, as arising from field experience, suggest at least the value of a particular type of approach. This latter involves a process in which the community itself is involved in determining the nature, method, and pace of change or innovation or reform. This process we call the community organization process and we will seek to define and describe it in the chapter which follows.

[26] Robert Lund, *Hour of Glory*, George G. Harrap, 1951, p. 275.

2

The Meaning of
Community Organization

DEFINITION

COMMUNITY organization, as the term is to be used in this book, is to mean a process by which a community identifies its needs or objectives, orders (or ranks) these needs or objectives, develops the confidence and will to work at these needs or objectives, finds the resources (internal and/or external) to deal with these needs or objectives, takes action in respect to them, and in so doing extends and develops coöperative and collaborative attitudes and practices in the community. Let us expand this definition somewhat.

By "process" we mean simply the conscious or unconscious, voluntary or involuntary, movement from identification of a problem or objective to solution of the problem or attainment of the objective in the community. There are other processes for dealing with community problems, but here we call the community organization process that by which the capacity of the community to function as an integrated unit grows as it deals with one or more community problems. Sometimes it may be a deliberative process, at other times it may simply be the way people choose (because of tradition, because it is comfortable, because this is "the way it happens") to work together. The process may therefore evolve without the assistance of the professional worker—it (the process) is something apart from him.[1] But the task of the professional worker in community organization is to help initiate, nourish, and develop this process. To do this he uses certain methods (on which we will elaborate later). But it must be emphasized here, because of the tendency to confuse process and method, that we are suggesting that the professional community worker uses certain methods to facilitate the community organization process, but that this latter may emerge and be active in the community without the professional worker's presence or without those involved being conscious of the precise nature of the process or the steps in the process. Part of the task of the worker in this field is to make the process conscious, deliberative, and understood.

"Community," in the sense in which it is used here, refers to two major groupings of people. (1) It may be all the people in a specific geographic area, i.e., a village, a town, a city, a neighborhood, or a district in a city. In the same manner it could refer also to all the people in a province or a state, a nation, or in the world. For instance, the task of the United Nations can be considered a community organization project, in part at least, for what is being attempted is development of coöperative working relations among nations around common problems and objectives, the most important of which is abolition of war and establishment of peace. While, therefore, community organization is usually carried on in small geographic areas, the process may be in operation in a much wider area. (2) But "community" is used here also to include groups

---

[1] In the Kibbutz (pl. Kibbutzim) described on pages 225–232, this process is prevalent in the community, and deviation from it is unusual. Similarly, in the Friends Society such a process is the usual means of operating. There are other geographic or functional communities in which this process occasionally or frequently evolves. Often the process is followed without consciousness of this as a unique or distinctive approach. And in many of these cases, no professional worker is present to stimulate or nourish the process.

of people who share some common interest or function, such as welfare, agriculture, education, religion. These interests do not include everyone in the geographic community but only those individuals and groups who have a particular interest or function in common. Community organization may be involved (indeed it regularly is) in bringing these persons together to develop some awareness of, and feeling for, their "community" and to work at common problems arising out of the interest or function they have in common.

Some of these functional communities, it should be said, fail to identify their true nature, and confuse themselves with the geographic community. Thus many welfare or recreation or adult education councils think of themselves as councils of the geographic community, and fail to distinguish their functions clearly. The welfare council and similar agencies have multiple and somewhat different objectives. These are (1) to create the "welfare community," i.e., bring into significant association those persons who are part of the social organization of the welfare community; (2) to make plans to meet the general needs of the welfare community and the welfare needs of the geographic community; and (3) to win support of the geographic community for its welfare plans. These objectives tend to be confused and often remain undifferentiated. But the difference is fundamental. The welfare council has one kind of task within the welfare community—coördination, identification of common needs, acting together in respect to common needs, setting standards and targets for welfare work, etc. There is a rather different task that the council performs relative to the whole geographic community (of which, of course, the welfare community is a part), i.e., identification of the "welfare needs" of this total community, development of plans to meet these needs, and enlisting support in the geographic community for implementation of these plans. Thus the objectives of the welfare council require it to utilize the "inner resources" approach (basic community organization process) within the "welfare community," but to utilize something like the approach we have described under the term "community relations" in the geographic community.[2]

There has been a tendency in welfare councils, as indeed in other highly specialized councils (such as adult education, housing, recreation, library, civil liberties, etc.) to confuse "functional community" and "geographic community." Failure to differentiate the two, and the different objective a council ought to have in each, has led to considerable confusion. Within the "functional community" the task is full development of the community organization process; in the "geographic community" the task is advancement of a specialized program which the "functional community" (a minority group) feels is useful and desirable for the "geographic community." These different tasks imply different objectives and different methods.

Those whose primary concern is that the geographic community develop sufficient cohesion and capacity to deal with its own problems have a focus for their work in the geographic community which is distinct from the work of the adult education or welfare council in the same geographic community. These latter councils may wish to see greater community integration and may coöperate to that end, but their primary effort is directed at advancement of their own program of welfare or adult education in the geographic community. This leads to quite different methods of work in the geographic community. The welfare council by a variety of methods sells, or gathers support for, or induces the acceptance of, a welfare program in the geographic community.

On the other hand, those who seek to use the community organization process in the geographic community (the "generalists" we will call them here) assume that conceptions of need and programs to meet these needs must be identified, formulated, and acted upon by the people in the geographic community. Therefore the methods

[2] A welfare council may, of course, take the initiative in stimulating the community organization process in the geographic community. See the illustration on pages 58–60 which describes the use of this process within both the welfare community and the geographic community.

developed to facilitate community development are focused on nourishing people's desire and will to act in respect to their own conception of need. Emphasis is placed wholly on the process, the outcome having two facets: the need in respect to which the community decides to act (a health center, a library, a playground) and the objective, which is concerned with increasing capacity of the community to act as a unit on such matters.

Special-interest councils, like the welfare council, thus have the same objective in their "functional community" as the generalists have in the geographic community. That is, the welfare council is concerned about development of the capacity of the welfare community to act coöperatively in respect to its common needs and objectives. It recognizes that this requires that the welfare community define its common problems and learn to function as a unit in respect to these problems. Therefore it uses methods similar to those whose objective is community integration or development of community capacity. But what must be recognized (and what is consistently ignored) is the fact that the field to which these objectives and methods apply is an entirely different field for specialized councils from that for the generalist in the geographic community. The field of the former is the "welfare" or the "recreation" or "civil liberties" community; for the generalist it is a whole geographic area. In the geographic community, the objective of the special council and the objective of the general council or generalist are quite different.

The process and principles in community organization are almost precisely the same in a geographic community and in a functional community, but confusion as to the community in which one is working can lead only to chaos. It is, for example, impossible to work with all the people in either community, and it is therefore essential to identify the major subgroups or subcultures in the community in which one is working. A welfare council confused about whether it is engaged in community organization in a geographic community or in a functional community will have no way of identifying clearly its subgroups, and the coöperative welfare organization it should be building will be handicapped by seeking (often in vain) to involve many subgroups from the geographic community who have little interest, desire, or need to be intimately involved in the welfare community.

The process of "identifying its needs or objectives" means simply the way the community locates or focuses upon the problems in the community about which it is disturbed, establishes goals for community achievement, or both. This requires some amplification. As implied above, there is no expectation that all the people in the community will come together to establish goals, although subgroup meetings, house-to-house canvass, opinion polls, referendum votes, etc. may all make it possible for a large majority of people to express opinions. But the group that meets to "identify" the problems consists usually of the leaders of the various subgroups in the community. A good deal more will be said later in this book about the way subgroups and their leaders are located. Suffice here to say, that the representative leaders, in consultation with members of their groups, identify a problem or problems about which they wish something might be done. It is simply a process of becoming conscious of "things we don't like," "things we need here," "things we wish we could do," etc. Elementary as this may sound, it is of great importance in community organization, for it is from the feelings which surround these expressions of opinion that will come the motivation for action. Many workers in the field take too much for granted that consciousness of these problems or needs on the part of people in the community already exists. Actually many people live with their problems for such a long period that they adjust to them, build defences to protect themselves from consciousness of them, or learn to accept them to such a degree that their feelings about them lie deeply buried. In community organization the problems, needs, concerns, and hopes of the community come to consciousness, feeling about them is expressed, emotion is discharged and harnessed. A canvass of any street in any neighborhood can elicit quick replies to "what are the problems of this neighborhood?" These quick and often superficial replies may indicate precisely what the people really feel needs attention; often, however, it is only in a less formal atmosphere that people will reveal long-buried feelings about their neighbors, their city government, their schools, their houses, their jobs, which constitute problems or goals which are probably the matters of fundamental importance to the people concerned.

To say that the community "orders (or ranks) these needs or objectives" is simply to indicate the necessity of establishing some order of priority. Among the host of problems or objectives, some will represent ideas about which there is much feeling, great conviction, and unanimity of opinion. These are the things for first attention. At this point the worker can assist greatly in processing the expressions of desire or need. But he does not determine content. This latter is dependent upon the community. It is a need because they feel it is a need, not because it is reasonable, logical, or scientific. The "feeling about" is a prime determinant of the importance of a problem for community action. Now every professional worker will have his own conception of the community's need and problems. He will have inevitable biases. Some feel he should be completely objective (which is impossible) or that he should not reveal his own conception of the problem (which is hardly honest). Our own conviction here is that the professional worker has a right, if not a responsibility, to reveal his own appraisal of the community and its needs. This responsibility is not unlike that of the psychiatrist who does analysis and interpretation at appropriate times but does not claim infallibility and does not insist on acceptance of his ideas. Similarly, the community organization worker has the privilege of contributing his conception of needs. But rather than press for acceptance of his formulation, his emphasis is on having the people rank his objectives along with the many others which may be suggested. If, therefore, the emphasis is on "how will we rank these various needs?" rather than on "this is the problem as I see it," we will have the kind of process we are seeking to detail here.

Many communities, like individuals, identify problems with

which they feel incompetent to deal or objectives they feel they cannot reach. This is particularly true of those communities in which apathy, indifference, and the conditions of *anomie* have set in. Hope for any improvement in life seems long ago to have been lost. In such circumstances identifying and focusing upon needs is of little use if the community, through its leaders, does not find both the will to attempt movement and the confidence that such movement can be successful. In some communities, of course, there is an abundance of such confidence; in others there are individuals whose sense of security and confidence is contagious and provides support for others. Communities lacking these circumstances find difficulty in mobilizing for action—the desire, will, hope seem to be lacking. Sometimes a crisis shakes people from their lethargy, and new movement is possible. Often the support must come from an external agent, such as the community organization worker, whose stimulation, encouragement, and support make possible development of a conviction that "something can be done here" and "we can do it."

Finding the resources (internal and/or external) to deal with these problems involves (beyond the will and confidence necessary) discovery of the other tools, instruments, persons, techniques, materials, etc. necessary to do that which is felt to be important to do. It involves not merely the resources of the people within the community but, where necessary, drawing upon resources outside the community. Here is a little village in India which decides it must develop a more effective water supply. Part of the task is finding the source for the supply, securing and laying pipe lines, providing for distribution within the community, and regulating the use of water in the village to maintain a consistent supply. Another part of the task is securing permission to use water from this source, discovering the technique of using the supply economically, and laying the pipes properly. Most of the first group of tasks, the villagers can and will do, but the second group may require outside advice and assistance. Similarly, a neighborhood council in the United States may decide that its major problem is housing and that it wishes to do something about this. The complexities of the housing problem in most large urban centers would make this seem an insoluble problem for a small neighborhood. Certainly it would be without outside resources—resources which help the group to understand the nature of the problem, the sources of aid available (private and governmental), the other agencies and groups with the same interests and concerns as the council, the points at which the housing problem can be most effectively tackled, and ways in which short-term plans for conservation and neighborhood improvement may be developed along with long-term plans for slum clearance. What is required in most community problems is an awareness of "what we can do for ourselves," "where we need outside help," and a knowledge of resources available. To attempt to deal with problems for which local resources are inadequate may simply cause frustration and a sense of failure—and create or recreate a state of apathy in respect to all other problems. A wise group will be able to utilize fully its own resources and at the same time recognize the points at which outside help, or a different kind of action, is required.

It should be added parenthetically that communities, like individuals, seldom use their own resources to the full. In communities in which a process of community organization has been initiated and continued, people are often surprised at their own capacities, and those of their fellows, to take part in community endeavors. Almost every professional worker, whether in slum, suburban, or primitive communities, has testified to the wide variety of capacities found among the peoples of these communities.

The proposition "takes action in respect to these" is perhaps self-explanatory. It may be added, however, that this is a vital aspect of the process. To neglect it is to encourage the feeling, probably prevalent in many North American communities, of "another organization that never gets anything done." Now, many organizations that do little more than encourage people to sit around and talk are valuable and useful, and we should have the maturity to understand and support such a process. But because of the predisposition in

North America to want to see obvious results, and because the community organization process identifies a problem about which something "needs doing," action needs to be taken in respect to the problem and reported back to those who marked the problem out for action. In some cases "simply talking" is the only action feasible; in most cases there can be tangible, "practical" action. But what is important is that the process leads to some achievement, partial though it may be. For it is this achievement that for many persons, certainly in the first projects attempted, tests the validity of the process. If something is accomplished, the difficulties will be suffered gladly, a glow of satisfaction will emerge, new confidence and a strengthened resolve will develop.

While all stages in the process are important and in fact inseparable, certainly none is more important than the final qualifying phrase in our definition that "in so doing (it) extends and develops coöperative and collaborative attitudes and practices in the community." What is implied here, in the simplest terms, is that as the process evolves and progresses, people in the community will come to understand, accept, and work with one another; that in the process of identifying and dealing with a common problem, subgroups and their leaders will become disposed to coöperate with other subgroups in common endeavors, and will develop skills in overcoming the inevitable conflicts and difficulties which emerge in such collective tasks. Without this qualification, and indeed essential element, a community may achieve a specific goal with no more skill and capacity at the conclusion of its task than it had when it began—in fact, there may be less disposition and capacity to work together. What community organization as a conscious process is directed at achieving is not simply a new nursery, water system, or housing project, but more important, an increased capacity to undertake other coöperative projects in the community. As Elliott Jaques suggests of the workers in a factory who initiated such a process: ". . . they have set in motion a process and an institution which will ensure for them that, however the new methods work out, it is likely that they will be able to deal more readily with similar problems in the future by being able to recognize them earlier, and by being better equipped to cope with them as they arise." [3] The result of the community organization process, at any stage, is that the community should be better equipped than at some previous stage, or before the process began, to identify and deal coöperatively and skillfully with its common problems.

This emphasis on collaborative and coöperative attitudes and practices does not imply elimination of differences, of tension, of conflict. Indeed, these latter are the forces which give life and vitality to a movement. It must be recognized, however, that such conflict can be disruptive and destructive, or it can be positive and creative. It can move through a community leaving bitterness, distrust, and hatred. Or conflict can lead to increased understanding, tolerance, and community strength. The difference in the effects of conflict in particular situations is undoubtedly the result of many factors, but we suggest that none is more important than the attitude of the people involved toward, and their skill in dealing with, conflict. Tension and conflict can be used for constructive ends [4] by people with understanding of community processes; with a devotion to community goals; with skill in committee and community participation; with a disposition to find a *modus operandi*. Coöperative and collaborative work requires people who can endure, welcome, and move comfortably with diversity and tension. The problem of initiating and sustaining the community organization process in such a way that it will acquire increasing strength and power in any setting is precisely that of finding or developing enough people of this kind. In most situations it is a slow process and one which will become dynamic only as the area of shared concern, and the capacity for coöperative work, are spread throughout the community. This is the "added dimension" in the community organization process. It is not simply getting a particular task accomplished: it is the achievement of such insights and skills by members of the

[3] Elliott Jaques, *The Changing Culture of a Factory*, Tavistock Publications, 1951, p. 105.

[4] See Lewis Coser, *The Functions of Social Conflict*, The Free Press, 1956.

community as will permit a creative use of tension and conflict in the community.

Many persons participating in community organization will see the practical steps to action as the essence of the process, and for the professional worker this will also be important, but for him (the worker) the fundamental and dominant long-term goal is development in the community of the capacity to function as a unit with respect to its needs, problems, and common objectives. This goal may gradually be understood by the participants, but it is not unusual for the community, like the patient in therapy, to be primarily concerned with the immediate problem, and for the professional worker, like the therapist, to be primarily concerned with long-term objectives of adjustment and integration.

PLANNING AND COMMUNITY INTEGRATION

It will be seen from the above that there are essentially two aspects to the community organization process: one having to do with planning, and the second with community integration. In our view these two essential aspects of community organization, each important in its own right, are inseparable parts of the one process—in fact, one can state that only when these two aspects are interlocked and merged into one process is community organization, as we used the term here, present.

"Planning" we use here as an inclusive term to take in all aspects of the act, from identification of a problem to action in respect to it. Some may prefer a phrase such as "task orientation," or "project," or "action process." The choice of terms is a matter of preference. But what is involved is the process of locating and defining a problem (or set of problems), exploring the nature and scope of the problem, considering various solutions to it, selecting what appears to be a feasible solution, and taking action in respect to the solution chosen. This is obviously a complex process in itself, and as suggested, constitutes for some professional community workers, and for many people in the community, the whole of community organization. If the planning process (as defined here) is carried through effectively and efficiently, they feel community organization has been successfully undertaken. In the view taken in this book, these are necessary, but not sufficient, steps.

The second aspect of community organization we term "community integration." Some would prefer to call this development of "community morale" or "community capacity" or "the spiritual community." Again this is simply a matter of terminology preference. In the sense in which it is used here, community integration is a process in which the exercise of coöperative and collaborative attitudes and practices leads to greater (1) identification with the community, (2) interest and participation in the affairs of the community, and (3) sharing of common values and means for expressing these values. This implies a process at work in the community which facilitates the growth of awareness of, and loyalty to, the larger community of which the individual is a part; development of a sense of responsibility for the condition and status of the community; emergence of attitudes which permit coöperation with people who are "different"; and growth of common values, symbols, and rituals in the community as a whole.

This does not mean a community in which all norms, beliefs, values, and ways of life are standardized. But it does suggest that community means a "common life" of some kind, and that there is value in identifying oneself with, and sharing in, this common life. Implicit in much that has been said is the assumption that association with, and feeling "part of," this common life not only is an experience which provides the individual with certain psychological security, and his life with certain meaning it might not otherwise have, but that it builds a community capable of dealing with common problems which, if they were not solved, would lead to deterioration of the physical or social community, or both. These assumptions will be discussed in greater detail in the next chapter, but it may be well to state here that belief in a process of community organization is based on certain value-preferences which all do not share. It may be well also to stress that this process should not lead to eradication of differences among subgroups and subcultures in the community. A welfare council composed of sixty welfare agencies is not seeking to make all the agencies alike or to standardize all procedures within them. What it is seeking is identification of common problems with which all are concerned and with promotion of capacity of these sixty agencies to work coöperatively in solving these problems. Similarly the neighborhood council is not devoted to having the Polish group and the Mexican group, for example, eat and dress alike and observe identical festive days. Nor does it seek eradication of differences among church groups. What is sought is an understanding of these differences, acceptance of them by all in the community, but at the same time, development of a common frame of reference within which all can work together for common ends. "Diversity within unity" is a popular slogan, but in many North American communities "diversity" is more readily apparent than "unity."

While there are therefore two dominant tasks in, or aspects of, community organization (planning and community integration), it is essential that these two be considered integral aspects of the same process. For the writer, by far the more important objective is community integration. But community integration is not something that is developed by itself, or by good-will meetings, or by wishing and talking about it. It is a quality of community life that emerges in action, as people rub shoulders in common tasks, as people share consciously in common projects, as they seek common goals. And it appears that the more important these latter tasks and goals are to the people concerned, the more intensely they share in the project, the more significant the process of sharing becomes, and the deeper the "feeling" for community that results.[5] For this reason, planning in respect to problems that the people of the community feel to be of the greatest importance is an essential element of the community

[5] Something like this has been suggested by several studies of morale in which a prime condition is said to be the sharing of common goals considered to be of the greatest importance. (See Goodwin Watson, *Civilian Morale*, Reynal & Hitchcock, 1942.)

organization process. There has been a tendency among social workers to deprecate the methods and efforts of some urban neighborhood councils that deal with such matters as rat control, traffic safety, housing, child-rearing, and liquor-law enforcement in their neighborhoods. Yet here we see concern with issues which are of supreme importance to the residents of these neighborhoods. One can almost say that the degree of relevance of the projects chosen to the primary concerns of the people in the community determines the significance of the process for the community and the possibilities for developing a common life that has meaning and importance to the people in the community.

Thus the view here is that planning and community integration are inseparable parts of the community organization process and that both constitute elements which must be carefully cultivated and nourished in every step of the process. We intend later to detail the way in which this may be achieved, but at this point we may illustrate briefly how these two parts of the process affect work in the field of community organization.

Example A is a small neighborhood council in a city in the United States that has been considering opening a community nursery school for children of working mothers. At a previous meeting there was general approval of the plan, and the only question raised was by a Roman Catholic member, Mr. M, who reported he believed his church had been considering opening such a nursery for members of the church. He was asked to investigate, consult with officials of the church, and if possible bring Father R to the next meeting. At this meeting the plan was ready for implementation, all present favored immediate action, but neither Father R nor the man who raised the original question was present. The question raised by the chairman was, "Should we go ahead in view of their absence?" Now, simple as this question appears, the answer may have profound significance for the community. As far as carrying out the plan is concerned, there was no obvious reason for delaying action—the funds, location, and leadership were all ready. But in terms of developing community integration, it was of vast importance for future coöperative work that the plan be one that all are agreed was right and proper. In this case, the council decided to ask a subcommittee to meet with Father R, Mr. M, and other church officials to discuss the matter; if they approved, the plan would be put into immediate action; if not, it would be referred back to a special meeting of the council. It so happened that the Catholics did want to open their own school, but when the subcommittee met with Father R and Mr. M, the discussions were friendly, and the Catholic leaders agreed to come to the special meeting of the council. At this meeting Father R explained the position of his church and its desire to assume responsibility for its own children. The matter had been discussed in the parish, however, and it was felt that one nursery school was sufficient for this particular neighborhood. Therefore he wished to support, and coöperate with, the council school, but requested that Catholic children be permitted to come to his church for half an hour on two mornings each week. The reason for this request was explained, the matter discussed at length, and the new coöperative plan was agreed upon. The nursery school was opened with the support of all major groups in the community.

It cannot be claimed, from this brief report, that community integration was increased by this project. Nonetheless, one may speculate that the course taken by the council tended to make for greater understanding in the community of diverse points of view, for greater unity of feeling around the plan developed, and for greater community integration than would be the case if the council had moved without consulting leaders of the Roman Catholic church. Elementary as this illustration may seem, it suggests that consciousness of the need for community integration in the community organization process may lead to increased good will in, and capacity on the part of, the community.

Example B is a small village of recent settlers in Israel, a village in which there was a fairly rigid power structure with three families serving as the traditional leaders of the sixty families who constituted the village. The government social worker assigned to work with these people (and several other villages) moved slowly and carefully. It was soon apparent to her that the leaders of the village were more concerned with their own gain than with the welfare of their people; that while their leadership was tolerated and accepted as inevitable, they were neither liked nor trusted by the people; and that much of the apathy which characterized the life of the village could be attributed to these facts. Nevertheless, the traditional way of getting action in the village was through these leaders, and if the government was to secure coöperation from the village in raising certain crops and getting the village established on a self-supporting basis, it seemed apparent that they would have to work with and through these leaders. The worker, herself, felt she could not be part of this inequitable power structure. Gradually as she became acquainted with the people she was able to discover persons who were liked, respected, and trusted by the villagers. Without neglecting the formal leaders, she gradually spread her area of consultation on welfare needs to include the informal leaders, and she eventually held several meetings at which both formal and informal leaders were present. These latter, silent at first, soon learned with the support of the social worker to speak at meetings. A much more realistic picture of village needs and resources was developed. The formal leaders, feeling their power slipping, fought the movement that included consultation with informal leaders. This the worker tried to handle in long private discussions with the formal leaders, but as power moved more and more into the hands of the villagers, two of the formal leaders left the village, while the third formal leader adjusted to the situation and became an accepted leader in the new village organization. This latter took the form of a council elected by all the villagers each year; three years after its initiation, it was making a good deal of progress both in terms of developing community life and in terms of material (mainly agricultural) gain.

Now, it is conceivable (especially if the formal leaders had been more responsible people) that agriculture and welfare problems could have been handled with greater dispatch and with as much efficiency if there had simply been acceptance of the existing power structure and a disposition to work through the traditional leaders. But, again, if community integration—development of the capacity of a community of people to function in respect to their problems— is a goal of the worker, then some such steps as reported above are essential. The result in this case was completely satisfactory; in other cases it might be far less so. Nonetheless, the objectives implicit in community organization require an attempt to release the potentialities of the community, and this cannot be achieved, it is submitted here, by acceptance of a dictatorship, however benevolent.[6] Thus the planning goal must be considered along with the goal of community integration, and this latter requires conscious development of coöperative and collaborative attitudes and practices throughout the community.

A third example is the consideration given by the board of directors of a large Community Chest to the recommendation of its budget committee. The latter had recommended that the Chest terminate its grant to Agency C, a home for unmarried mothers. The reason for the budget committee's action stemmed from an agreement reached by all agencies serving unmarried mothers that they would serve only women who had been resident in the city six months prior to their request for service or help. The representative of Agency C had agreed to this policy, but since that time its board had discussed the matter further and had decided they could not follow such a regulation and would continue to accept unmarried mothers from out of the city. Actually Agency C was a small organization; they received only partial support from the Community Chest. The budget committee's recommendation was based on the views expressed by such statements as, "If we agree on policy, we have to stand back of that policy," and "What is the use of planning if we don't implement our plans?"

Such action must be evaluated in the light of the actors' objectives: if planning and uniform action are the paramount objective, the recommendation of the budget committee is probably sound. But if the objective is to develop the capacity of the community to work together on matters of common concern, then surely such action as was proposed by the budget committee is destructive and arbitrary. In this situation, the board of the Chest delayed action, investigated the situation by meeting with the board of Agency C, and found that this agency, which was an agency of a religious sect, felt an obligation to provide services to girls sent to them by their members in nearby small towns where no such services were offered. In view of this, an agreement was reached with all concerned, whereby the Chest would continue its grant, but Agency C would provide special funds (on a *per diem* basis) to care for out-of-town clients.

Again, obvious and sensible as such action appears, it underlines the primary function of a community organization agency, which is to facilitate mutual understandings, identify common areas for work, and nourish coöperative work in these areas. It is not simply to develop efficient planning, and not at all to eradicate differences, nor to set up a superstructure to which all other parts of the community are lesser in importance; it is to draw together subgroups of the community in coöperative enterprises which the subgroups feel are important, to the end that there is good will, understanding, and capacity for united action when necessary.

The final illustration is that of a welfare council in which two members of the board of the council became interested in the treatment of juvenile offenders in the city. This interest was expressed at a board meeting, with the suggestion that civic officials be approached to remedy present practices. The matter, which was presented in the dying moments of the board meeting, was approved with but cursory consideration, and a committee composed of the two interested members and the council secretary was appointed and given power to act. The small committee was free to approach civic officials, and might well have done so with modest success. The committee felt, however, that (1) they were hardly competent themselves to decide the precise nature of the remedy to be proposed, (2) changes would come only as a result of vigorous community protest, and (3) this was an opportunity for collaboration on the part of all member agencies of the council. The committee therefore increased its membership to include several experts in the field, began intensive study of treatment of juvenile law offenders, and developed a full report with appropriate recommendations for improving practices in the local community. At the same time, the committee sent two letters to the member agencies of the council. The first letter outlined the nature of the problem and urged agency interest and support; the second letter, written as the committee's report reached its final stage of drafting, asked agencies to send representatives to a meeting to consider the committee's report. It was hoped a large and enthusiastic meeting would endorse and support the report and join in sending a delegation to the city hall to urge acceptance of the committee's recommendations. Unfortunately less than half of the agencies responded, the meeting was small and apathetic, and although the committee's report was approved, there appeared little enthusiasm for it. The committee could now go directly to city hall with what they were certain was a valuable plan for changed practices. But they felt they had failed to arouse the agencies to the seriousness of the problem, and had therefore failed to provide opportunity for coöperative work on an issue of great importance. After some exploration, the committee decided on a new approach to agencies: a series of six case histories of juvenile offenders was prepared; these were rewritten and illustrated by a public relations firm. Each case described simply the experience of one child, his appearance in an adult court, his stay in the city jail with adult offenders, his exposure to indifferent officials and hardened criminals. There was no evaluation of the experience (although the lesson was obvious) but each case concluded with the question: "Are you proud of the way _____ cares for its children?" These case histories were sent to the agencies, one each week for six weeks. Copies were sent to the local newspapers, all of which treated the matter in their editorial columns, and one of which ran several articles with photographs of a small boy in court, in the city jail, being led to a car by burly policemen. The effect was dramatic. Before the end of the six-week period the council was being urged by the agencies to call a meeting on this matter. When the meeting was held, every member agency was strongly represented. The problem was discussed, the committee's report was considered and slightly modified, and a plan for implementation was developed. This latter recognized that the welfare community was united in its desire for change, but called for coöperation with other organizations and groups in the geographic community in securing the desired change. A conference was called, therefore, of representatives of all churches, service clubs, and ethnic groups to consider the issue. This conference called quickly was nevertheless well attended. Again the problem was outlined, the proposals for change submitted, and a plan for action was discussed. There was unanimous agreement on the plan, and a delegation was appointed to appear before the municipal council. This latter meeting resulted in full acceptance by the city of the proposals of the conference, and rapid action on these proposals followed.

It may be claimed that the two original members might have taken direct action and secured results with an expenditure of a good deal less time and energy than in this lengthy process. Or it may be suggested that the committee simply used agency representatives to secure support for the committee's proposals. But one may also propose the hypothesis that this committee was concerned with stimulating first the welfare community, and later the geographic community, to act in respect to a common problem. True, the plan was developed by experts, but the plan was modified and accepted by the welfare community as a sensible way of dealing with an issue about which all were concerned. And it may likewise be claimed that the procedure followed took adequate account of the need to nourish the dual processes of planning and community integration, and that this approach led to the development of capacity of both the welfare and the geographical communities to function in respect to their common problems.

COMMUNITY ORGANIZATION AS A
SOCIAL WORK PROCESS

Community organization, as it is defined and described here, is one of the basic social work processes, being used to attain the same basic objectives, and using many of the same methods, as casework and group work. It has in fact moved through some of the same stages as casework and has only recently (and in a limited way) been able to identify itself with these other processes.

A number of years ago, there was what was sometimes called the "religious counselor," a person who certainly knew the answer to, if not the nature of, the problem even before he saw the client; in community organization we have had the worker who knew the problem and the solution to the problem before he arrived in the community, and who proceeded to organize the community around his conception of the need and the goal. Later, in counseling we had a phase of "scientific psychological tests" on the basis of which the counselor could tell the client not only what his problems were but what he should do about them; in community organization we have used some of the insights and tools of social science to show where and how changes could be made with the least social dislocation and with the greatest support in the community. Now, in casework there is recognition that the client himself must be involved in identifying his problem and mastering it, and that if the process is successful, the client will be better equipped to deal, not only with his original conscious problem, but with many other life situations. Similarly, in community organization we are coming to realize that the community itself must struggle and strive to deal with its own conception of its needs, and that in doing this the community can increase its capacity to deal not only with these problems but with many other problems as they arise.

Thus, while the context in which the caseworker, group worker, or the worker in community organization operates is quite different, fundamentally the objectives they seek and the means they use to achieve these ends have a good deal in common. If we were to adapt to casework our statement defining community organization, it would read: "The caseworker seeks to help the individual identify his problems, develop the confidence and will to deal with these problems, find the resources (internal and external) to deal with these problems, take action in respect to these problems, and in so doing increase his understanding of himself and his capacity for integration." We should then be defining approximately what the caseworker or psychotherapist attempts with an individual. client.

Such an analogy must not, of course, be carried to extremes, for the caseworker deals with an individual, operates from a basis of psychodynamic theory, seeks to relate diverse threads of individual behavior. The community organization worker deals with a whole community and its major subcultures, operates from a basis of sociocultural theory, deals with such accounts of need as people can express in meetings, seeks to relate diverse groups to one another. One could therefore easily overemphasize the similar nature of these processes. With this caution, it may be useful, nonetheless, to explore briefly some of the fundamental similarities.

The objectives of all social work methods, for example, are similar. All are concerned with removal of blocks to growth, release of potentialities, full use of inner resources, development of capacity to manage one's own (the individual, group, or community) life, ability to function as an integrated unit. As already implied, these have somewhat different application in the face-to-face, group, and community situation. But essentially what is sought by all social workers is this same general end. In community organization, what is desired is initiation of that process which will enable a community to overcome those blocks (apathy, vested interests, discrimination) which prevent the community from working together; release of potentialities and use of indigenous resources (which emerge as the community struggles and strives to deal with its needs or goals) and growth of those coöperative attitudes and skills which make possible achievement of increasingly difficult ends. This, as implied, is merely application to the community situation of objectives analogous to those of casework and group work.

It is natural, also, that these processes should rest on similar assumptions, namely, the inherent dignity and worth of the individual, the resources possessed by each to deal with his own problems, the inherent capacity for growth, the ability of the individual (or group or community) to choose wisely in the management of his own affairs. In addition there is the assumption that people overwhelmed by the complexities of life often become psychologically paralyzed, but with help this stage can be overcome and normal processes of growth resumed. Some extension of these assumptions is required for community organization, and these will be detailed in the chapter that follows. It may be stated here, however, that the above apply, with some adaptation, for community organization. For example, communities are also subjected to great forces which paralyze their capacity for action and in some cases self-preservation. The condition of *anomie* is not unknown in our society, but it is assumed that even here with help a community can emerge from this situation and develop capacity for coöperative action.

Further, somewhat similar methods are used to facilitate casework, group work, and community organization processes. In casework there is the need to accept the client, to develop a professional relationship with the client, to start at the point where the client now is, to provide him with understanding and support, to help him make decisions and to take action, to help him struggle to overcome his problems, to interpret the nature of the process in which he is involved, to help him achieve independence, etc. If the community is considered as the client, these identical concepts are all applicable. For the worker in community organization (as will be pointed out in detail in Chapter 8) has the same general orientation and approach, i.e., accepting the community as it is, helping it move in the direction and at a pace which it finds both comfortable and challenging, encouraging it to struggle, supporting it in times of stress and discouragement, interpreting the short- and long-term goals of the community organization process, etc. There are common methods, as there are common objectives and assumptions, for all social workers.

But while there is this common base and a common core of philosophy and method, there are significant differences in casework, group work, and community organization. For example, how does each deal with such a problem as hostility? In all situations the worker must be prepared to accept the expression of hostility with calmness and objectivity and to understand its meaning. But the caseworker deals with it in a face-to-face situation, the group worker in a small-group setting, and the community organization worker in the context of a whole community. The caseworker asks herself such questions as: To what degree is this expression of hostility relevant to the problem on which we are working? Is this a matter which should be explored with the client now or at another time? Should it be ignored? To what extent is the client ready and able to explore the cause and meaning of his hostility? The group worker is also, of course, concerned about the cause of the hostility, but he asks himself: Does this hostility represent a reaction to group structure, group process, or group program? To what extent is such hostility damaging to the group as a whole? Can the group handle such hostility or does the hostile individual require special treatment? Can the situation be altered in such a way as to help the hostile person find greater satisfaction in the group? The worker in community organization is similarly interested in the causes of hostility, but he asks himself such questions as: Does this represent a reaction to a threatening situation or process? Does it reflect deep-seated feeling of one group toward another? Does it relate to particular group values or orientation? Is this hostility merely the expression of the individual or is it representative of the group of which he is a member? What effect has this on the community organization process? Can it be handled by people in the community or is it likely to destroy the process in which we are engaged? How may this be best handled?

In terms of treatment, the caseworker is most likely to work out this problem in face-to-face contacts. She may refer the client to a psychiatrist if the problem is severe, she may attempt to adjust a home situation if the root of the problem lies there, but in most cases the hostility, if it requires exploration, will be examined by the client and worker in a regularly scheduled face-to-face interview. The group worker may see the problem of the hostile individual as one which requires personal help and refer the individual to a caseworker or psychiatrist; he may, if he feels the continued expression of hostility is destructive to the group, either move the hostile person to another group or insist that the hostility be contained;[7] but probably he will seek to adjust the situation so that the need which the hostility expresses (e.g., for affection, recognition, status, etc.) is met in, and by, the group. The worker in community organization does not make referrals or shift a member out of the group or organization. He must deal with the hostility through the people who lead and operate the organization. He may help the group to accept calmly such expressions of hostility; he may help the group or community to work its way through such expressions of hostility but at the same time move consistently toward the real issues. The worker's effort is directed at helping the community develop the elementary insights necessary to face, accept, and work through deep expressions of feeling in meetings and conferences; he helps the community to recognize that in the process of working together there will be inevitable conflicts and expressions of hostility, and that the essence of the process is development of capacity to work these through in meetings and conferences. Occasionally there will be the severe neurotic who consistently blocks progress, but even here the group must learn to deal with this, even though the action taken must be consultation with the neurotic's subgroup so that another person will represent them, or promotion of the neurotic to some position where his talents are used and his weaknesses are not accentuated.

The differences in diagnosis and treatment suggested above are stated in general terms and could be greatly amplified. Enough

---

[7] Gisela Konopka, *Social Group Work*, Prentice-Hall, 1963, p. 64.

has been said, perhaps, to indicate certain fundamental differences not merely in context but in method of dealing with the problem. Primarily, the caseworker works the problem out with the individual; primarily, the group worker seeks to have the problem handled, with his help, in the regular program of the group; primarily, the worker in community organization attempts to help the community understand and work through the problem itself. This, of course, is subject to modification in many specific situations, but in general it defines some major differences.

It is sometimes suggested that the real difference in casework, group work, and community organization is the level at which the worker in each specialization functions. Some feel the caseworker carries diagnosis to deeper levels, often probes the unconscious, and provides therapeutic treatment, whereas the group worker or community organization worker deals at a relatively superficial level. In the writer's view this is a fallacious argument. Advanced workers in all three specializations approach at times the therapeutic level of work (although some question their right or competence to work at this level) and there are not only individual therapists but group therapists (who bring to light factors and forces in the group situation of which members of the group are unaware), and as we will show later, social therapists. The distinction between casework, group work, and community organization is not the level at which the worker functions, but certain fundamental distinctions in context, objective, and method.

It may be evident from the above that while all social workers must learn to accept and deal with hostility, the way this is done varies as between caseworkers, group workers, and workers in community organization. What is true of dealing with the problem of hostility is true of many other similar problems. There is a common objective; there are common assumptions and certain common methods in social work; but there are also significant differences in objectives and methods in casework, group work, and community organization. All three processes move from the same general field and have a similar orientation; but when they move from the general into a specific field, they each develop distinctive ways of dealing with problems of the individual, the group, the community. In addition to the fact that some of the same insights and methods develop differently in a specific setting (e.g., casework, group work, etc.), each process has distinctive insights and methods of its own. While increasingly, for example, the psychology of individual behavior has moved to a consideration of group and cultural factors, and caseworkers recognize the need to be aware of such matters in dealing with a client, these factors are matters of dominant concern for the worker in community organization. But further, his interest in these matters is of a quite different nature. He is interested in the various subgroupings and subcultures in the community; the value systems, behavior patterns, and social organization in each; the formal and informal leaders in each group; the interests, problems, or concerns these groups have in common; the degree of coöperation and competition between the groups; the conception of status each group has of itself and of others; the kinds of frames of reference within which all might work comfortably; the values, symbols, and rituals which all share or might share. The worker in community organization is interested in the social forces playing on the community which facilitate or block community integration, and which help or prevent individuals from identifying themselves with the community as a whole, which facilitate or handicap coöperative work, which create or ease social tension. His is a large canvas and he is concerned with the relationships of the major parts of the picture. His methods of diagnosis are therefore different; his methods of operation are also distinctive. These latter will be outlined in detail in Chapter 8 and need not be expanded here. But sufficient has been said, perhaps, to suggest that while all social work has a common philosophy and methods, there are distinctive refinements of methods in the specific settings of casework, group work, and community organization, and each of these processes has unique features which are not shared by the others.

There remains one other relationship between casework, group work, and community organization which requires identification. It is frequently said that all caseworkers and group workers are involved in community organization. What is often implied here is that all *should* be involved, for it can hardly be claimed that they all are. A caseworker may, for example, perform adequately with clients and neglect, or even resist, participating in coöperative work of any other kind.

But what is often meant by community organization is what we have described under community relations, and in this sense it is probably true that all agency workers presumably have some responsibilities for public relations, community services,˙ and community participation. Certainly these are important and responsible activities, but they do not necessarily involve the worker in community organization as it has been defined here.

In an important sense all social workers should be involved in community organization, for all are members of the welfare community, all are members of a geographic community, and all are probably members of several other "interest communities," such as professional societies. It would seem important, therefore, that all social workers understand the nature of the community organization process and be capable of playing a constructive role in this process.

One might expect the caseworker and group worker to understand something of the forces which make coöperative work difficult, to be able to support a community as it strives to solve a problem with which it is confronted, to be able to recognize the long-term goals of developing responsibility and coöperation in the community, and to facilitate this process. Many social workers, unfortunately, are not able to perform in this way, and their failure to do so should be instructive to social work educators. Apparently, for example, while caseworkers have been trained to accept hostility in a casework situation, many find this difficult to do in a group or community situation; while they are conscious of process and of long-term goals in dealing with a client, many become absorbed in the content of a meeting and fail to recognize (or ignore) the process in which they are involved in a group meeting; while able to see the need to support the client in a face-to-face situation, many are unable to provide similar support for individuals or groups in the community setting. What this suggests is that there has not been tranference from one area, such as casework, to another area, such as community organization; or that the generic aspects of social work have not been sufficiently well taught. In any case, many social workers are inept in a community organization setting. As suggested, this poses a problem of considerable importance for social work education—a problem which fortunately we do not have to consider here.

A legitimate question to be asked here, however, is what may be expected of a caseworker or group worker participating in a community organization project (but not as a professional community organization worker)? We should expect that they would:

1. Understand the objectives of community organization—i.e., not simply the planning objectives for a nursery school, or a public assistance program, or slum clearance program, but the community integration objective which seeks to develop in the community attitudes and practices of social responsibility and coöperative work. It is so easy to see the obvious planning objectives and be hypnotized by these, as opposed to seeing the long-range objectives.

2. Be in sympathy with and support these objectives. Often discerning and skillful people in casework or group work see the community organization process as unrealistic or idealistic—"if you need something in this kind of society, you have to fight for it." These persons fail to recognize a rather different approach to social action, one which is more concerned with long-term results than with immediate gains; one which, in the interests of solving the whole or ultimate problem, is content to delay the solution of the immediate problem. This difference must be clear, and the long-term objective must be supported. This does not mean, of course, that the social worker does not take part in minority group action in the community. The worker may join with others for higher wages, may be part of a church group which fights against a city ordinance, may be a member of a minority political party. And as a member of

the "welfare community," itself a minority group in the larger geographic community, he may press for vigorous social action. But within a given community structure, be it geographic or functional, the worker should understand and support those processes which make for mutual understanding, appreciation, willingness and ability to work with others, capacity to function as a cohesive unit.

3. Be able objectively to regard behavior in the community setting. Just as social workers learn to be objective in the casework or group work situation, so they should learn to play the participant-observer role in the community organization setting. This means the capacity to understand the behavior of certain group representatives; the sudden rise of tempers in a meeting; the reason for apathy at points in the process; the rise and fall in enthusiasm in the community organization process; the reason why strong feelings arise in respect to certain issues; the way people, unconsciously but with reason, move away from the subject and pursue "rabbit trails"; the needs which are seeking satisfaction in the behavior of the domineering, the overly active, the passive participant; the historic, cultural, and status factors which make it difficult for certain groups and their representatives to work together; etc. These requirements of objectivity make it possible for the worker to understand some of the forces operating in the community setting and to lay the groundwork for more effective participation.

4. Be skillful in associating himself with the community organization process. This does not mean playing the role of the community organization worker (as will be defined in Chapter 8) but it does mean ability to play a constructive part in the process, that is, ability to help the group to define and clarify goals; to encourage the group (as a group) to rank these goals and view them realistically; to encourage frank exchange of views and full participation by all present; to understand, accept, and identify oneself with diverse subcultures in which the worker may not share; to support and help to clarify the expression of opinion of the inarticulate or insecure; to secure, and help others secure, satisfaction in the

achievement of consensus and community goals; to endure, and help others endure, the painful occasions when agreement seems impossible; to regard calmly, and help others accept, the inevitable conflicts which occur in this process; etc. All these skills and many others, it seems not unreasonable to suppose, all social workers might display in a community organization setting.

5. Be able to contribute effectively in respect to content. In many cases the social worker will have a specialized knowledge far beyond that of many others in the community with regard to certain issues about which there is concern. This makes it possible for him to become the "main figure" in the situation, and perhaps to secure the kind of recognition that he may wish or need. Needless to say the role of a social worker, unless he is invited in as an expert adviser, is hardly that of "explaining" or "lecturing." His role as a participant is that of helping to clarify the problem, of contributing factual information, of reporting experiences in other centers, etc. Essential in such a contribution—and it can be one of great importance—is ability to communicate with people in the community. The "jargon" or technical language social workers have developed is useful and time-saving to them, but it is a block to communication with those not acquainted with it. Therefore, ability to state simply and clearly the issues, the facts, the experience, is especially important in the community field. A second aspect of this communication is a degree of humility—many of the assumptions upon which social work rests are still assumptions; they are not yet unassailable facts and hardly provide a foundation for dogmatism. It would be useful for social workers to make their contribution, then, not only clearly but in such a way that people are less encouraged to feel they are receiving a divine message than that they are being stimulated to think, to strive, and to find for themselves what they believe to be the best possible answers to their problems. The effort is always directed at helping the community find its way, rather than showing it the way.

As implied several times, most of these objectives and skills are common to all fields of social work, but apparently the differences in the setting lead some social workers to feel they apply in one situation but not in another. These professional insights and skills must be mastered, it is true, in one setting, but their application in a variety of fields and situations would greatly facilitate work in community organization.

3

Basic Assumptions in Community Organization

CRITICAL VIEWS

IT CANNOT be said that the conception of community organization as outlined in the last chapter is widely accepted. The assumption that somehow life will be better if this process is activated in the community is questioned by many. "Better for whom?" they ask. "Are the people of a village or urban neighborhood happier, more content, or more secure because some technician or professional worker persuades them that they should organize to change their way of life?" "Are welfare agencies likely to show more initiative, offer better and more humane services, have more freedom because they are induced to join a welfare council or community chest?" Or, to shift the argument, "Even if one were able to initiate such a process, does it deal with the problems of a society in which technological development moves far faster than people can be organized to meet and adapt to changing conditions?" In light of these and other such questions, it seems necessary to attempt to clarify our position further and to deal as adequately as possible with these issues.

THREE CONTRARY VIEWS

Roughly, there are three main strands in these criticisms. The first is concerned with the emphasis placed on *coöperation* in our conception of community organization. There would be some who would suggest that there is little evidence to indicate that coöperative work brings the kind of results we imply in all, or even a majority of, situations. Further, it could be argued that the emphasis on coöperation as a primary good, which seems implicit in our thesis, is hardly justifiable in light of competing goods (e.g., the value of the individual personality). Therefore, some would suggest that our interpretation of community organization overvalues and overstresses coöperation. A friend writes, for example,

I have no desire to be deeply involved in the community in the way you suggest but would prefer to be left alone to do the things I do well and in the area where I can make a special contribution. Further, to impute progress solely or primarily to coöperative work is a fallacy. Many of the great ideas and discoveries in the past were the product of individuals. Who has shaped our thinking in the past century—Marx, Freud, Darwin, Edison, Ford? Why, so, emphasize coöperation?

A second critical view is that community organization interferes with the way people choose, desire, or want to live, and that in many situations it tends to manipulate ideas and people to secure the ends of a professional elite. Further, this is all done in the name of democracy, when it is quite clear that a movement that is "democratic" and "manipulative" is highly self-contradictory. Thus, a minister, obviously disturbed by the work of a neighborhood council, says:

That man came in here (a neighborhood) and got all the people stirred up about their problems—real and imagined. Before long he was using the organization to do the things he wanted, raise money for the Chest, oppose the churches on Sunday sports, etc., and to make a reputation for himself. The people never wanted this organization and would be better off without it.

A third strand of criticism implies that however justifiable the community organization process may be in philosophical terms, it is not practical in a society in which "cultural lag" becomes more pronounced every day. Change in our way of living must come quickly, it can be imposed, and people will adjust to the new objective situation.

Carl Becker in his *Progress and Power* writes:

Never before have men made relatively greater progress in the rational control of physical force or relatively less in rational control of social relations. The fundamental reason for this discrepancy is clear: it is that forces of nature have been discovered and applied by a few exceptional individuals, whereas every effort to ameliorate human relations has been frustrated by the fact that society cannot be transformed without the compliance of the untutored masses. . . . It is therefore not enough that a few individuals should have discovered the advantages to be derived from rational social arrangements; *in addition the masses who compose society must be persuaded or compelled to adapt their activities to the proposed changes, and the means of persuasion or compulsion must be suited to the apprehension of common men.*[1]

In other words, the means for a better social organization are at hand; to await for their acceptance by "the masses" would be to wait in vain, for by the time adjustment was made, a whole new set of problems would confront us. Therefore forceful, if not compulsory, action must be taken.

Robert Lynd makes a similar point (if we interpret community organization to be a process of learning or education) when he says:

There is a widespread tendency to steady ourselves in the face of the functional inadequacies of our culture by a comforting reliance upon education. "What we need," we are prone to say, "is to intensify education; and, as education makes people better-informed, many of the problems that now beset us will disappear." . . . But this great faith in gradualness implies a largely static view of culture; it assumes what may be called the haystack theory of social problems, that is, that our culture confronts a fixed quantum of problems which are being slowly carted away by "progress," each load reducing the total awaiting removal.

[1] Carl Becker, *Progress and Power*, Stanford University Press, 1936, pp. 91–92 (italics supplied).

Actually, however, the culture appears to be piling up problems faster than the slow horse-and-haywagon process of liberal change through education and reform is able to dispose of them. . . .

. . . one cannot get an operation performed by setting out to teach the masses about appendicitis. The same point applies to teaching ethics and citizenship, and organizing businessmen in clubs devoted to "service," while the institutional straitjacket is left essentially unaltered. While all possible improvements in education and personnel must be pushed for all they are worth, the basic responsibility remains squarely upon the shoulders of social science to discover where fundamental changes in the cultural structure are needed and to blueprint the ways of achieving them.[2]

This implies that mass man cannot expect to keep up with the problems with which he is confronted in the modern world, and must therefore increasingly expect direction from the social scientist or an elite who acts on the advice of the social scientist.

Further support for the practicality of planned, induced, and forced change comes from some social psychologists who sharply question the assumption that social change may be brought about only through prior changes in the attitudes of individuals. The study of *Desegregation* suggests a contrary position, and the author says:

The data reveal that desired changes in the behavior of individuals and groups can be brought about by a change in the social situation in which they are required to function. Changes in the social situation are effected and reinforced by individuals with authority, prestige, power, and the control over the media of communication and important areas of life. . . . Lewin, Festinger, and others have contributed to a newer theoretical understanding of the nature of social change by emphasizing that there are objective as well as subjective determinants of such change and by pointing out that changes in behavior might produce compatible subjective changes.[3]

Thus, psychologically speaking, if it appears to the planners, or

[2] Robert S. Lynd, *Knowledge for What?*, Princeton University Press, 1948, pp. 236–237.

[3] Kenneth B. Clark, "Some Implications for a Theory of Social Change," *The Journal of Social Issues,* IX (1953), 72–73. See also Robert A. Dahl, *Who Governs?*, Yale University Press, 1963, pp. 316–325.

scientists, or technicians that certain rapid changes in the customary ways of living are indicated, such changes could be made with some expectation that the changes would be accepted, and even that appropriate modifications in attitude might follow the objective change. The argument here is directed less at deprecating the importance of subjective change than at raising questions of those who tend to rely exclusively on gradualism, education, and the people themselves developing a movement for change.

VALUE ASSUMPTIONS

A simple response to these counterviews would be that community organization, as it is defined here, does not make coöperation an ultimate good, does not deny the value of individual effort, does not insist that all goals can be achieved only in coöperative work. Similarly, it could be said that the particular conception of community organization outlined here has no tolerance for manipulation but is disposed towards "open covenants openly arrived at." Nor does this interpretation of community organization imply denial of the validity and value of other approaches to the solution of the problems of community life (e.g., the need for planning by social scientists, housing, traffic, zoning, and other types of experts) but asserts that the development of "community" (both geographic and functional), as interpreted here, is essential if the values implicit in the concept of democracy are to be maintained. This, however, is not an adequate reply to those who hold contrary views, and it is necessary therefore to restate and amplify the basic assumptions on which our conception of community organization rests and to define that which it specifically seeks to do.

First, however, we should seek to avoid the confusion of what Max Weber distinguishes as "preference statements" and "fact statements." This is the distinction between "what we prefer to see" and "what is"; between the way "we want to move" and "the only possible ways to move." Now, it is quite clear that community organization, as indeed all social work, rests on preferences (as well as facts). We seek a position or objective we prefer; we value what we think enhances human dignity. There are no data to prove that this is "right," "better," "an ultimate good." It is largely a matter of choice based upon preference for a particular configuration of "goods." Similarly, many of those who choose other positions or objectives rest their choice on their own conception of "value" or of "good." In each case, of course, there is a combination of wisdom, experiences, and facts, which to the advocates seem to support their position, but the ultimate position or objective selected is a matter of choice.

Community organization derives from a unique frame of reference, the nature of which may now be examined. The framework takes its special form as a result of (1) a particular value orientation which stems from traditional religious values which have been expanded to form the basis of social work philosophy, (2) a particular conception of the problems confronting modern man in his community and social life, and (3) certain assumptions that influence method, which derive in part from the value orientation of, and in part from experience in, social work. This frame of reference limits, conditions, and provides the focus for workers in community organization. What is attempted, what is done, what is valued has its source in this framework. The adequacy of the community organization process as a means of dealing with problems of the modern community, in light of counterviews and criticisms, can most conveniently be evaluated as one investigates in detail the nature of its frame of reference. This we now propose to do by examining the value system, the conception of the problem, and the broad assumptions about method which constitute this frame of reference.

The value orientation of community organization (and, indeed, of all social work) derives from acceptance of certain concepts and facts as a foundation for work with people. Among these articles of faith are: the essential dignity and ethical worth of the individual, the possession by each individual of potentialities and resources for managing his own life, the importance of freedom to express one's individuality, the great capacity for growth within all social beings, the right of the individual to those basic physical necessities (food, shelter, and clothing) without which fulfillment of life is often blocked, the need for the individual to struggle and strive to improve his own life and environment, the right of the individual to help in time of need and crisis, the importance of a social organization for which the individual feels responsible and which is responsive to individual feeling, the need of a social climate which encourages individual growth and development, the right and responsibility of the individual to participate in the affairs of his community, the practicability of discussion, conference, and consultation as methods for the solution of individual and social problems, "self-help" as the essential base of any program of aid, etc.

These and other similar orientations constitute the "bias" of social work, condition its goals, and preclude certain types of action felt to be more useful by its critics. There are some who think of social work as a science, but it is necessarily value-oriented and is dedicated to implementation of those goals implicit in the outline above. Quite definitely and clearly it is a program which seeks to "influence" and to secure certain "value-laden" ends. It uses the knowledge and insights provided by social science, but it is not a social science.

THE COMMUNITY PROBLEM

Given this value orientation, the next step is a general appraisal or diagnosis of community life to ascertain to what extent these goals are being secured in the community and what might be done by social work to further their attainment. Without giving a complete analysis, the following points may be said to be relevant.

(1) The dominant impetus for change today is technological,[4]

---

[4] It can be argued that this impetus for change is ideological and that technological development is merely the manifestation of a particular ideology. We can accept this point of view without yielding to the temptation of entering into a discussion which would lead us far from the purpose of this brief summary of some of the obvious symptoms of our disordered society.

is pressing toward increased industrialization and urbanization, with comparatively little consideration of the effects of such movement on social relations. Cybernation and automotive processes have helped to produce advanced technologies in western countries. In the developing countries the pressure is "to catch up," to "move a century in ten years," and one finds, as a result of both external and internal pressures, acceleration of movement toward industrialization and use of modern machines and methods. Behind this movement, of course, is the tense international situation, the need for the most effective means of destruction, the need for strong allies, etc., but this merely gives further stimulation to forces already in operation. The result, throughout the world, is movement away from traditional patterns of earning a living, from the traditional farm, village or small-town community, from a pattern of relatively simple social relationships, to a situation in which, as the old patterns disappear, there is confusion, uncertainty, and loss of identity. While the effects of these trends are more obvious in the United States, the same picture is to be seen, or is likely to be seen, in other countries throughout the world. As T. N. Whitehead of the Harvard School of Business Administration puts it:

> Every advance of industry has so far been accompanied by a corresponding impoverishment in social living. The rise of organized industry has reduced the importance of other institutions as integrators of society, without shouldering these functions itself. And the resulting social instability is so great as to threaten the industries themselves.[5]

To which Lynd adds:

> It is this structural distortion, with the elements so unequal and out of balance that the sheer preservation of the going system becomes a monopolizing preoccupation, that presents one of the most striking aspects of our culture. To the resulting general sense of strain may be traced the compulsive overemphasis upon aggression rather than affectionate mutuality, upon action rather than upon repose, and upon doing rather than feeling.[6]

[5] Quoted in Lynd, *op. cit.*, p. 70.
[6] *Ibid.*

(2) The processes of urbanization have almost destroyed man's "feeling of belonging" to a community. To Tolstoi's phrase "the political nonexistent" we might add "social" and say that cities are heavily populated with "the politically and socially nonexistent." Annually, one out of four families in the United States makes a major move of residence, and as Morris and Rein further point out, no more than five out of every hundred Americans die in the community of their birth.[7] Recent decades have seen a rapid increase in urbanization throughout the world. This trend is vividly seen in the United States where, in 1940, some 51 percent of the population lived in standard metropolitan areas· (i.e., cities of 50,000 or more people). By 1960 the figure had risen to 63 percent.[8]

The rough generalization may be made that, as the size of a community grows arithmetically, the need for deliberate (as over against unplanned, casual) organization that weaves the individual into the group life increases in something like a geometrical progression.... Citizenship ties are weakening in our urban world to the point that they are largely neglected by large masses of people. Neighborhood and community ties are not only optional but generally growing less strong; and along with them is disappearing the important network of intimate, informal social controls traditionally associated with living closely with others.[9]

(3) The problem of developing and maintaining common or shared values (the basic ingredient for cohesion) is made vastly more difficult by industrialization and urbanization. Society, as MacIver indicates, does not need common rules for everything; and the limits of incompatibility of beliefs and values that can exist in cultures short of disappearance of a meaningful system are, as we know, rather wide ones. But we also know that without "a set of

---

[7] Robert Morris and Martin Rein, "Emerging Patterns in Community Planning," in *Social Work Practice, 1963,* Columbia University Press, 1963.

[8] Roland L. Warren, *The Community in America,* Rand McNally, 1963, p. 75.

[9] Lynd, *op. cit.,* pp. 82–83.

common understandings" among the members of society there would be chaos. As Lindeman indicates, "diversity 'gone wild,' uncoördinated and divisive, leads to chaos. Difference carries value only when viewed in the light of probable unity. Where there is no prospect of functional unity, diversity becomes a liability, not an asset." [10] The question is how wide and deep do these understandings need to be? In a useful analysis of the sociology of Louis Wirth, Richard Bendix points out that Wirth,[11] while desiring to enlarge the sphere of individual freedom, saw the central focus of sociology as the analysis of consensus. This latter he conceived as perhaps the central problem of our society, since its attainment is made increasingly difficult by the forces unleashed in urban society. In one of his last addresses Wirth referred to the condition of mass society which militates against that consensus reached by continued negotiation, persuasion, and compromise.[12] At another point Wirth suggested that in modern society "agreement is neither imposed by coercion nor fixed by custom so as no longer to be subject to discussion. It is always partial and developing and has constantly to be won. It results from the interpenetration of views based upon mutual consent and upon feeling as well as thinking together." [13]

What is being suggested here is that while we have no answer for the question of how much diversity or how much unity there is to be in the ideal community, forces at present are dissipating "common values" or "common understandings"; that persistence of such a trend would lead to a chaotic community; and that emphasis today, as Wirth implies, can well be placed on means of obtaining consensus, for this latter is "always partial and developing and has constantly to be won." Or as another writer has said, "Both normative consensus and individual conformity can be maintained only by incessant effort and active social evaluation." [14]

[10] T. V. Smith and Eduard C. Lindeman, *The Democratic Way of Life*, Mentor Books, 1951, p. 144.

[11] Richard Bendix, "Social Theory and Social Action in the Sociology of Louis Wirth," *American Journal of Sociology*, LIX (May 1954), 526.

[12] *Ibid.*, p. 529.

[13] *Ibid.*, p. 527.

[14] Robin M. Williams, Jr., *American Society*, Knopf, 1952, p. 353.

(4) The tendency for large subgroups to develop cohesion as separate entities in the community produces social tension, potentially dangerous in any community. When one finds ethnic or cultural groups constituting themselves psychological and sociological islands in the community, one finds not a static situation but one which inevitably must lead to increased tension between these groups or a serious attempt at organizing their interdependence. Robin Williams makes this point when he writes with characteristic caution:

> The possibilities for the smooth functioning of such a "mosaic" society are not, to say the least, very great in the modern world. Diverse subcultures have been linked together through the extraordinary development of transportation and communication, occasioning widespread mutual awareness of other groups and their cultures, as well as much direct personal contact. *This awareness of differing or similar values and specific patterns of conduct is rarely a matter of emotional neutrality;* the presence of conflicting normative standards is typically not taken in a purely "factual" way, but on the contrary produces some degree of social tension. When originally segmental groups interact with others and begin to lose their closed, quasi-autonomous character, what were at first conflicts between the standards of different groups tend to become intrapersonality conflicts for the individual.[15]

Increasingly groups will find it difficult to live apart, they must by the force of circumstances interact, and the problem is whether they can organize this interaction in such a way as will minimize tension (both group and individual) and increase capacity to function with some degree of unity in respect to common concerns.

(5) Democracy will weaken, if not perish, unless supporting institutions are supported and new institutions (to meet new ways of living) are developed. Democracy implies decentralization and distribution of power; the kind of unity which supports diversity; participation in conference and discussion to produce genuine consensus; the right to be a part, and influence the direction, of the social life of the community. Sir Oliver Frank suggests that

[15] *Ibid.,* pp. 350–351 (italics supplied).

democracy is derived from three basic ideas: "the value of the individual human personality, a real sense of belonging, and the basic like-mindedness of society which is the root of democratic life." [16] As already implied, forces in mass society are tending to weaken this idea in practice—"the political nonexistent" has no vital share in the conduct of public affairs. Participation in municipal affairs in the large cities of North America is consistently meager, and the separation of the average man from the larger issues of national and world affairs seems to increase daily. The movement in almost all major forms of association (e.g., industry, labor unions, etc.) is toward centralization and amalgamation, and this tends to decrease the significance of the role of the individual in these associations. The huge metropolitan centers grow and the individual continues to shrink. The question of whether such trends are inevitable, or whether new forms that will provide opportunity for the practice of democracy will arise, is surely a crucial one for our day.

(6) The barriers that prevent active participation in the direction of social change inhibit personal development. While there exist in most urban communities a host of reform agencies and associations, the fact remains, as many studies have shown, that only a small percentage of the people in any community participate in these. These associations have not been able to develop a structure and frame of reference which is hospitable to large numbers of the "political nonexistent." And yet to be denied such opportunities shrinks and limits the horizon of the individual. In suggesting criteria for mental health, one writer has stated as the first criterion "active adjustment or attempts at mastering of his environment, as distinct both from his inability to adjust and from his indiscriminate adjustment through passive acceptance of environmental conditions." [17] Masses of people are frustrated at this point because they

[16] Quoted in "Management and Human Relations," address by William Blackie to 9th Annual Congress on Industrial Health, American Medical Association, Chicago, January 8, 1949.

[17] Marie Jahoda, "Towards a Social Psychology of Mental Health," Research Clinic for Human Problems, New York University, 1950, p. 12. See also Alexander H. Leighton, *My Name Is Legion*, Basic Books, 1959, pp. 157–159.

have failed to find an adequate means (method or association) through which they can express their views with security. And consistent blocking at this point has resulted, not just in frustration, but also in an apathetic acceptance of this situation as inevitable.

Now the above points constitute facets of a central problem in our society and in rapidly changing cultures in less-developed countries. This is the problem of man's loss of his essential human dignity. For surely man is being overwhelmed by forces of which he is only dimly aware, which subjugate him to a role of decreasing importance and present him with problems with which he has no means to cope. Aspects of this central problem are the difficulty of full expression of a democratic philosophy and the threats to the mental health of individual members of societies such as we have described.

Given the particular value-orientation of social work and the situation in the community as interpreted here, use of the process of community organization follows as an inevitable attempt to apply social work objectives in the community. Were the social milieu entirely different, a rather different expression of social work would undoubtedly appear in the community. But the present conception of community organization clearly emerges from these two factors, namely, the values sought and the context in which they are sought. An interesting question, which we will have to leave to the student of the sociology of social work, is whether if the social situation were quite different, the values or the objectives of social work would not be quite different. Society and the objectives of any group in society unquestionably interact and influence one another. And the dominant values sought by social work may arise simply from a temporary tendency in society to neglect these values. This may be. It does not detract, however, from our main thesis, which is that community organization is an attempt to develop and expand practices which seem to nourish a particular conception of life in a society all too prone to ignore these values.

ASSUMPTIONS REGARDING METHOD

We have attempted to identify values and problems, and have now to examine the third aspect of our frame of reference, namely, the assumptions which condition method. Methods may stem from what is scientifically valid, from what is feasible, from what "one can get away with," from what one can make work. But if means are to be consistent with ends, methods must arise from a particularization of objectives in any setting. Thus casework, group work, and community organization may have common and basic objectives, but as problems in a particular setting (with an individual or with a group or in a community) are dealt with, these objectives have to be focused, and appropriate means of achieving them have to be developed. In other words, a particular frame of reference must be developed for each setting. This frame of reference brings together certain assumptions that stem from one's general conception of values and one's analysis of the problem. In the community setting the assumptions which influence method may be stated as follows:

(1) We assume communities of people can develop capacity to deal with their own problems. This implies that communities of people, even those in situations which many people feel hopeless, can develop attitudes and skills which permit them to work effectively at the task of shaping their community more adequately to meet their needs. Angell's study of integration in American cities [18] suggests marked differences in the manner in which communities have been able to mobilize their resources to deal with problems in the community. This difference is sometimes a matter of chance, but we assume here that deliberate effort by the lower-ranking cities could gradually eradicate many of these differences. The progress made by many neighborhood councils suggests how a whole neighborhood of depressed people has been able to come to grips with many of its problems. Many of the councils have

[18] Robert C. Angell, "The Moral Integration of American Cities," *American Journal of Sociology*, LVII (July 1951), Part 2.

suffered from lack of skill and capacity to organize, yet a British observer studying such councils in the United States has said:

> Even where actual local participation by membership in the Council is at its lowest, public meetings have been held for the discussion of such topics as housing, sanitation, health, and recreation, and some degree of interest has been aroused. . . . It becomes a factor in the common daily life of the area. . . . (It) may render a very important service by creating in a depressed minority group in a "less-chance area" a sense of power and worthwhileness.[19]

Even in depressed neighborhoods, people have shown capacity to function as a unit. In functional communities, such as welfare communities, the record is quite clear, and where consideration has been given to development of skill in coöperative work, the achievements over a period of time have been considerable.

Perhaps a notable example of people's capacity to function effectively as a community comes from Africa, where a British Colonial officer describes the change in the way of life of one tribe. He describes their way of life as he first knew them in the following way:

> Their towns and villages are little more than fishing settlements along the sides of the creeks. From May to October, the season of the rains, the little dry land there is is almost submerged and all the houses there are depressing and dark and squalid, a state of affairs which has, over a period of years, engendered in the Ilajes a state of complete lethargy and apathy, so that now the average Ilaji is interested in doing little beyond the minimum of work and in sitting and drinking palm wine and illicit gin, and in making an occasional expedition to catch a few fish when he is hungry.

Later this tribe had difficulty with the administrative officer, and was forced to move to a much less suitable site, but the change—plus a religious conversion—set them to work at building their new village. The new life is described by the same, but somewhat surprised, Colonial officer thus:

[19] Elizabeth Handasyde, *City or Community*, The National Council of Social Service, 1949, pp. 48–49.

They have organized themselves for working and everyone has his or her job; one party of women may be trading at a certain market, where they will go by canoe, taking fish and selling it and buying other types of food, cloth, salt, or kerosene; others will be cutting wood for the fish-drying sheds; some are washing clothes, weaving cloth or dyeing it; some are preparing fish for drying and some are working in the drying sheds. The men are mostly engaged in fishing in the sea, for which they have some twenty large canoes. The children are taken in a hall by one or two of the more educated Apostles and are taught to read and write and to sing hymns. They also get their daily task of mending nets or some other petty job. . . . All the village organization is communal, and is run by a committee of about ten senior men, who are the trustees of the church. Those who are married live in their own houses and draw their food from the central ration store daily and cook it at home; for the others there is a central cookhouse and the food is drawn cooked according to the messes of workers. There is a tailors' shop with some ten Singer treadle-type sewing machines, and anyone whose clothes are a little worn gets sent for a new lot. There is also a separate washing and ironing house, run like a laundry; there is, too, a carpenter's shop and net-making parties. The really astonishing thing about all this is the ready and willing manner in which everyone goes about doing his or her job, which is a complete antithesis to the other Ilajes. As far as one can see there is no question of compulsion, merely the fact that they have found that by hard work they can find satisfaction and a better way of life. Everyone who has gone with me to this village has been incredulous of the whole thing, thinking that Africans could never develop on these lines unaided, but it is indubitably a fact that this has been organized all by themselves, even despite the fact of there being only some half-dozen who have gone to school, and none of these has read above Standard V, and, moreover, the organization is something of which no efficiency expert should be ashamed.[20]

(2) We assume people want change and can change. The tendency is to assume that all people are contented with the *status quo*, do not want change, and will resist change. But surely the evidence is not only that communities of people constantly change their ways of life but are rather consistently interested in "making

[20] C. E. E. B. Simpson, "An African Village Undertakes Community Develop-Education, II (December 1950), 7–9.

things a little better." This will to change is often paralyzed by those social forces which, as Toynbee suggests, present a challenge which is so overwhelming that retreat is the only possible response. In such circumstances apathy, indifference, and reliance on the security of the *status quo* are inevitable. But our assumption here is that if such blocks to free thinking and feeling are removed, all people everywhere will participate in changes which promise to meet their communal needs more adequately.

This is supported in part by Spicer when he says:

It has become something of a commonplace to say, "People resist change," but a generalization that has many more facts to support it is the opposite: "People accept change." The notion that people tend to resist rather than accept change may be a special idea of our era, formulated by those who are especially conscious of cultural differences or by those who are engaged in trying to bring about change. To the latter, certainly, the fact of resistance is more striking than acceptance. The truth is, however, that people everywhere constantly change their ways. Language, domestic animal breeds, tools, ways of growing crops, methods of curing, and forms of political organization have changed steadily through the centuries, not only among Europeans but also among the Congolese, the Japanese, the Chinese, and all the other peoples of the earth. No generation seems to behave precisely like a former generation. Rates of change, comparing one people with another or one aspect of culture with another, show great differences, but the outstanding fact of constant change nevertheless remains. . . . It seems possible, for instance, despite our ignorance, to support the following generalizations: people resist changes that appear to threaten basic securities; they resist proposed changes they do not understand; they resist being forced to change.[21]

(3) We assume that people should participate in making, adjusting, or controlling the major changes taking place in their communities. This is not to suggest that changes cannot take place without voluntary participation of people. Clearly the opposite is true. Nor is it assumed that any neighborhood group or welfare council can control all the forces that impinge on the collective

---

[21] Edward H. Spicer, ed., *Human Problems in Technological Change*, Russell Sage Foundation, 1952, pp. 17–18. See also Dr. P. J. A. ter Hoeven, *Attitude Change: A Dynamic Process*, Ministry for Social Work, The Hague, 1964, pp. 21–29.

lives of these people. Rather it is that people should have an opportunity to organize to secure their own communal goals and to plan the adjustments which must be made to changes over which they have no control, and to regulate as far as possible their own communities, be they geographic or functional. The need and right to participate in this way is based on the subassumptions that (1) man grows and fulfills himself as he participates in the regulation of his own life, (2) unless man so participates, he becomes entirely subjected to the whim of forces which leave him socially and politically isolated and his life meaningless, and (3) without such participation, democracy has no life or vitality.

(4) We assume that changes in community living that are self-imposed or self-developed have a meaning and a permanence that imposed changes do not have. "Man, in so far as he acts on nature to change it, changes his own nature," said Hegel. In the community, people as they define and work towards their goals, modify and develop attitudes and capacities consistent with these goals, so that the culture as a whole adjusts to the changes that are taking place. The dangers of adjustment to rapid and imposed changes have been persistently emphasized, especially by anthropologists, who see the intricate web of social organization the whole of which is affected by change in any part. It is not that such changes cannot be imposed and made permanent; it is that a community without any sense of participating in, or conscious planning of adjusting to, imposed changes, may become completely disoriented. Margaret Mead writes on this point:

If, in order to use a certain type of machine, it is necessary to adopt all the attitudes towards punctuality of Western factories and school systems, absorbing this alien type of education may act selectively within the new culture, so that only the deviant or only the obedient and frightened learn, and the gifted and creative may turn away. An alien technology, supported by forms of education and interpersonal relations which are also alien, is likely to separate the practitioner of the new skill from his cultural roots, prevent the new practice from becoming integrated in the living habits of the mass of the people, and produce populations who are confused and disoriented because they do not participate meaningfully in the new forms of their society. We see this happening every day in workers who emigrate from country to city, from a peasant to an industrial country, who learn to comply with the alien ritual of factory or clinic, but who are themselves lost and disoriented.[22]

(5) We assume that a "holistic approach" can deal successfully with problems with which a "fragmented approach" cannot cope. This implies that a neighborhood council in changing the character of its neighborhood can do more to combat delinquency than any specific program such as recreation; or that a welfare council can do more to solve social problems by developing a coördinated attack on these than can separate social agencies working apart from each other. Most of the problems of the community have multiple roots. A single specialized approach to the problem is often of limited value. The community's effort to cope with the problem and/or its roots often creates those changes in attitude necessary to any successful approach to the problem. Thus the effort to work coöperatively at the problem in its total setting may be the most significant step in the solution of the problem.

(6) We assume that democracy requires coöperative participation and action in the affairs of the community, and that people must learn the skills which make this possible. Between individuals in the community there must be active participation in a communication process which makes possible the identification of common goals and areas for collective action. Without this, democracy is threatened.

Since consensus conditions and is the product of the participation of persons in a common life, the limits of consensus are marked by the range of effective communication. Consensus may disintegrate because communication between the individuals and the groups who are expected to act collectively is reduced to a minimum. As John Dewey has pointed out, "Everything which bars freedom and fullness of communication sets up barriers which divide human beings into sects and cliques, into

[22] Margaret Mead (ed.), *Cultural Patterns and Technical Change*, UNESCO, Paris, 1953, p. 309.

antagonistic sects and factions, and the democratic way of life is undermined." [23]

But such communication is seldom a matter of chance, it requires motivation and skill to initiate and sustain. Therefore people need practice and expert help in establishing and maintaining democratic institutions in the community.

(7) We assume that frequently communities of people need help in organizing to deal with their needs, just as many individuals require help in coping with their individual problems. The help required by communities, as with individuals, may be of many different kinds. It may be need for refinancing, for advice on road construction, a program for the school system, recreational program, etc. While all these may be necessary and desirable, our assumption is that most communities need help in organizing themselves to cope with the problems in their midst, so that not all decisions are made by a small group at city hall or by the representatives of a few agencies but represent the real desires of the people. Some communities have been fairly effective in operating without help, but most communities need help in this respect, and many would function better if such help were available. In essence, the assumption here is that while people have resources and capacities, they may often need professional help in finding ways to mobilize these effectively in the modern world.

This brief outline of assumptions that impinge on method will probably suffice to emphasize and supplement other statements of assumptions throughout the book. And it may suggest the foundation from which community organization develops its unique character. Based on values common to social work, it sees these values thwarted in modern community developments, and seeks therefore to develop an approach that is as realistic and consistent as possible with its objectives. It posits, therefore, certain assumptions which seem to emerge from analysis of its values and the problems in the community. These assumptions condition the nature

[23] Bendix, *loc. cit.*

of community organization, the methods used by the worker in the field, and the principles applicable in the process. Every step in procedure—identification of goals, diagnosis of the problem present, and assumptions regarding what are the resources and needs available for dealing with this problem in light of goals—must be constantly reëxamined in view of fresh knowledge and new insights. For all three are interrelated aspects of the foundation from which community organization emerges. It has a certain value preference for dealing with the problems of the community. This preference and the problem it seeks to solve lead to a set of assumptions affecting method (which we have attempted to identify) which constitute a framework or a frame of reference for community organization and determine its nature and method. *Community organization* is, then, a process by which a community identifies its needs or objectives, orders (or ranks) these needs or objectives, develops the confidence and will to work at these needs or objectives, finds the resources (internal and/or external) to deal with these needs or objectives, takes action in respect to these, and in so doing extends and develops coöperative and collaborative attitudes and practices in the community.

LIMITATIONS

We should now be able to return briefly, but with profit, to deal with some of the contrary views expressed at the beginning of this chapter. Some of these viewpoints have already been dealt with, by implication at least, for it should be apparent that this conception of community organization is not designed as a cure-all for the problems of our day, but is an experimental approach, resting on quite tentative foundations, to deal with special aspects of the problem of social organization; that it is not a substitute for a political system, but a supplement to it; that it does not deny the need for individual differences, for conflicting ideas, for tension with respect to competing proposals, but claims that without an arena for the development of some common understandings and agreements, individualism and conflict may run wild and social disruption may ensue. This may be made clearer as we deal briefly with the critical views more directly.

With respect to the first criticism, it is claimed that too great emphasis is placed on coöperation, on the gentler values of the middle class with its desire that "things run smoothly and peacefully," and the value of group, as against individual, thought and effort. Such a view ignores the point that on his own, mass man stands to be completely submerged by complex forces which he does not understand and over which he has no control. If he is to have anything to say about his future, he must join with others to gather the strength necessary to influence in any significant way the conditions under which he will live now and in the future. In this very effort he may not only achieve such an influence, but may as an individual acquire the sense of worthwhileness and develop the capacities that make him a mature citizen with dignity, rights, and responsibilities. Without deprecating the value of individualism, we can say with Murphy:

Individualism is so ingrained in our own society that it is impossible for us to imagine that personality might be at its richest where group identification is strongly accented, and where people stress the things they have in common, not their distinctive differences. . . . There is a place for individuality even in the sharing of a homogeneous task.[24]

The values of freedom and consensus, of individualism and community are neither contrary nor separate. But it is easy to stress freedom of enterprise, freedom to hold property, freedom of religion, and to forget these are sometimes accompanied with the isolation, loneliness, squalor, and a sense of ineffectiveness, in which matters the individual may have little choice. It is widely recognized that, as MacIver said years ago,

Community is simply common life, and that common life is more or less adequate as it more or less completely fulfills in a social harmony the

[24] Gardner Murphy, *Personality, A Biosocial Approach to Origins and Structure,* Harper & Row, 1947, p. 909.

needs and personalities of its members, according as it more or less completely takes up into itself the necessary differences which individuality implies, so that they become differences within a unity and not contradictions of that unity . . . socialization and individualism are two sides of a single process.[25]

If our analysis of current social forces is even partially correct, it permits error, when action is contemplated, in the direction of communal thinking, for many industrial societies are so highly individualistic that the philosophy "if each before his own door sweeps, the village will be clean" is dominant. In such a society freedom runs riot, and the devil takes the hindmost. Again, as Louis Wirth said: "Without some measure of agreement among the members of a society, there would be chaos. But without the freedom of the individual to enter into agreement with other members of his community, there would be tyranny." [26] It is our view that individual freedom is possible only in a community in which there is also some unity, some consensus, some conception of common values. These latter are missing in many communities, and as we have implied, development of common values is an achievement which has constantly to be won. Therefore, when we assume that communities must be constantly seeking and sharpening the area of "common understandings," we are not assuming diminution of individual freedom, but rather pressing for one of the conditions which make freedom possible, realistic, and meaningful.

Further, to stress coöperation does not mean elimination of tension and conflict, both of which are essential aspects of a dynamic society. Within the neighborhood council, the welfare council, the council of churches, the council of manufacturers, there will be the constant struggle of ideas, of competing programs, of individuals for recognition. But this struggle will go on within a framework of common agreement and common purpose. In the larger community, the struggle between different functional com-

[25] R. M. MacIver, *Society—Its Structure and Changes*, R. Long & R. R. Smith, 1933, pp. 167, 214.
[26] Bendix, *loc. cit.*

munities will be carried on, but as skills in conference and collaborative work increase, this struggle will be less irrational and explosive and more considerate of conflicting points of view, more disposed to seek consensus, and where this latter is not possible, more tolerant of the rights of both majorities and minorities. As small towns and urban neighborhood communities learn to work together in their councils and community associations, and as functional communities in urban areas learn to collaborate, there may develop that basic like-mindedness that makes diversity within unity a reality.

The second strand of criticism is that workers in this field interfere with communities and their affairs when their help has not been requested and further, that they manipulate people and events to secure their own private ends. Now in social casework it is generally assumed that help cannot profitably be given until the client is ready and willing to use and accept help. This applies to community organization with one important modification. To wait until a highly disorganized neighborhood or a number of competitive welfare agencies asks for help in developing a coöperative organization would be to wait in vain. Therefore community organization seeks to create the awareness of need—of need, not for external help, but for self-movement. In some cases, as with individuals, such awareness may not develop in the community or neighborhood, and there is no possibility of initiating community organization at the level at which it is being described in this book. When the sense of need does not arise, the worker in this field does not press further. But community organization clearly implies the effort to have people look searchingly at their communities for common needs and objectives. This may be called "interference" as long as the term does not imply imposition of ideas. It is an attempt to motivate people to act if certain conditions are present—if the people feel no such conditions exist, there is no basis for action. The disposition of the worker in community organization is to stimulate people to think and become aware of their common life.

As to manipulation, it is quite clear that the worker who manipulates ideas, people, and events secretly and maliciously does not operate within the framework outlined in the main body of this chapter. What the worker seeks to do is to awaken and encourage local initiative, feelings of responsibility, skill in participation, self-development, and growth. Interference, beyond that described above, or manipulation in the sense of secret covenants and use of others for one's own purpose, is quite contrary to the goals implicit in the conception of community organization as we have defined it here.

The third level of criticism is that community organization involves a slow process, the results of which can be felt only in long terms. The critics argue that problems of "cultural lag" are tumbling over our heads and smothering us, and that some quicker method is required. Here we must emphasize again that social work (or one of its specializations, community organization) is not to be considered a panacea or a cure-all, or the only way to deal with problems of the community. It may well be that groups of scientists and/or groups of expert planners are required to deal with immediate and long-term problems of restructuring required in mass society. But it is submitted that this procedure, without such participation as community organization implies, may speed the loss of values of belonging. But with such participation, the work of scientists and experts can be greatly facilitated. That is to say, permitting imposition of plans by small groups may provide for alleviation of some problems but increase the tendency toward centralization, which already endangers individual freedom and moves man even further away from a sense of control over his own destiny. If, however, we have a society in which there are large citizens' groups planning in respect to their community needs (either in geographic or functional communities), we have a network of democratic institutions which may be used by the planners for consultation. Even if they are not so used, these citizen groups may still constitute a potential force to criticize the work of planners, to adapt the results of planning to their own circumstances, to integrate it into their own planning. In England the

National Council of Social Service, and in Canada the Canadian Welfare Council, constitute such communities (in these cases the welfare communities) which are often consulted by government planners in respect to welfare measures but which reserve the right to criticize and mobilize opinion for or against the measures prepared by the planners. Such procedures seem essential for preservation of democracy. And while there will undoubtedly need to be large-scale and technical planning, such planning without the checks implied by the community organization process may in the long run prove disastrous.

Actually, it is premature to advocate any one method of work in the community to the exclusion of all others. There are those who see the need for revitalization of the political system, or decentralization of industry, or restructuring of urban life, or development of primary group life, etc. All these may make a contribution, and each has specific objectives in mind. A good deal of experimentation is required before we can state with certainty what methods and instruments will nourish and sustain those values which a community of people believe important. But community organization is a process which, however slow, deserves to be thoroughly tried and evaluated.

We have already indicated that community organization is not a science; presumably it is an art—the art of building consensus within a democratic framework. But this art, if such it can be called, can utilize many of the contributions of the social sciences, and can benefit greatly by the kind of disciplined study social sciences can make of community organization projects. These latter, indeed, provide a common ground for social workers and social scientists. As Robert Lynd states:

The central assumption becomes that men want to do, to be, to feel certain identifiable things . . . as they live along together; and the derivative assumption regarding the role of social science is that its task is to find out ever more clearly what these things are that human beings persist in wanting, and how these things can be built into culture. If man's cravings are ambivalent, if he is but sporadically rational and intelligent, the task of social science becomes the discovery of what forms of culturally-structured learned behavior can maximize opportunities for rational behavior where it appears to be essential for human well-being, and at the same time provide opportunity for expression of his deep emotional spontaneities where those, too, are important.[27]

Thus it may be that the social workers and social scientists may find an area of mutual interest. The former may concentrate on the practical problem of initiating the community organization process, the latter in developing instruments for measuring the effect of social work processes and undertaking such measurements. But both may coöperate in developing theory, in establishing experimental and research designs, and in the refinement of techniques and procedures.

[27] Lynd, *op. cit.*, p. 200. For an interesting approach to rational change, see Milton Lebowitz, *The Process of Planned Community Change,* D.S.W. dissertation, Columbia University, 1961, University Microfilms, Ann Arbor, Mich.

Part Two

Factors Impinging on Community Organization Methods

4

Some Hypotheses About Community Life

BEFORE we proceed to identification of principles of community organization and the role of the professional worker in this field, we shall summarize some hypotheses about community life and about the process of planning which will help us to establish the principles. As we have indicated in the previous chapter, we begin with a frame of reference which provides a guide for community organization effort. But within this framework, that which is feasible is determined in considerable degree by the nature of the situation, the worker's understanding of it, and his skill in working in this situation. Just as the caseworker must know a good deal about individual psychodynamics and the process of interviewing, so the worker in community organization must know a good deal about the forces in the community which make for or hinder community integration, and about the techniques of planning.

It is at this point that the social sciences could contribute a good deal to the social worker, for the former provide tested hypotheses which suggest to the social worker insights and clues which influence the steps he may take in seeking to reach his objectives. Social science theories are not, of course, the sole determinant of method, this latter being dependent on the values and assumptions mentioned in previous chapters. But these two—social science theory and social work values—serve as the codeterminants of method. Indeed, the constant modification of social work method is partly (if not largely) the result of social science research. The influence is consistent and significant, but the changes are made within the framework social work has established for itself. In other words, social workers, like other professionals, are constantly seeking more effective ways of performing their task, and draw heavily upon the social sciences for help in this respect.

What we are concerned about in this chapter, then, is an understanding of some aspects of community life which will help us in shaping principles and methods of work in community organization. There are innumerable textbooks on the community, and it is not our purpose to summarize these here. What we will do is to indicate briefly some aspects of community life which have implications for community integration, as we have previously defined that term. We wish here to provide at least a partial answer to the question: What do we need to know about the community which will help those who are concerned about developing a kind of community life in which people feel a sense of belonging, participate in the life of the community, achieve a set of common understandings, and work coöperatively at their common problems? Again, of necessity the factors we identify will have to be more in the nature of an illustrative sample than a complete listing, but they should serve to suggest the variety of factors about which there must be awareness. While we will deal primarily with the geographic communities, readers interested primarily in functional communities will recognize many points which have significance for their work. Almost everything that is said about subgroups, leadership, symbols and rituals, apathy, etc. has relevance not just for the community council or the neighborhood council but for the recreation council, the adult education council, or the welfare council.

THE MULTIPLE-FACTOR THEORY

There is no single factor which, by itself, makes for community integration. The community is a complex whole, all parts of which are related, interact, and influence one another. To select one part of this whole and identify it as the primary cause of integration or disintegration is not possible. Just as we have come to recognize the fact that there are multiple causes of discrimination, delinquency, crime, or economic progress, we are led by the weight of logic and evidence to recognize that we cannot pluck out a single force or circumstance and attribute the attainment of "maturity" in the individual or community to that single factor.

Even accepting the "multiple theory" of causation, it is difficult to identify the group of forces which produces community integration. In his study of "The Moral Integration of American Cities," Angell writes:

It is one thing to demonstrate that cities are different with respect to moral integration; it is quite another to determine what the causal factors are . . . for cities differ in size, in age, in background of their population, in the natural resources they have available, in mobility, in history and tradition, in leadership, and in many other respects. But even if some of these could be identified as significant, . . . there is the problem of whether a particular feature, even if shown to be related to moral integration, is cause or effect of that integration. For instance, it can be argued that the organizations possessed by a city are influenced by the degree of solidarity of the community as well as being a cause of that solidarity.[1]

This evidence points to both the complexity of causal factors and the difficulty of identifying them as cause rather than effect.

[1] Robert C. Angell, "The Moral Integration of American Cities," *American Journal of Sociology*, LVII (July 1951), Part 2.

Angell does indicate relationships between "moral integration" and certain factors tested in the communities in which he carried on his studies. He does not, as pointed out, suggest these to be cause-and-effect relationships, but their association or lack of association may be significant. For example, high mobility rates, a heterogeneous population, a high crime index, a low welfare index, a large population, tend to be present in the cities of low moral integration. On the other hand, economic development, absentee ownership, church membership, the percentage of Roman Catholics in the total population, and other factors were found not to be significant factors. The result is, therefore, a few modest generalizations such as the following: the greater the mixture of races and nationalities, the more difficult is moral integration; the economic factor is unimportant for moral integration; mobility scores increase as the integration scores fall; social problems tend to multiply, not only absolutely but relatively, with increase in community size.[2]

Such generalizations are hardly unexpected and suggest that we are far from identifying all, or even the major, factors of importance here. Some of these will emerge as individual studies proceed, and will later require collating and testing. For example, is physical distance between neighbors important? To what extent? In what kinds of communities? A report of one such study indicates:

Perhaps most striking is the way in which friendships and group-formation within this homogeneous community were determined by physical distance and functional distance, i.e., positional relationships and features of design that determine which people will meet by chance. The units of physical distance which showed up in the study as important were incredibly small, for example, the difference between houses 22 feet and 44 feet apart; such physical and functional distances are shown to play a significant part in the creation of social isolates.[3]

It is likely that the many on-going studies in the social sciences will

[2] *Ibid.*, pp. 15–21.
[3] Isabel Menzies, review of *Social Processes in Informal Groups,* by Leon Festinger, Stanley Schachter, and Kurt Black, in *Human Relations,* IV (1951), 104. See also William H. Whyte, Jr., *The Organization Man,* Doubleday, 1957, pp. 365–386.

eventually permit testing of hypotheses about community integration in a variety of communities.

For the moment, however, we have to recognize that while there are many factors which make for, or prevent, community integration, we can only generalize loosely about these, and can say only in specific situations, and after careful study, which forces are of major importance in a given situation. It seems not unreasonable to suggest the hypothesis that instead of single factors, there are clusters of factors that interlock and reinforce one another and influence the degree of community integration.

Thus an economic system may stimulate great differences in economic power, competitiveness, special symbols by which status is recognized, rigid class and caste structure, a particular kind of educational system, etc. But the economic system is in turn influenced by these same factors; indeed, it is difficult to separate these from the economic system. All these aspects of community life are inextricably linked together, and while a change in one aspect will affect other aspects, the reaction to change in one area may well be resistance, rather than adaptation, in other areas. The assumption that once prevailed in the Soviet Union, for example, that if collective farms were enforced, people would soon adapt their customs and habits to the collective life, proved quite unfounded, and enforced participation in collective farms was, as a policy, in effect abandoned.[4]

The problem of identifying forces which make for community integration is one of considerable complexity. While we will in the pages to follow suggest certain factors which appear to be significant, it must not be forgotten that we cannot with assurance state that these factors are fundamental in all situations. Nor should it be forgotten that these factors have only partial significance when taken singly: it is this group of factors, together with others, that influences community integration.

[4] Harry Schwartz, "Soviet Heeds Malthus as well as Karl Marx," *New York Times*, Sunday, September 20, 1953, p. 4E.

SOCIAL STRUCTURE

The social structure of a community is undoubtedly positively related to the degree of integration existing or possible in the community. It is easy to see the marked differences in the social structure of the small coöperative village in Israel and that of an American industrial city, and the differences in attitude and behavior which seem to stem from the differences in organization and orientation of these two communities. Similarly, obvious differences can be seen between the "company town" in which almost all the employment, housing, and work are provided by one industry and the coöperative fishing village where each owns a share of the fishing ship and the cannery, or the highly competitive industrial town, and the old New England town in which kinship relations predominate. Each of these is structured differently with somewhat different value systems, customs and mores, and degree of integration.

But even in towns and cities that appear similar, as Angell has shown, there are significant differences in integration, and some of these differences may well stem from unique (but hardly distinguishable) social structures. An interesting example of the different effects produced by social structure (in community response to identical stimuli) is given in an analysis of activity in two towns of about the same size, and within fifty miles of each other, in southwestern United States. The study reported a number of similar projects initiated in these two towns, and a description is given of the development in each town. The consistency of the action within each of the two towns is high, and the following description of a street-paving project may be considered typical:

The streets of Rimrock were in bad repair in the fall of 1950. That summer a construction company had brought much large equipment into the area to build and gravel a section of a state highway which runs through the village. Before this company left, taking its equipment with it, villagers, again acting through the Church organization, decided that the village should avail itself of the opportunity and have the town's streets graveled. This was discussed in the Sunday priesthood meeting and announced at the Sunday sacrament meeting. A meeting was called for Monday evening, and each household was asked to send a representative. The meeting was well attended, and although not every family had a member present, practically all were represented at least by proxy. There was considerable discussion, and it was finally decided to pay 800 dollars for the job, which meant a 20-dollar donation from each family. The local trader paid a larger amount, and, within a few days after the meeting, the total amount was collected. Only one villager raised objections to the proceedings. Although he was a man of importance locally, he was soon silenced by a much poorer man who invoked Mormon values of progress and coöperation and pledged to give 25 dollars, which was 5 dollars above the norm.[5]

The report of action in the adjoining town of Homestead reads as follows:

During the winter of 1949–50 the construction company which was building the highway through Rimrock was also building a small section of highway north of Homestead. The construction company offered to gravel the streets of Homestead center if the residents who lived in the village would coöperatively contribute enough funds for the purpose. This community plan was rejected by the homesteaders, and an alternative plan was followed. Each of the operators of several of the service institutions—including the two stores, the bar, and the post office—independently hired the construction company truck drivers to haul a few loads of gravel to be placed in front of his own place of business, which still left the rest of the village streets a sea of mud in rainy weather.[6]

In a number of other problems reported, the reaction is similar: the town of Rimrock meeting to discuss the matter finds in conference a method of coöperatively dealing with the problem, while the town of Homestead, a few miles distant, finds coöperative decision, let alone coöperative action, extremely difficult to secure. Why do such profound differences exist between two adjoining towns which, on the surface, appear similar?

[5] Evon Z. Vogt and Thomas F. O'Dea, "A Comparative Study of the Role of Values in Social Action in Two Southwestern Communities," *American Sociological Review*, XVIII (December 1953), 649.
[6] *Ibid.*, p. 650.

What is important are the causes of this marked difference in community action in Rimrock and Homestead. The authors describe it thus:

The stress upon *community coöperation* in Rimrock contrasts markedly with the stress upon *individual independence* found in Homestead. This contrast is one of emphasis, for individual initiative is important in Rimrock, especially in family farming and cattle raising, whereas coöperative activity does occur in Homestead. In Rimrock, however, the expectations are such that one must show his fellows or at least convince himself that he has good cause for *not* committing his time and resources to community efforts, while in Homestead coöperative action takes place *only* after certainty has been reached that the claims of other individuals upon one's time and resources are legitimate. Rimrock was a coöperative venture from the start, and very early the irrigation company, a mutual nonprofit corporation chartered under state law, emerged from the early water association informally developed around—and in a sense within— the Church. In all situations which transcend the capacities of individual families or family combinations, Rimrock Mormons have recourse to coöperative techniques. . . .

The value-stress upon individual independence of action has deep roots in the history of the homesteader group. The homesteaders were part of the westward migration from the hill country of the Southern Appalachians to the Panhandle country of Texas and Oklahoma and from there to the Southwest and California. Throughout their historical experience there has been an emphasis upon a rough and ready self-reliance and individualism, the Jacksonianism of the frontier West. The move to western New Mexico from the South Plains was made predominantly by isolated nuclear families, and Homestead became a community of scattered, individually owned farmsteads—a geographical situation and a settlement pattern which reinforced the stress upon individualism.[7]

The differences in the patterns of behavior and the social organization in these two communities derive from quite different systems of beliefs and values, and these differences have been structured in such a way that the character of each is quite distinct from the other.

What is important for us here is not simply the idea that com-

7 *Ibid.*, pp. 648, 650.

munities are structured differently. For the practitioner in community organization it must also be recognized that this difference in social structure conditions to some extent the degree of social integration, the nature of the response of the community to any community problem, and the manner and pace with which it will deal with such a problem. Like the educator who adapts himself to the need, level, and capacity of a student, the worker in the community must not only recognize differences in social structure but must adapt his methods to these differences.

It may be pointed out here, also, that the social structure of a community constitutes a whole, and that change in any one part of the structure reacts on all other parts. The writer recalls, for example, the efforts toward church union in his home town. The attempt was made to bring two relatively similar Protestant groups into one church. These seemingly like-minded, God-fearing, and friendly people fought with great heat and bitterness over this issue. What was not recognized was that these separate churches supported a good many other aspects of the social structure, such as class structure, historical and national associations, clerical interests, certain "in-group" traditions, etc. The issue was fought on purely theological grounds, but it was quite clear that the churches as separate entities were such, not simply for theological reasons, but also because the separate bodies incorporated many other facets of life about which the members were largely unaware but which were as important as the differences in theology, if not more important. Wilson makes this point when he suggests that integrative processes in the community may be immobilized or blocked because "unrecognized mechanisms in group life . . . resist change. Such resistance may be strong, persistent, and completely inconsistent with the manifest goals and striving of groups."[8] This suggests the intricacies of the social structure and the difficulty of analyzing all the parts, and relationships between parts, which may facilitate or block any proposed change in the community. It

[8] A. T. M. Wilson, "Some Aspects of Social Process," *The Journal of Social Issues*, Supplement Series No. 5 (November 1951), p. 22.

implies also the importance of the people of the community being involved in planning major changes, for they will feel, even though they may not be able to verbalize it well, what changes are desirable, feasible, and at what cost they may be secured. And if the community itself is thoroughly involved in a process of change, the change will take place in the whole community and not just in one part.

Margaret Mead emphasizes the complexity of the problem in the following:

. . . as an individual's behaviour, belief, and attitudes are shared with members of his cultural group, it may be necessary to effect a change in the goals or systems of behaviour of the whole group before any given individual's behaviour will change in some particular respect. . . . No knowledge of the way an individual of a given constitution and capacity may be able to accept or reject change can ever be used alone, without giving due weight to the nature of the culture of which he is a part, and his position in the particular social group within which he lives.[9]

All this is to emphasize the fact that all communities are structured uniquely, although the differences may be small in some instances; that the parts of these structures are closely related, and change in one part affects other parts; that the relationship between parts of a culture is often difficult to recognize and identify; and that planning in respect to change in any part of the community must consider its effect on the whole community.

SOCIOCULTURAL PATTERNS

In every community, certain traditional ways of behaving develop which determine to some extent whether the people will participate actively and coöperatively in community affairs, and determine almost competely the manner in which they will coöperate or resist. This has been implied above but requires some amplification.

[9] Margaret Mead (ed.), *Cultural Patterns and Technical Change*, UNESCO, Paris, 1953, p. 309.

A community study in Greece points out that Greeks are "born into a group," to which group they are tremendously loyal. Further, they are used to coöperating with members of this group and, at great personal sacrifice, will carry out group projects that have meaning for the group. But the government seeking coöperation for large impersonal objectives finds resistance to its ideas.

It (the government) tries to put this coöperation on a par with war, both in the title of its bi-weekly publication, and in the phrasing of its admonition. But the disrupting centralization, the hated interference, remains. "Compulsory free labour" is demanded of the farmers, and there is a whole class of compulsory coöperatives for the betterment of the villages. These are circumvented with the ingenuity born of long experience. However, we also have a recent report of a village where everyone gets up when the church bell rings at four in the morning, to work, without compulsion, on some village project, with pride and enthusiasm. The work is done under the leadership of a villager respected for his ability and disinterestedness. It appears that when the coöperative pattern which is already present is utilized, the villagers will work together for the common welfare.[10]

Most communities have practices which determine which groups will coöperate with certain other groups, on what kind of project, and in what particular way. The writer recalls one community in which almost every project initiated by a community council received full support from every church but the Anglican. At first glance it appeared to be merely the resistance of the Anglican clergyman, but on closer study it was evident that the Anglicans were an exclusive upper-class group who traditionally remained aloof and were particularly suspicious of the Roman Catholic church. In fact, the wise men of the community would say, "This is the way it has always been; if the Roman Catholics come in, the Anglicans stay out." In other communities it will be other churches, other classes, and other groups who will be disposed to stay apart. But most communities have their own peculiar ways of operating, their own conception of what is a "right and proper" method of

[10] *Ibid.*, pp. 111–114. See also Herbert J. Gans, *The Urban Villagers*, The Free Press, 1962, pp. 74–119.

procedure, and their own feelings as to what is a proper pace for movement.

An analysis of committee behavior in four cultures may be instructive at this point.[11] This study shows quite different responsibilities assumed by the chairmen and by committee members and rather different ways of conducting business in committee in China, the United States, the Near East, and South America. What is less easy to recognize is that some differences also exist within the United States and Canada among different groups of people. There is a general impression among progressive educators, for example, that the permissive chairman is the most acceptable chairman. Actually some recent studies have shown that some groups expect more direction from the chairman and are uncomfortable with a permissive leader.[12]

An interesting illustration of cultural influences on behavior in community projects is the degree to which people in most large North American cities act "the congenial, good-hearted guy" on community committees. Often, even on matters on which they have strong contrary feeling, they will support a motion or action simply because "I can't afford not to," "It doesn't look good," "It's going to pass anyway and why should I stick my neck out." One realizes that for many such men this is part of a larger game of getting on in the community, making a good impression, offending no one, building up one's personal reputation. This is consistent with Riesman's observation that business and professional life and play have become extensively fused in American society.[13] Activities formerly sharply isolated from work, such as entertainment, have become part of business relations. Aspects of the personality, such as pleasingness or likability, formerly regarded as irrelevant to work efficiency, have been increasingly called into play in working life.

[11] John Gyr, "Analysis of Committee Member Behavior in Four Cultures," *Human Relations*, IV (1951), 194–195.   195 (1951).
[12] Leonard Berkowitz, "Sharing Leadership in Small Decision-Making Groups," *The Journal of Abnormal and Social Psychology*, XLVIII (April 1953).
[13] David Riesman, *The Lonely Crowd*, Yale University Press, 1952.

The tendency in this culture is to ask in all situations: Did they like me? Did I make a good impression? Am I doing as well as I should?

Another tendency, pointed out in Wolfenstein's article on "The Emergence of Fun Morality," is the current American conviction that life ought to be fun and the resulting efforts that are made to make it so.

Not having fun is not merely an occasion for regret but involves a loss of self-esteem. I ask myself: What is wrong with me that I am not having fun? To admit that one did not have fun when one was expected to, arouses feelings of shame. Where formerly it might have been thought that a young woman who went out a great deal might be doing wrong, currently we would wonder what is wrong with a girl who is not going out. Fun and play have assumed a new obligatory aspect. While gratification of forbidden impulses traditionally aroused guilt, failure to have fun currently occasions lowered self-esteem. One is apt to feel inadequate, impotent, and also unwanted. One fears the pity of one's contemporaries rather than, as formerly, possible condemnation by moral authorities.[14]

These are, of course, merely illustrative of the multiplicity of forces which emerge from, and play upon, the community, influencing the behavior of individuals, relations between individuals, relations between groups, and patterns of behavior in committee, conference, and community life. All these condition a process such as community organization, and constitute social facts which the professional worker must understand and be prepared to cope with.

SUBGROUP RELATIONSHIPS

Subgroups, and the relationship between subgroups, are probably factors which strongly influence community integration. If, for example, one finds in a community a Protestant group whose marked cohesiveness is primarily an aspect of their opposition and hostility to the Roman Catholic group in the same community, there

[14] Martha Wolfenstein, "The Emergence of Fun Morality," *The Journal of Social Issues,* VII (1951), 22.

is a subgroup configuration which makes community integration very difficult, as does also a subcultural pattern which supports "differences" at the expense of "similarities" or which accentuates competitiveness as opposed to coöperation.

It seems likely that physical proximity or coexistence does not, in itself, determine integration or the lack of it. One finds a Polish group in one community isolated and separate from much of the life in the larger community, while in another city the Polish group may live in a particular area, have their own churches and clubs, yet are identified and associated with the life and social organization of the city. If one may assume that coexistence does not in itself make for greater mutual acceptability of subgroups, is it possible to identify factors which do make for greater acceptance, for greater coöperation, for a social climate which supports coöperative attitudes? There is some evidence here to suggest tentative hypotheses at this point.

Eisenstadt's work on immigrant groups in Israel [15] is useful here. His study sought to identify the conditions required to be present if a new immigrant group is to adjust to, and identify with, the larger community of which it is now a part. There are three major factors, apparently, that influence such adjustment. One is internal —within the subgroup. Immigrants who were members of highly cohesive groups (kinship, ethnic, neighborhood, etc.) tended to be more flexible, more disposed to identify with the whole community, more likely to participate in community affairs. This is quite contrary to the usual assumption that strong subgroups make for "in-groups" which develop and maintain their solidarity in opposition to other community groups. Rather, it suggests a theory (plausible from the theory of individual psychology) that the secure and well integrated may have less fear of the "outside world" and more freedom to venture into it than do the insecure. If this were so, it would, of course, suggest that the community organization process

[15] S. N. Eisenstadt, "The Process of Absorption of New Immigrants in Israel," *Human Relations*, V (1952), 223–245.

would flourish best in communities in which there were few weak and many strong subgroups.

A second factor, which will not be reported at length here, relates to the attitudes and practices of government administrative officers who deal with the new groups. Consistency of explanation, of promise, of discipline are factors of importance. Close personal relations, such as the ability and willingness of the officer to identify with the group, to share their problems and their conditions of living, to provide friendliness, are characteristic of government personnel who seemed to facilitate adjustment to, and identification with, the new community.

The third condition of adjustment of the part to the whole—the subgroup to the community—is a group of factors which may be met in varying degrees but of which it may be said that the greater the degree of fulfillment of these conditions the greater degree of community integration. These are:

DEVELOPMENT OF GROUP VALUES AND ASPIRATIONS COMPATIBLE WITH THE COMMON VALUES IN THE COMMUNITY

This implies that the group or subculture will develop values not inconsistent with those prevalent in the community of which it is a part. Thus the Dukhobors, or even the Mennonite group, seldom integrate in Canadian communities because their conception of what is "right, proper, and good" in respect to education, the meaning of community and nationhood, the use of money, differs radically from the ideas of the majority of the people in Canada. Pronounced and doctrinal differences on fundamental issues may be permitted, and subgroups allowed to flourish, but these differences present a substantial block to the development of community integration. A subgroup, however, whose beliefs and practices (with respect to matters of prime importance in the larger community) are not inconsistent with those of the community will, other things being equal, facilitate community integration.

EXTENSION OF THE SCOPE OF ACTIVITIES FROM WITHIN THE GROUP EXCLUSIVELY, TO INCLUDE VARIOUS COMMUNITY-WIDE ACTIVITIES

That is, there will be more opportunity for development of coöperative work if members of a subgroup begin to participate in the activities of the larger community. Activities here may cover a considerable range from reading the local newspaper, listening to local radio programs, to taking part in war-bond drives, salvage collection, clearing areas for playgrounds, etc. Various groups may have their own newspapers, carry on their own activities with little reference to other groups in the community. To the extent that they operate in this way—isolated and exclusive—development of the community organization process will be difficult. There must be some communication between the group and the community, and it is being suggested here that participation by members of various groups in community activities is one way in which such communication may be made meaningful.

THE EXTENT TO WHICH MEMBERS OF SUBGROUPS ARE ORIENTED TOWARDS "REFERENCE GROUPS" IN THE WIDER COMMUNITY AND THE DEGREE TO WHICH THESE "REFERENCE GROUPS" ACCEPT THESE MEMBERS OF SUBGROUPS

A simple example of this is the desire, or lack of desire, of Negro doctors to be members of, and participate in the affairs of, the local medical association; and of equal importance, the desire, or lack of desire, of the local medical association (who, we are assuming, are mostly white) to have these Negro doctors as members. If Negro doctors are oriented in the direction of participation, and if the medical association wants and welcomes them, this, it is being suggested, facilitates integration of the whole Negro group into the community. But if the Negro doctors do not want to belong or if the medical association does not want them, a block to community integration is being set up. This point is one that is often overlooked in community affairs and one hears frequently the dominant groups in session say, "Those Poles (or any minority group) live by themselves, they won't take part in anything." What Eisenstadt is suggesting is that not only must the minority groups want to participate, but the other groups in the community must also want them and be willing to accept them.

THE EXTENT OF DEVELOPMENT OF RELATIONSHIPS OF SUBGROUP MEMBERS WITH "OLDER PRESTIGE" MEMBERS OF THE COMMUNITY

In every community there is probably a special kind of elite— older citizens whose age and status mark them as symbols of importance in the community. To be denied any contact or association with such persons handicaps community integration; and development of such contacts and relationships may facilitate this process. The tours of British monarchs to various Commonwealth countries undoubtedly is arranged by the British government to stimulate integration in the British Commonwealth of Nations.

THE EXTENT TO WHICH THE LARGER COMMUNITY PERMITS FULFILLMENT OF THE ROLE EXPECTATIONS AND ASPIRATIONS OF SUBGROUPS

There are many implications of this concept; let us take one example. Here is a small Jewish group in a largely Gentile community. The former are conscious of their community responsibilities, are aware of the contribution they can make to the larger community, and are anxious to participate in the community chest, the welfare council, the community concert series, etc. Their role-expectations and aspirations are such that they see several of the Jewish group playing a leading role in these endeavors. Presumably the conditions—in the form of these organizations—are present for utilizing the ambitions and services of this group. But if there is resistance by present members of the controlling groups in these organizations to the participation of Jewish people, there will be frustration and withdrawal, *unless* these aspirations can be fulfilled in another way, e.g., by service on subcommittees, by service in other organizations, etc. Or the ambitions of the Jewish group may be modified to the extent that they see themselves concentrating their effort in one organization, and later giving help to the other organizations. Thus if the aspirations of a group are utilized or modified (without rejection), there exist more favorable conditions for integration than might otherwise be the case.

THE EXTENT OF IDENTIFICATION WITH THE LARGER COMMUNITY

This point has already been implied in several others above. But it needs to be said that identification exclusively with the subgroup will prevent integration, whereas identification with the "common life" of the community will facilitate integration.

It appears, therefore, that coexistence of subgroups does not by itself necessarily make for better relations between these groups. Apparently development of coöperative relations between subgroups depends upon a series of complex factors in which the attitudes and behavior of members of all groups—within the group and with respect to other groups—are decisive.[16]

LEADERSHIP

Community and subgroup leaders appear to play an important role in determining the degree of community integration. Angell in his study to which reference has already been made, found leadership to be an important factor in moral integration. In his conclusion he writes:

According to our findings, an optimal leadership group would be: (1) Composed of well-educated persons; (2) Composed of those whose original involvement in community affairs sprang from their own interest, the involvement of their friends, or the nature of their profession; (3) Widely representative of socioeconomic groups within the city; (4) Made up in somewhat equal proportions of those who were born in the city, those who were born elsewhere but have lived in the community a long

[16] *Ibid.* For further discussion of subgroup relationships, see Herbert J. Gans, *op. cit.*, pp. 229–262.

time, and those who have lived in the community a decade or so; (5) Composed of those who have had enough contacts with other segments of the population to enable them to understand their points of view (social realism); (6) Marked by congeniality but not "cliquishness"; (7) Composed of those who realize the importance of effort and informal organization in overcoming public apathy toward community problems.[17]

These generalizations Angell believes to be not just plausible hypotheses but fairly reliable principles. It is at this point that he feels most secure about his findings. While some of his results must be considered tentative, he states:

With respect to leadership, our knowledge is fuller. A city would be well advised, according to our findings, not to depend on a few, over-burdened leaders, but to develop a large but coöperative leadership group, continually recruited from the well-educated younger persons in various occupational and ethnic segments of the population who have close contacts with problem situations and strong motivation to improve them.[18]

Most workers in the community field would accept these generalizations as both safe and feasible, yet would wish the analysis to proceed further. Is the generalization to select from "various occupational and ethnic segments" adequate? Does this mean all segments of the community or just some of the segments? And in selecting from these segments, does one choose only "the well-educated younger persons" irrespective of whether these persons have a position of leadership, are accepted and trusted by this segment of the community? These questions are of considerable importance, yet the above generalizations provide little help in securing adequate answers.

It seems reasonable to suppose, however, that the "segments" or groups to be included in a community association will be dependent upon the size and character of the community. In a large urban community with a relatively small Jewish population, one subgroup may be the Jewish community, but in another city in which the

---

[17] Angell, *op. cit.*, pp. 108–109.
[18] *Ibid.*, p. 122.

Jewish population is much greater relative to the whole population, one subgroup may be the Orthodox Jews, another subgroup the Reformed Jews, and so on. Similarly in one community, labor may be represented through the larger unions but in others it may be represented by members of neighborhood groups which include both union and nonunion workers from many different fields. In many small communities, especially in developing countries, there is not the same fabrication of group life. There will, however, be segments often based on kinship groups, sometimes informal grouping around friends, leaders, or "central figures." While little definitive information is available here, it at least suggests the necessity of careful study of the social organization of the community if the "segments" or subgroups to be involved in community affairs are to be identified.

As to who will be selected from these subgroups to take a position of leadership in the community, it must be clear that a good deal depends upon the purpose for which they are to be selected. If the purpose is to initiate a community playground or library, perhaps, as Angell suggests, the "well-educated younger men" can accomplish this as efficiently and effectively as any group. But if we are concerned (as we are in community organization) with bringing the major subgroups together in the community to identify, and take action with respect to, common needs and objectives, then arbitrary selection of educated young men can hardly be considered adequate. For the end postulated is not simply achievement of a project (like a playground or library) but initiation and development of a process which brings diverse elements in the community together. The association of well-educated younger persons from various segments of the community may simply be the organization of a group of "like-minded persons" who, however well they perform their task, may do nothing to further integration in the community.

Community organization must be concerned not only with an adequate identification of group life in the community, but with identification of those leaders whose participation in community activity will encourage the involvement and participation of other members of the group of which they are the leaders. In most groups we will find both informal and formal leaders. The latter are leaders who hold their positions by virtue of some office such as teacher, priest, judge, the president of a business, the mayor. Informal leaders are leaders by virtue of the fact that some individuals or some group look upon them as persons upon whom "one can count," "whose opinions must be respected," "who can help you when you are in a jam." Informal leaders depend on a "following" for their status, while formal leaders may have prestige without a close loyal following. Both types of leaders, of course, wield an influence; the attitudes of both are important in moving subgroups into closer contact with the larger community.

Eisenstadt's work [19] is again instructive at this point. His studies indicate that the leader's influence in relating his group positively to the whole community is dependent upon the leader's own positive identification with his group. If the leader finds his group related to (not blocking) his own mobility aspirations, if the leader accepts and can live comfortably with his group, and if in turn he is accepted by his group—given these conditions, the leader's positive influence towards community integration may be considerable. This type of leader, whom Eisenstadt calls the "positively identified leader," may not only help to develop cohesion within his group but may also help to "integrate the group in the larger community."

The "negatively identified leader" who finds, or feels, his own aspirations are being blocked or modified by association with his group, whose identification with his group is weak, who in turn is not an object of identification by the group and may even be rejected by them—this type of leader not only adversely affects group cohesion, but even if he tries to move the group into the wider community, is usually unsuccessful. The "negatively identified leader" is often a "marginal man," not really belonging to any subgroup, for he is attempting to move away from one group and into a group with greater status. Such leaders, because their

[19] S. N. Eisenstadt, "Social Mobility, Group Cohesion and Solidarity," unpublished paper, Jerusalem, 1954. See also Alexander H. Leighton, *My Name Is Legion,* Basic Books, 1959, p. 313.

mobility aspirations stimulate them to move around in the community, are often noted by other subgroups as "the natural leader of Group X that we need in this community council." Actually, the implication of Eisenstadt's study is that such leaders are a hindrance to the community organization process.

Angell has provided us with some safe assumptions about leadership in the community. Beyond this our findings must be tentative, but it appears that those concerned with community integration must be aware of the complex social organization of the community, be able to identify the major subgroups in the community, and must discover the "positively identified leaders" of these subgroups.[20]

SYMBOLS AND RITUALS

Community-wide symbols, values, institutions, celebrations, etc. are a stimulus to community integration. Alexander Leighton[21] has indicated that all people everywhere have systems of belief which influence their behavior and which are in part: (1) logical, i.e., based on experience and reason, (2) cultural, i.e., based on the pressure of other people's opinions, and (3) personal—emotional, i.e., serving to satisfy the aspirations and allay the fears of the individual. The most deeply ingrained and unchangeable beliefs, he asserts, are predominantly those rooted in the two last mentioned.

There is a tendency to believe that development of community life is the product of experience and reason applied to this particular problem. But while one may wish to increase the area in which rational decisions are made and work toward this end, it would be fallacious to ignore the reality of the situation in which cultural and emotional factors play such an important part. These latter are often the prime determinants of whether people will relate to the community or not. In a somewhat different context, Margaret Mead has written:

[20] For an extensive treatment of the question of leadership, see Murray G. Ross and Charles E. Hendry, *New Understandings of Leadership*, Association Press, 1957.

[21] Alexander H. Leighton, *Human Relations in a Changing World; Observations on the Use of the Social Sciences*, E. P. Dutton, 1949.

Over and over again we see that attempts to remedy such conditions chiefly by knowledge and logic (as seen by the agents of change) fail. Those failures can be better understood if it is recognized that explanation and logical interpretation *alone* are often ineffective in changing behaviour because their application is blocked by the emotional satisfaction which the individual achieves through his present mode of life. The new knowledge can be put to use only as the old behaviours, beliefs and attitudes are unlearned and the appropriate new behaviours, beliefs and attitudes are learned.[22]

This suggests not only the importance of subgroup symbols and rituals, which may constitute a substantial block to community integration, but also, and of more importance at this point, of community-wide values, symbols, institutions, and rituals with which all groups may identify, which provide a common emotional experience, and which serve as integrative forces in the community. There is, of course, a great range of such forces. There is the local baseball team, symphony orchestra, the old and trusted leader, the newspaper, radio station, and the "local character." There are also common ideas, which, however inadequate if judged by common definition, do serve as cohesive forces. The "American way of life," the "Christian tradition," "British justice," and other such phrases apparently are meaningful and real to many people and serve, as Myrdal has pointed out, as common objectives. There are local events and celebrations—the centennial celebration, the community festival, the opening of the new subway, the Santa Claus parade, etc., which seem to provide some opportunity for the expression of a "common interest."

But it is assumed here, as well, that if the major subgroups of a community can come together to identify and deal with common problems, this process may produce symbols and rituals that have meaning and possibilities for integration. Thus the Red Feather, the sign of the Community Chest campaign, can become such a symbol in the community, although often it represents only some of the segments of community life. The annual cleanup day of a neighborhood council, the opening of a new village school, the folk

[22] Mead (ed.), *op. cit.*, p. 292.

festival of a community council, etc., possess potentialities for providing expression of deep feelings in which all in the community share.

APATHY AND PREJUDICE

Traditional practices of apathy, prejudice, and discrimination present obstacles to a process leading to community integration. A community in which apathy prevails in respect to community affairs, or in which prejudice and discrimination are customarily directed at minority groups, is likely to be a community with a low level of integration and one in which these attitudes and practices constitute forces which resist any tendency to develop active coöperation around common projects with all parts of the community involved.

The causes of apathy are complex and will likely vary from situation to situation. Social structure undoubtedly influences the degree of interest in the community; the "company town" is likely to be more apathetic than a town of homeowners; a series of unsuccessful efforts to carry out community projects may cause withdrawal and resistance to further participation; high mobility rates probably decrease interest and participation in the affairs of the community. Merton has pointed out, in this connection, the importance of goals and means of obtaining goals in a given social structure. If goals are not clear, or if goals are clear but achievement of them is limited to a few, or if goals are clear but means of obtaining them are ill-defined, a society becomes relatively unstable; dissatisfaction, apathy, and lack of participation may result.[23] One may find in such situations what is often called "mass apathy."

Riesman and Glazer, in an analysis of political participation, review the many historical, socioeconomic, class, and regional factors which are related to political interest or apathy. One of their observations, of special interest here, is that the complexity

[23] Robert K. Merton, *Social Theory and Social Structure,* The Free Press, 1949.

and incomprehensibility of twentieth-century political activities so obscures the individual's self-interest that "self-interest, in its variety of traditional meanings, will not suffice to justify, from the standpoint of the individual, his concern with politics today." [24]

Mussen and Wyszynski in a study of personality and political participation report:

Stated very generally, our findings lead us to conclude that political apathy and activity are specific manifestations of more deep-lying, and pervasive passive and active orientations. Thus, one of the outstanding characteristics of the politically active individual is his attempt to understand himself, i.e., his awareness, examination, and acceptance of his own emotions, conflicts, and feelings, including feelings of inadequacy and inferiority. He is concerned with ego-satisfying personal experiences and emotional and intellectual expression rather than with conventional values and general social standards. His social consciousness and orientation are apparent in his emphasis on love-giving and social contribution, his respect for the rights and feelings of others, and his admiration for social scientists and liberal political leaders.

The politically apathetic individual, on the other hand, seems to be generally passive, dissatisfied and generally threatened. Although he gives evidence that he is fundamentally hostile, he cannot accept his hostile impulses. Instead he appears to be completely submissive and unchallenging to authority, rigid, and incapable of enjoying deep emotional experiences. . . . Conformity with social conventions, refusal to become aware of deep feelings, and submissiveness may all be devices which aid the apathetic individual to cope with basic insecurities in what he sees as a threatening environment.[25]

It is evident even from these brief references to theory and research in this area that the causes of apathy are manifold, and probably combine to produce different degrees of both individual and community apathy. Similarly in the case of prejudice, a variety of causal factors have been identified ranging from historical forces

[24] David Riesman and Nathan Glazer, "Criteria for Political Apathy," in Alvin W. Gouldner (ed.), *Studies in Leadership,* Harper & Row, 1950, pp. 505–559.

[25] Paul H. Mussen and Anne B. Wyszynski, "Personality and Political Participation," *Human Relations,* V (1952), 80.

to individual psychology. As in the case of apathy, a good deal of attention has been given to the various psychic factors which produce prejudice and hostility in the individual. Bettelheim and Janowitz, in their study of this phenomenon,[26] found some support for their four main hypotheses that (1) hostility towards out-groups is a function of a hostile individual's feeling that he has suffered deprivations in the past; (2) this hostility is also a function of the individual's anxiety about his future; (3) the individual blames the out-groups for past failures and future fears, projecting undesirable characteristics in himself onto the out-group, this behavior being indicative of a lack of ego strength and of inadequate internal controls; (4) ethnic intolerance is related more to the individual's movement within society than to his position at a particular moment of the investigation.

Apparently, there are deep psychological needs which some people meet by being apathetic or hostile and prejudiced towards others. It seems reasonable to assume that when the social climate makes the expression of these dispositions safe and acceptable, they will become more pronounced than in a community where such expressions of feeling are frowned upon. Further, the development of community feeling for or against these attitudes will determine to a considerable extent whether they spread, i.e., whether apathy or prejudice becomes a standard to which one conforms or whether such attitudes are repressed by the weight of community norms. Marie Jahoda [27] reports on a British study of young factory workers who moved as a group from a school in which the main values were intelligence, industriousness, respect for the teachers and older people in general. This group of schoolgirls in which these characteristics seemed to be fully accepted and practiced, moved to a factory where "intelligence was useless, hard work frowned upon by one's colleagues, and respect for age out of place." A few weeks after the schoolgirls had made this transition "they had adapted

[26] Bruno Bettelheim and Morris Janowitz, *The Dynamics of Prejudice,* Harper & Row, 1950.

[27] Marie Jahoda, "Some Socio-Psychological Problems of Factory Life," *British Journal of Psychology* (January 1942).

completely to the new set of norms." While not all adaptation is so dramatic as this, there are numerous illustrations of the way in which community pressures encourage or repress specific individual and social traits.

The problems of apathy and prejudice, it is clear, are complex, and require treatment at a variety of levels. The relevant question here is how the worker can deal with these at the community level? Obviously in the community in which these attitudes are acceptable and approved, the process of change in the community will be long and arduous. But as change begins, as apathy and/or prejudice become less acceptable, the social climate will be less favorable to these attitudes, new satisfactions may be developed and found in coöperative work, and a gradual change in community rates of apathy and prejudice may occur. But it is quite clear that a community approach will not eradicate those feelings which have deep psychological roots. The intensely hostile individual will inevitably find a scapegoat. Experience has indicated that the "climate" in respect to these matters can change in the community, that fewer people will be apathetic or hostile, that more people will repress prejudice, that expressions of apathy and hostility may be reduced, that individuals and groups may learn to work together in a relatively congenial atmosphere but that there will remain a "hard core" of withdrawn, hostile, and insecure individuals who will change only with therapeutic help. But change in the community as a whole, meager though it may be, may effect a change in the social climate, which may affect the second generation who may develop with less apathy and fewer prejudices, and the process of change in long terms may have a profound effect on the character of community life.

INDIVIDUAL'S PREDISPOSITION

The disposition of the individual to participate in community affairs is dependent upon a wide variety of factors, a few of which have relevance here.

Angell has performed a useful service by reporting the tendencies of different segments in the community to participate. On the basis of replies to the general question, "Do you feel you are doing as much for the community as you want to, or should you be taking a more active part?" an order of replies was developed, values were assigned, averages taken, and index numbers given to each group of replies. Significant differences were found in respect to: (1) age, e.g., "the moral order of a community is shared more completely by middle-aged people than by any other group"; (2) income, e.g., "families with higher incomes participate more fully in community affairs"; (3) occupation—"those in higher occupations definitely do participate more" although here it should be noted that the index figure for Unskilled and Service (1.55) is much lower than for Skilled and Semiskilled (2.56) and for White-Collar workers (3.20); (4) schooling—the higher grades attained, the more participation; (5) voting—"it is striking that nonvoting is strongly linked with lack of interest in other kinds of community participation"; (6) nationality—the foreign-born feel a greater obligation and desire to participate than the native-born; (7) race—"it is evident that Negroes want to carry their share of community responsibility and are even more inclined to participation than are the whites"; (8) length of residence—"evidently the more deeply one is rooted in a community, the more one participates in its affairs." [28]

In addition to these tendencies, it is possible to offer certain other rough generalizations in respect to community participation.

THE STATUS IMAGE WHICH AN INDIVIDUAL DEVELOPS FOR HIMSELF

Eisenstadt distinguishes between those with flexible status image and those with a ritual status image. The former, he suggests, have three major orientations: (1) attainment of various personal goals, (2) attainment of cultural goals, and (3) attainment of cohesive primary group relations of mutual affection and response. The indi-

[28] Angell, *op. cit.*, pp. 93–100.

vidual with a ritual status image tends to focus on certain goals and amenities such as money, job, and type of home. Eisenstadt finds that:

> Those with ritual status images could not distinguish very much between the attainment of the various types of goals and social relations. The attainment of social solidarity is, for them, conditioned by the attainment of a specific type of instrumental goals and pattern of life. Hence, they cannot differentiate to any large extent between various reference groups, finding within each one the satisfaction of a particular type of goal, but focus all their aspirations on one undifferentiated field with which they identify their overall status aspirations. . . . On the basis of this analysis, it can be postulated that those with ritual status image tend to choose their reference groups and standards in such a way as to maximize overall disintegrative tendencies . . . while those with open status image tend to choose their reference group so as to spread out the risks between different types of disintegrative behavior and to maximize the possibilities of adjustment within the social system.[29]

TIME PERSPECTIVE

If an individual sees himself as a permanent member of a community, all other things being equal, he will tend to be more identified and involved than if he sees himself as merely living in the community temporarily. This, of course, has been implied in the discussion of mobility, but the emphasis here is on future perspective, i.e., the individual's conception of his future in the community. In industry it has been suggested that the worker who looks forward to spending the rest of his working life in a particular firm is more disposed to participate in solving problems arising in his work than the worker who sees himself moving in the near future to another firm or industry.[30] This, it is suggested here, may be equally applicable in community affairs, and indeed Angell's data seem to support this point.

[29] S. N. Eisenstadt, "Reference Group Behavior and Social Integration," *American Sociological Review*, XIX (April 1954), 180–181.

[30] David Ketchum, Annual Address, Canadian Psychological Association, *Canadian Journal of Psychology* (1951).

RECOGNITION

The degree of recognition the individual receives for his participation in community projects apparently influences the degree of his satisfaction in these projects, his attitudes to these and other projects, and his disposition to participate in other community projects. This phenomenon has been mentioned by several social scientists (Kleinberg, Williams, Mead) [31] as a fairly safe generalization. It seems reasonable that a person who secures recognition that provides him with real satisfaction in community activity will be favorably disposed to such activity and will have a tendency to continue or to engage in other similar activities. The difficulty is, as Angell points out, that too few persons in the community have such opportunities for satisfaction, with the result that leadership and participation become concentrated in a few hands.

FRAME OF REFERENCE

If the individual's own frame of reference excludes all but his own group or subculture, his tendency to move outside his group is thereby lessened. The individual whose sole aspirations are limited to his own group resists participation in the community, whereas the individual whose aspirations are broader is much more disposed to venture forth from the group and into the life of the larger community.

BACKGROUND

The individual with childhood experiences (in the home, school, gang, neighborhood) which encouraged active participation in the life of the group or community is more disposed to greater

[31] Otto Kleinberg, *Tensions Affecting International Understanding,* Social Science Research Council, New York, 1950; Robin M. Williams, *The Reduction of Inter-Group Tensions,* Social Science Research Council, New York, 1947; Mead (ed.), *op. cit.*

participation in community activities than the individual who has not had such experiences. Several studies of children who attended progressive schools in which participation was encouraged seem to suggest that a disposition to take part in school and community affairs tends to carry over into university life,[32] and one may postulate the hypothesis that it probably carries over into post-university life.

The identification of these generalizations suggests the variety of factors, in addition to others mentioned in this chapter, which may determine the extent, nature, and scope of the individual's participation in community activities.

We have outlined here some illustrative material on community life which forms a background for workers in community organization and conditions the principles and methods they use. As indicated at the beginning of the chapter, it was not our purpose to develop a comprehensive picture of community life, but to select a few factors which serve to illustrate the worker's dependence on an understanding of the dynamics of community life, if he is to work with some degree of perspective, understanding, and competence at his task.[33]

[32] R. Freeman Butts, *A Cultural History of Education*, McGraw-Hill, 1947, pp. 649–650.

[33] Ben Lappin, *The Redeemed Children*, University of Toronto Press, 1963, pp. 36–156.

5

Some Aspects of Planning

PREREQUISITES TO PLANNING

WE HAVE suggested that the two fundamental and interrelated processes in community organization are planning and community integration. We have identified some aspects of community life that impinge on community integration, and we turn now to the concept and nature of planning. Here we face considerable difficulty. For while a great deal of planning goes on in every sphere of life, and while plans are produced in the thousands by groups, communities, and nations, there has not been the systematic and careful study of planning as a process that there has been, for example, of procedures and behavior in groups and communities. It has been claimed by some that rigid rules cannot be laid down for planning, that planning always begins with a set of circumstances (in terms of people, stage of development, nature of the problem, etc.) which vary greatly from situation to situation, and that the "clean slate" assumed by many planners never has existed, and never will exist.[1]

---

[1] David E. Lilienthal, *T.V.A.—Democracy on the March*, Pocket Books, Inc., p. 213. See also Milton Lebowitz, *The Process of Planned Community Change*, D.S.W. dissertation, Columbia University, 1961, University Microfilms, Ann Arbor, Mich.

It is possible to accept this latter point of view, yet to postulate certain hypotheses about planning which may have relevance in all situations. Every individual seen by the psychiatrists is different, each individual presents a problem the roots of which constitute a configuration quite unlike that of any other person, each requires different treatment and a different kind of help. Yet the psychiatrist has a specific set of hypotheses which influences the way he deals with all patients and provides a consistent guide for his work. Similarly we are assuming here that there are certain basic ideas in planning which, although their application and usefulness will vary from one situation to another, provide a consistent guide for planners. In other words, it is possible to have a conception of the nature of planning and the steps by which it proceeds, without being bound in all circumstances by rigid procedures.

PRELIMINARY CONSIDERATIONS

Certain generalizations, however elementary, have wide application and usefulness. For example, we would suggest that one must plan for planning. This is not a play on words but the essence of what has been implied about flexibility in planning. One does not begin to follow route-like certain steps in planning in a given situation, but rather one begins with some appraisal of the situation: some estimate is made of where one begins, with what objectives, with what resources, with what limiting conditions, etc. Thus one generalization would be that planning begins with consideration of what the situation is; how much planning is desirable, necessary, feasible; what plan for planning is most useful.

However, even if one grants that certain useful generalizations may be made, one confronts the fact that most such generalizations, at present, rest on widely divergent experiences which have not been compared, tested, or carefully evaluated. Interest has tended to center on either the plan (i.e., the product of planning) or the human factors involved in planning (i.e., the variety of human conditions which must be considered if planning is to take place), and little attention has been given to planning as a whole process.

That such study needs to be undertaken can hardly be doubted. But we must be content here with identifying those stages in planning now commonly accepted as necessary, and to leave to others, or to another time, exploration of more basic data in this area.

Two points may be made in preface to an elaboration of steps in community planning.

Planning, as it is conceived here, represents the whole act, from the stirring of consciousness about a problem to the action taken to resolve that problem. Planning is not, therefore, merely development of a "solution"; it is development of a solution relative to a given problem in a given social milieu, and active application of that solution. Viewed in this way, planning is focused on active resolution of a problem, and means are adjusted not to the end of developing a plan (a "paper solution") but to attainment of the objective (resolution of the problem). This rather different conception of ends implies, as indicated, a difference in means. Throughout the process there is less concern about "the ideal plan" than with a plan that is applicable, that is feasible, that will be supported. The "dusty plan stored away in the files" is the subject of scorn by many so-called practical people. Actually such plans— conceptions of things as they "might be"—have more value than is often imputed to them, for they constitute the insight of the expert and the dreamer and set long-term goals that are often less unrealistic than the "practical people" imagine. Surely there is a place for such planning—and one would hope that some of it would find expression in the community planning we are discussing. But, essentially, here we are concerned with "action planning"—planning which leads to action in respect to a problem. For this reason some of the steps to be taken, some of the people to be involved, and some of the considerations allowed to condition the solution differ from those present when action in respect to a problem is hoped for, but the possibility of such action is not permitted to affect the purity of the plan.

A secondary preliminary consideration relates to the motivation for planning. For some, and this may be particularly true of the dreamers or the planning experts, a general experimental attitude or an image of potentiality may be the dominant motivation for planning.[2] But the primary motivation for planning as we conceive it here is sensitivity to, awareness of, disturbance about a problem. Such differentiation of motives into discrete units is probably not feasible, since motives are usually multiple and interlocked. But the dominant motives in action planning should, we suggest, stem from dissatisfaction with conditions as they now exist and with a desire to change these conditions. A neat dilemma confronts us here. The planning process, often a long and tiresome one, which we are suggesting should be initiated, nourished, and sustained by a real sense of need for change in respect to a particular problem situation. If such feelings about the problem do not exist, the matter can easily be referred to a subcommittee, and no one is much disturbed if the matter is not heard of again. On the other hand, those people with strong feelings about a problem often want "immediate action" and are impatient with the necessarily slow steps in planning. It is essential in community planning to find some way of sustaining the feeling of need for change while working through the many aspects of action planning.

This latter establishes another condition for successful planning. A group feeling keenly about a problem will not be able to go through the long, difficult, and often frustrating experience of planning in respect to this problem if the group does not have good morale. The common feeling about the problem gives considerable impetus to working together, but there must be sufficient group strength and capacity to withstand the many difficulties involved. Once having achieved this strength and capacity, however, morale in the group may rise even higher. Thus high morale contributes to, and in turn is strengthened by, successful planning.

Elliott Jaques, in his classic study, *The Changing Culture of a Factory*, develops a somewhat similar theme when he writes:

[2] Rensis Likert and Ronald Lippitt, "The Utilization of Social Science," in Leon Festinger and Daniel Katz (eds.), *Research Methods in the Behavioral Sciences*, The Dryden Press, 1953.

Two interrelated factors are necessary in any successful process of working-through of group problems. . . . The necessaries are a group with a problem severe and painful enough for its members to wish to do something about it; but also of a sufficient cohesion of purpose, or morale, to render them capable of tackling it and of seeking and tolerating necessary changes. It is this combination of pain and morale that induces understanding acceptance of the illumination of difficulties unconsciously concealed because too devastating to admit; but it is only the giving of genuine understanding of such difficulties that permits resolution of the underlying stresses and their symptoms.[3]

Now it is obvious from this that Jaques is oriented in the field of psychiatry; but he is not writing here about group therapy in a mental health clinic, but of committees and councils of industrial workers charged with developing plans and policies for a factory. True, considerable weight is given to the need for self-understanding and awareness of unconscious forces operating in groups before they can successfully work their way through difficult problems, but this merely implies a level of operation which most would admit to be desirable, but feel not feasible, in many community situations. But the basic points emphasized, and arrived at independently, deserve careful consideration. Jaques uses the word "pain" as a prerequisite to effective group planning, probably in the way that psychiatrists use the concept of pain as a necessary condition of personality change. Undoubtedly he considers pain as a condition of fundamental change in the nature and character of the group. We are, perhaps, less concerned here with such fundamental change, yet subscribe to the conviction that such deep-seated feeling may frequently be necessary to sustain the planning process. This will vary with the situation, some problems being relatively unimportant and not demanding much involvement. Yet it is being suggested here that the most significant opportunity for successful action planning arises around those problems about which the planning group feel greatly disturbed—about which they are deeply con-

[3] Elliot Jaques, *The Changing Culture of a Factory*, Tavistock Publications, 1951, p. 310.

vinced, about which they feel "something must be done." The "pain" felt may only occasionally be comparable to the "pain" of the emotionally disturbed, but we suggest as a tentative hypothesis that it is the most powerful motivating force for action planning.

Lest the reader be misled into an impression that we are, in this chapter, dealing with community organization process, it is necessary to emphasize again that we are here discussing planning, and that community organization and planning are not identical processes. Indeed, there are presented in this chapter ideas and illustrations which cannot be accepted by community organization workers without some modification. The broad principles of planning are, of course, of value, but in community organization these must be merged with principles relating to community integration. The way planners take action on their plan, for example, is conditioned in community organization by considerations of community involvement in, identification with, and disposition to support fully, the plan. While principles of community organization derive in part from that which has been said about the community and that which is being said about planning, they are not entirely dependent on these data, but also depend upon the values and assumptions previously identified. The material in this chapter, then, is relevant to, but not the sole determinant of, community organization principles.

With this word of caution, we wish now to identify what appear to be rather widely accepted "steps in planning" and to discuss these briefly. These steps are: (1) definition of the problem; (2) study of the nature, meaning, and implications of the problem; (3) decision regarding ultimate solutions; and (4) action on the solution agreed upon.

DEFINITION OF THE PROBLEM

The first stage in planning is development of a clear definition of the problem with which the group is concerned. Elementary as this may appear to be, it is of vital importance and is frequently neglected.

At a recent meeting of a neighborhood council which the writer attended, a woman rose to speak with considerable feeling about the deterioration of the neighborhood. Her feeling was apparently shared by others in the meeting, it was decided the matter should be investigated, and a ·committee was appointed to study the problem: "What can be done to prevent deterioration of the neighborhood?" In the discussion leading to the motion, it was obvious, however, that there were a number of conceptions of this problem: one person was thinking of the dilapidated condition of the houses, another of the messy condition of the streets, another of what appeared to be the spread of delinquency, another of the number of "dives" appearing in the neighborhood, another of the character of the officials appointed by the neighborhood. In an informal discussion after the meeting it turned out that what the original speaker was most concerned about, and this was evidently shared by some of the others, was the movement of Negroes into the neighborhood. But this latter conception of the problem was never once mentioned at the meeting. This presents an interesting example of a practice too frequently found in committees and councils. It is conceivable here that the committee appointed might define and proceed to work on a problem quite different from that which represented the real concern of the group present.

Either because of fear, semantics, or inability to articulate intelligibly, the problem is never clearly stated, and planning proceeds on some basis other than that desired. This implies the need for a chairman, an individual member, or a subgroup to spend some time attempting to formulate and articulate clearly the precise meaning of the problem. Most planners agree that time given to formulating and reformulating the statement of the problem brings adequate rewards in the sense that work is focused on that which is of real concern to the group.

To cite another example, we turn to the chairman of the budget committee of a Community Chest who is disturbed about the low fees charged by agencies who are members of the Chest. He feels these fees could be increased considerably and that there should be a much more consistent fee policy for Chest agencies. The matter is discussed and a committee is appointed "to study the fee policies of Chest agencies and to recommend suitable action." Now the discussion revealed a variety of views as to the nature of the problem: (1) the budget chairman felt agencies were leaning too heavily on the Chest, that the Chest was reaching its maximum income, and some agencies must anticipate a cut in their budget allocation which, however, they could meet by an increase of fees; (2) most of those present felt it unusual that there should be such inconsistencies in fee policies as reported and agreed that it would be useful to study the matter; (3) several agency representatives felt that in addition to receiving an increased allocation from the Chest, which most agencies had requested, some agencies might get additional income from higher fees. The committee appointed studied the fee policies of Chest agencies, reported that they were indeed inconsistent, but that since such policies were a matter for individual agency decision, each agency board should be asked to study the matter in light of the facts gathered by the committee. The report was adopted but no one felt stimulated or happy about the matter. Part of the reason for this weak planning effort was, of course, that such concern as existed was not clearly focused, and therefore the group never became conscious of the real issue or deeply disturbed about the matter. Like hundreds of other problems that come before such groups it was disposed of with great inefficiency, and waste of time and effort. Actually there was here a problem of great moment to all: there was not enough money to provide the services considered essential. Some felt the Chest should raise more money; some felt the agencies could raise more by increasing their fees; others felt both could be done. But the heart of the Chest operation was the need to secure enough money to provide the services necessary. All were concerned with this issue. Failure to solve it meant bickering, conflict, loss of morale. Instead of facing the central problem of how much money was really needed and how it could be provided in the present situation, the problem was introduced in partial form, watered down and somewhat distorted, and dealt with without enthusiasm or conviction. No significant change resulted except perhap a decrease in morale in the whole organization. This is but one more illustration of the need to clarify the problem before launching into other phases of planning.

IMPLICATIONS OF THE PROBLEM

The second phase of planning requires exploration of the nature, meaning, scope, and implications of the problem. Even if the problem has been well defined, there is the often difficult task of seeing the problem in all its manifestations and relationships. If the neighborhood council mentioned earlier was concerned, not with Negro infiltration but with all aspects of deterioration, they would begin to see how complex a problem had been selected. For they would be studying housing, street clearing, child training; attitudes and other social forces that permit deterioration of a neighborhood; city ordinances that affect housing, garbage collection, taverns; the after-school programs of agencies and public playgrounds in the neighborhood, etc. The problem is therefore one of some dimensions, requires to be organized in appropriate sections, and appropriate personnel assigned to each part of the whole.

But what is soon recognized is that most such problems are larger in scope than at first realized; that they impinge upon, and in turn are influenced by, many other problems.[4] This is the point at which a planning group must face a dilemma of sorts. To ignore the manifold relationships of this problem to many others is to be unrealistic and to tackle a part of a problem which can be treated only as a whole. But to deal with all relationships and implications would be to begin an endless task which could never be completed with the resources available. Therefore, while the problem must be seen as completely as possible, judgments must be made as to what precisely will be the facets of the problem with which the planning group will concern itself. For example, a community group may become concerned with juvenile delinquency. They will (unless

[4] See Peter M. Blau and W. Richard Scott, *Formal Organizations*, Chandler, 1962, p. 250.

they subscribe to the single-factor theory and proceed to deal with one factor) find at least five aspects of the problem: (1) the quality and the strength of family life in the community; (2) the resources required by all children, i.e., adequate food, shelter, clothing, education, recreation, leadership, church programs; (3) the services available to children who are particularly vulnerable to behavior problems, e.g., those whose mothers work, whose fathers are in prison, etc.; (4) the harmful influences in the community, e.g., the "dives," vice dens, gambling dens; (5) the treatment services available for problem and delinquent children. Pursuit of all facets of this problem may well take the council into such matters as consideration of the adequacy of an economic system that does not provide a twelve-month wage for all, the requirements for the selection of teachers and the kind of training teachers require, the reasons that seem to produce corruption in civic government, and many other complex problems. The planning group may simply become overwhelmed as they pursue some of these matters to ultimate questions. Therefore some refinement, delineation, and focusing of the problem is required. What is it we are primarily disturbed about? How much of this problem can we reasonably tackle? Who could or should be dealing with other aspects of the problem? How can we do our part, yet press for more adequate consideration of other parts of the problem? These and other questions require study and decisions at this point in the planning process.

It is here that two relevant considerations may arise. These may, it should be emphasized, come up before this point is reached, after it has passed, or may arise afresh at many stages in the process and be relevant at each point. These considerations have to do with use of experts or research personnel and involvement of other people in the community in the planning process.

Experts or research personnel may be useful in helping to delimit the problem, sharing experiences as to what occurred in other similar situations, in gathering data in respect to the problem, or in formulating the problem so that research is possible. Likert and Lippitt describe a number of ways in which the research personnel and planning group can share their concerns so that their meeting can be mutually helpful.[5] Obviously each needs to try to understand the thinking and orientation of the other, and to find common ground. The meeting at which the planning group describes its problem in detail with the research personnel listening, with the latter trying to break these questions down and reformulate them for scientific analysis, has proven useful. But occasionally the opposite process is followed: the research team outlines research projects similar to the central interest of the planning group and the latter then attempt to indicate the similarity of their problems to some of the research programs.

While it is obvious that technical experts and research personnel can make an important contribution to the planning group, some real dangers may reside in this relationship. At many points, certainly in dealing with a complex problem, the planning group may feel frustrated and baffled. Certain experts and research persons may appear to be so calm, knowledgeable, and confident that they will be permitted to define the problem or "take over" the direction of the work. On the whole, it seems indicated that the planning group must be the group to determine the course of their work; that experts may advise, suggest, and recommend, but that their role is a subordinate one; and that responsibility for determining direction must lie with the group who must eventually take appropriate action in respect to the problem. In slightly different context Jaques makes this point:

How the T-group leader forms his task-policy is a matter of considerable importance for group relationships in his command. On some aspects he will receive advice from outside. . . . but it is just becoming accepted at Glacier (Metal Works) that such outside advice can only be a recommendation, and that it is entirely up to the manager concerned whether he follows it. So long as he is held responsible for the task assigned to him he must be given the authority to carry it out in his own way. . . . It is only on this condition that a manager is in a position to take on the responsibility of building good teamwork, whether he proceeds by setting

[5] Likert and Lippitt, *op. cit.*

his local policy by himself, or reaches it through two-way discussion with his subordinates.[6]

The common assertion here is that a group or individual responsible for continuing action in a particular operation should not have responsibility for direction of the operation taken over by experts or research personnel. The importance of this relates to morale, feelings of responsibility, motivation for action. If the group relinquishes the responsibility for the major direction of the operation, they relinquish some of their sense of responsibility, some of their feeling of need to act in respect to the problem, some aspects of their status as leaders in this particular operation.

It should be added here that the control of the main direction of the planning process does not necessarily mean assuming responsibility for, or participating in, all aspects of the project. Lewin[7] and others have emphasized the importance of involving persons in each stage of decision-making in the planning process. His studies seem to suggest, at points, that only when individuals are deeply involved in planning procedures will adequate and supportable action ensue. Involvement in all stages of the process which produces a specific recommendation apparently leads to identification with the recommendation and a disposition to implement it. Some persons have interpreted this to mean that all must be involved in actually gathering data, in sitting in on all meetings, in being part of all decisions made. These latter practices, which lead to an incredible mismanagement of time and manpower in some welfare councils, human relations clinics, and university faculties, have little to validate them. No studies have been made of the number of people who have withdrawn (either physically or psychologically) because they did not have the time, energy, or disposition to follow the minutiae of detail involved in such a

[6] Jaques, *op. cit.*, pp. 286–287. See also Jack Rothman, "Goals and Roles in Community Organization," *Social Work,* IX (April 1964), 24–31.

[7] Kurt Lewin, "Group Decision and Social Change," in T. M. Newcomb and E. L. Hartley (eds.), *Readings in Social Psychology,* Holt, Rinehart & Winston, 1947, pp. 330–344; Gertrud Weiss Lewin, (ed.), *Resolving Social Conflict,* Harper & Row, 1948.

process, but it is suggested here that the carrying of the principle of involvement to its ultimate end (as some organizations do) leads to a loss of interest, efficiency, and morale. The task seems to be that of applying the principle of involvement wisely. This would suggest that responsibility for the direction of the process lies with the planning group, who may sanction authority for small task groups and research teams to proceed with work on various aspects of the problem. These latter would report back with data and recommendations which would be used, as the planning group see fit, in developing its policy and plan of action. What is fundamental is that the planning group assume and maintain responsibility for the whole project but that they be able to delegate authority to others and to use wisely the products of the work of their subgroups.

The second major consideration here has to do with addition of other people in the community to the planning group. This is usually done for one of two reasons: (1) the planning group feels the need for people who know a good deal about the subject and would strengthen the committee or planning group by virtue of their familiarity with the subject; or (2) the planning group sees ahead the need for action and feels the desirability of involving prestige figures, persons likely to be affected by their plan of action, persons whose support will "count in this particular area," etc., so that when the time for action comes, resistance will be partially overcome and considerable support will be ensured. These reasons are infrequently articulated, often confused, and their implications are seldom recognized. If expert help is required, some of the questions previously raised have relevance here. While the knowledge of experts may be valuable, it will be useful only if accompanied with an ability to control a probable bias; a capacity to sit through a process which will be slow enough to permit the layman to master the problem and all its implications; an ability to tolerate the expression of "crack-pot" ideas; and a firm reluctance to "take over" the planning group's responsibility. It may be that a wiser use of persons with technical knowledge would be as consultants at certain points in the process, or as members of a task force or a subcommittee to accomplish a certain part of the total job.

Involvement of community people so that support for the plan may be developed is quite a different matter. Here one must weigh against the importance of this support the implications of what Selznick calls "coöptation" and defines as "the process of absorbing new elements into the leadership or policy-determining structure of an organization as a means of averting threats to its stability or existence." [8] This is a common, and perhaps essential, practice in an organization dependent upon the support of the public for its existence. But it has its costs and these must be noted. For the "new elements"—the power figures and the vested interest figures—bring to the planning group their own conception of the problem, their own problems and purposes. These modify, often in a profound way, the structure, policy, and plans of the organization.

A few years ago, a local neighborhood council planning for more adequate recreation facilities for their children, and seeing the need of using the neighborhood school for evening activity, and recognizing the need for support for these efforts, invited the local school principal to become a member of their council. When use of the schools for adults came up, the principal gave in great detail reasons why such a project was not practicable, and far from getting support in appearing before the Board of Education on this matter, the council felt they could not make such an appearance because of the division within their ranks. This is, of course, an unusual example, but it serves to emphasize some of the implications of coöptation. More often the planning process is modified to the extent that the plan produced is "acceptable." The advocates of such involvement agree, with considerable justification, that it is better to deal with such opposition as may arise in face-to-face contacts within the planning group than to produce a plan which will be met with overwhelming opposition when the time for action arises. Nonethe-

[8] Philip Selznick, *T.V.A. and the Grass Roots*, University of California Press, 1949, p. 13.

less the disadvantages, as well as advantages, of such involvement must be recognized.

At this stage in the process, then, the problem and all its ramifications are explored, the precise aspect of the problem to be attacked is selected, work and study on this aspect are undertaken, often with the use of a variety of experts and task groups, the resulting data processed, and the possible alternatives for solution spread out for group consideration. While situations and problems vary, such procedure as this is in most instances essential.

SOLUTION OF THE PROBLEM

The next step in planning is securing a firm decision as to which alternative solution is to be selected. In other words, the plan for action is established at this point.

It is unlikely that exploration of the problem will yield a ready answer. The facts, and circumstances surrounding the facts, will be viewed differently, and judgments in respect to them will vary. Therefore it may be necessary to posit two or more solutions from among which the planning group must choose or combine into one single program for action. Thus a community council which is seeking to build a community center may consider such alternatives as (1) building a Y.M.C.A. with a private grant from a large international firm known to support a Y.M.C.A. but not likely to give to a community center, (2) taking over and turning the old lodge hall into a community center with the aid of many small private gifts, (3) asking the city to contribute to the erection of a new community center to which the citizens would contribute and which they would operate, (4) asking the city to build and operate a community center with public funds. Each alternative listed by this group has many implications in terms of economic and social costs, and these latter must be clearly identified before a meaningful decision is reached.

There are some who believe that such a "spelling out" of alternatives merely complicates the issue, confuses people, and leads to inevitable conflict. Far better, they say, to throw all the evidence and weight behind one plan and to generate enthusiasm for it. Here again, as at almost all other points, the issue is one of objective. If the purpose is merely to get a job done quickly, the advocates of "one alternative" are probably correct. But if the objective is to develop both good working relations and the best decision possible, the working out of alternative plans may have validity. For it is possible for groups to work through and secure unanimous agreement in respect to complex issues. And where they cannot, perhaps a delay in action is advisable, since to rush through one plan may merely mean that the disagreements will arise later in the process, or after it has presumably been terminated. Thus in an industry in which workers and management participate in all policy decisions and where no decisions are made without unanimous decisions, it can be reported:

The members of the factory recognize that this unanimity rule may lead them into situations of stalemate. But they prefer to maintain it on the grounds that decisions so arrived at have the best chance of being both the most correct and the most acceptable. Their experience is that so long as group relations remain satisfactory, no stalemate occurs. People show themselves to be flexible enough to modify their views. On occasions when stresses between groups appear, the unanimity rule is still useful. Even should a stalemate occur, it is by this means that the unfortunate consequences are avoided of taking decisions without full agreement, for decisions of this kind are usually impossible to carry out successfully.[9]

In a discussion of this principle the author adds the comment that while the unanimity rule does not solve all questions,

. . . rather is it to be seen as a mechanism for facilitating more constructive relationships and ensuring more realistic compromises when the necessary motivations and skills exist in those concerned.[10]

And one objective of a planning group, as we conceive it, is devel-

[9] Jaques, *op. cit.*, p. 267.
[10] *Ibid.*, p. 266.

opment of those motivations and skills necessary to make the best decision in light of the judgment of all members of the group.

In weighing the alternatives and reaching a decision, a large number of factors must be considered by the group. These relate to systems of belief prevalent in the community, power factors present, vested interest that may be threatened, the degree of support likely in the community. It is relatively easy, for example, for a group who feel strongly about a problem, who have studied all aspects of the situation carefully, and who want to take action, to outline for themselves a solution to the problem that is quite unrealistic. The planning group must continually remind themselves of "accepted ways" in the community, and this of course is often a function performed well by those involved by coöptation. The more they are steeped in traditional ways of moving in the community, the greater will be their skill to move along new paths without setting up stress between themselves and their community. A self-sanctioning group seeking to plan and develop community projects is impossible; conformity and modification of views to be consistent with those prevalent in the community are enforced in innumerable ways.[11]

One of the difficulties faced by all planning groups is maintenance of agreement once it has been reached. All individuals tend to be driven by conflicting motives and to subscribe to a number of opposing and conflicting beliefs. This is the result of unconscious forces, the nature and insistence of which most of us do not recognize. However, they produce inconsistencies in behavior which move an individual enthusiastically to support a plan or project one day and confess grave reservations about it the next. Therefore the group must not only secure agreement but maintain agreement, by reiteration of its basic points of view (which led to the decision) and restatement of its decision.

Even then, there may be resistance to the plan by members who agreed to it but later had doubts about the wisdom of their agreement. This may take the form of withdrawal, resistance to action,

[11] *Ibid.*, p. 258.

petty arguments about small points in the plan, scapegoating, or attacking someone in the group or outside the group. At no point is the importance of morale more obvious than here. A group with low morale may simply disintegrate at this stage, whereas one with high morale will have the capacity to work out these stresses before they proceed with action.

The planning group, in addition, will have other considerations to take into account. The tendency is to seek for panaceas. But, as implied, realistic accounting of the situation and forces operating in the community may make for modification of such views. Often a plan may be developed in stages, with short- and long-term goals, recognizing that change comes slowly, and establishing modest and attainable goals for the immediate future but looking forward to full implementation of the plan through consistent action over the years. A plan may also recognize the principle of indirection, which implies some analysis of community life to discover "points of leverage" or "areas of flexibility" as points for initiating a particular program. Thus a group working for more equitable opportunities for the Negro may find what the whites fear most is the possibility of intermarriage, and that which they resist least is the betterment of educational opportunities for Negroes. The latter would then constitute a "point of leverage" for initiation of a program for improvement of conditions for Negroes in the community.

All these are factors which may confront a planning group as it makes a decision on its plan for action. They will occur in various patterns and at various times, and of course, rigid laws for dealing with them cannot be made. But conscious awareness of them, and decisions made in respect to them, in terms of costs to the planning group, their organization, their objective, and to community morale, are suggested by this brief analysis.

ACTION

The final phase of planning, as it is conceived here, relates to action. This phase, as is evident from the foregoing, is not separate from the other aspects of planning, yet it requires distinctive strategy and skill. Most workers in the field agree that a group must plan for action almost as one plans a campaign of any kind.

Failure to plan action carefully may well result in what is called the "boomerang" effect. A group may begin a program to alleviate discrimination but finish their work with increased intergroup hostility in the community. Another group seeks to secure action on some point in their program and begins to exert pressure on various political figures. They may find the result is not merely a feeling of neutrality but perhaps resistance or active opposition. Such "boomerang" effects are usually the result of indiscriminate action, of starting at the wrong point, of suggesting programs which stir uneasiness or suspicion or increase hostility, of putting undue pressure on people, of launching a program when people are deeply concerned with some other issue.

It is obvious that a program of action must be launched with some awareness of the context in which it is to operate. A "fair employment practice bill" is not to be secured by indiscriminate pressure on congressmen or members of Parliament. Action here begins with some understanding of the accepted ways of operating in Congress or Parliament, of the ways in which bills are sponsored, of the ways in which such bills gather informal support in the House, and the ways of exerting pressure which the members of these bodies consider acceptable. In light of this information a planning group can begin a campaign of action, moving with enthusiasm and vigor but always along a path which, in this case, is not determined by them, but by the group whom they wish to influence.

Although viewed with mixed feelings by many professional workers, the Back of the Yards Council in Chicago has a most impressive record of successful action on matters in which it is interested. Part of the reason for this success is indicated in the following report:

In order to carry out this fight, leaders of the Back of the Yards Council had to familiarize themselves with the governmental "matching" financial arrangements—the relationships of various departments of the government, such as the Department of Agriculture, to this project—the arguments pro and con on the issue of the appropriation, the governmental channels through which a bill has to proceed before it reaches the floor for a vote—the requirements within the national appropriation for a state subsidy, the securing of facts on the number of Hot Lunch projects throughout the country, and a wealth of other information dealing with government administration. Leaders of the Back of the Yards Council who went to Washington were so completely informed on the issue that many senators who were opposing the bill were surprised to learn from Back of the Yards leaders that they had such and such a number of Hot Lunch projects in their own states, and that such and such a number of families in their own states were desirous of the continuance of this project. The calm, sound, factual, pithy, and sincere testimony of Back of the Yards leaders before both the Senate and House committees captured the admiration not only of most of the senators and representatives, but of a good many of the newspaper correspondents and columnists.[12]

Later the group went to Springfield, where it is said of the Council leaders:

Their knowledge of parliamentary procedures, committee regulations, governmental red tape, legislative floor tactics, and general information on the issue by the Back of the Yards leaders evoked the admiration of the state legislators.[13]

It will be evidenced over and over again, that the plan of action must be carefully conceived and developed if it is to anticipate success. One council which sought increased pensions and allowances for the old people in the community were conscious of the prevalent conservative attitude in the community in respect to such allowances. It was felt that the community would oppose any such increase in allowances because "people should be able to get on by themselves." Before advancing their plan the council began a campaign to inform the public about the aged through news stories, pictures, radio talks, etc. and aimed these releases at three points

[12] Saul D. Alinsky, *Reveille for Radicals*, University of Chicago Press, 1946, pp. 186–187.
[13] *Ibid.*

they felt people would understand: (1) there were more old people today than ever before; (2) the old people were fine people, dignified, and living the last years of life gracefully; (3) they were caught in the spiral of inflation, most had money saved but it meant much less now than when it was saved. There was no word in any of these releases about what could be done about the problem, but a surprising amount of comment arose in the community. "Isn't it a shame what's happening to old people today," or "You'd think they could do something for those old folks." When the council came forward with their plan for increased allowances, there was surprising support for it, and the plan passed the municipal council unanimously. Consideration of the prevailing systems of belief and ways of developing a plan consistent with these beliefs is, in many cases, sound procedure.

From these few illustrations, it is apparent that planning for action [14] is itself an intricate process, and that if it is to be successful it requires careful study of the community; the probable reaction of the community; the customary procedures by which similar plans are accepted, adopted, or enacted; the persons who must support the plan if it is to be implemented; the costs of the plan and the sources from which these costs are to be drawn; the reasons why the plan is essential and why the arguments against it are not considered valid; the "proper" ways of approaching leaders and others in respect to the plan, etc. Anything less than such a thorough approach jeopardizes all the previous work that goes into planning.

[14] For a detailed treatment of the various aspects entailed in social planning for action, see *A Study of the Needs and Resources for Community-Supported Welfare, Health and Recreation Services in Metropolitan Toronto: A Community Self-Study,* The Social Planning Council of Metropolitan Toronto, 1963, pp. 132–163.

Part Three

Principles of Community Organization

6

Some Principles Relating to Organization

THE principles of community organization which will be discussed here and in the next two chapters emerge from, and are based upon, the analysis developed in the preceding discussion. In broad terms these principles are shaped and limited by the frame of reference for community organization which we have provided. This framework derives from a specific value system, certain conceptions of the problem of community, and some general assumptions as to method. Within this general field, however, principles are shaped and focused more sharply by some understanding of the social forces which impinge on the individual and the group in the community, some understanding of the planning process, and some knowledge of empirical work in groups and communities. All these influence or determine the principles of community organization.

All this has been outlined in some detail in the preceding chapters, and we turn now to a consideration of specific principles—the elementary or fundamental ideas regarding initiation and continuation of community organization processes. These principles will be discussed in terms of the nature of the organization or association and the role of the professional worker.

The process of community organization requires some kind of structure and social organization. The task, or problem, or project will be considered by some group, committee, council, commission, or other form of organization. This latter may be formal, with title, offices, and employed staff, or informal with a few persons meeting in a home or school room. But there will be some form of association through which are channeled the aims and efforts of the persons concerned. The character, structure, and method of operation of the association are of first importance to us, since the association becomes the main channel through which the community. organization process moves. The degree to which the objectives and the unique process we have imputed to community organization are fulfilled is consequently dependent on the way the association functions. The principles guiding its development and work are, therefore, relevant principles of community organization. The association and process are not separate; the association is an instrument that facilitates the process.

We have chosen to use the term "association" to designate the organization (be it a committee, a council, a corporation, a commission, etc.) that is established to secure the objectives of the individuals concerned.[1] As we use the term it will mean the structure, established by members of the community, to deal with a community problem or problems.

DISCONTENT WITH EXISTING CONDITIONS IN THE COMMUNITY MUST INITIATE AND/OR NOURISH THE DEVELOPMENT OF THE ASSOCIATION

The motives which lead people into community endeavors are many and complex. We have already referred in a previous chapter to the fact that an "image of potentiality" or a "general experimental

---

[1] "Organization" is a word more generally used for this purpose, but the frequent use of this term would undoubtedly cause confusion in a context in which the phrase "community organization" appears regularly.

attitude" may motivate people to work through many different kinds of problems. Or people may be motivated to participate in a community association because they may make contacts or friends in this setting, or because they will find some satisfaction for their need for power. Any one, or cluster, of these motives may move a person or an association to pursue with interest and enthusiasm a particular community project. But we wish to emphasize here that deep and widely shared feelings of discontent with respect to certain features of community life may well be a more effective springboard for creation and development of an association that will have sufficient motivation and dynamic to overcome the many difficulties that confront diverse individuals and groups seeking a common means of dealing with problems of their community.[2]

This view is, of course, similar to one prevalent in psychiatry in which pain is considered a prerequisite to change. The individual will resist change and will, indeed, change only if such alteration promises to be less uncomfortable than the individual's present state. Only if the individual feels more pain, discomfort, unhappiness now than will probably be the case if certain changes are made, will there be present a suitable condition for intensive therapy. But if motivated by pain, and even though suffering through the therapy process, the individual may find quicker and more permanent resolution of his difficulties than if he were motivated to consider change because of an interest in psychotherapy or because of casual acceptance of the prevailing view that "everyone should have an analysis." It is not that casual interest or enthusiasm will not lead the individual to therapy; it is that such motivation is hardly a sufficient preparation for the rigorous and difficult soul searching which must accompany, if not precede, the successful resolution of a problem or the adjustment necessary for change.

We have already implied that in the community field there are a variety of motives which may be found among the individuals who support, and work in, a community association. Obviously, discontent is not the only motive that leads to community participation and involvement. But we return to the thesis, largely accepted

2 See Robert Dahl, *Who Governs?*, Yale University Press, 1963, p. 197.

in psychiatry, that discontent leads to a more dynamic involvement than the other motives mentioned. And, we suggest, such involvement is desirable if the community association (the neighborhood council, the welfare council, the village council) is to work through the many difficulties that must be confronted in initiating and developing the community organization process. For the participants in this process are not simply a few friends meeting around a common interest, nor a professional staff developing a plan to "sell" to a passive committee or board, but rather representatives from diverse groups with quite different interests and beliefs, seeking to find a means of working together on a problem of mutual concern. This process is one that is fraught with difficulties—with tension, conflict, and jealousy. If there is a profound conviction about the common problem, a deep feeling that "this community situation is wrong and must be righted," the group has a common motivation which may not only make it possible to overcome some of the difficulties confronted in the process, but may provide the association with a dynamic and a quality of life not found in associations nourished by gentler or more moderate motives.

It should be said, of course, that such discontent cannot (at least, should not for our purposes) be artificially induced. But we assume, and indeed experience has shown it frequently to be the case, that such discontents may arise spontaneously or that freeing people to talk will bring to the surface discontents which have long lain dormant. It is when these discontents are verbalized and agreed upon that the community association may spring into life or may take on a new and dynamic quality which makes it possible for the community to resolve coöperatively some of its common problems. The association will not, of course, always operate with burning discontent pressing it forward. There will be times of dynamic activity and times of relaxation. But it is when the association, representing the major groups in the community, becomes deeply discontented with a situation in the community that it will find the resources and the capacity to use the community organization process in an energizing way.

Thus, with some modification, community organization may use for its purposes a concept prevalent in psychiatry. "Pain" is perhaps a too precise and limited term to apply in the community field. But "discontent" as we use it here is a comparable term. For it implies such dissatisfaction with the present situation that considerable sacrifice will be endured to relieve this situation. Where, therefore, the association grows from the seeds of discontent with existing conditions in the community, it begins with a "common feeling" of importance and a "common wish" of some intensity. The stronger the feeling, the deeper the disturbance, the more profound the conviction, the greater will be the motivation to use effectively the association in resolving the problem about which discontent exists.

The validity of this principle has been intuitively recognized in all large continuing organizations. The Y.M.C.A. has, for example, revived itself time and time again by creating among its leaders a profound sense of discontent with "the condition of young men in our cities"—or with their condition in the army, in lumber camps, in industry, in small towns, etc. The program developed to meet these conditions provided the Y.M.C.A. leaders with great satisfaction, but it was when the leaders became gripped with a feeling of some great need from which a great sense of mission emerged that the organization—the Y.M.C.A. as a whole—strove and struggled in a way which energized and revitalized it.[3] This is no less true of the Communist party, the Roman Catholic Church, the Red Cross, or innumerable other organizations. All these have had continuing programs which elicited support from their followers, but it was when they faced some desperate need, some new challenge or threat, some emergency situation which constituted for all members "a situation to be remedied" that the organization took on new vitality. Further, many of these organizations in their wisdom far exceed modern public relations men in their skill in winning continuing support among their followers. For they develop a picture of universal evil, of great dangers and tragedies, of tremendous need,

[3] Murray G. Ross, *The Y.M.C.A. in Canada* Ryerson Press, 1951.

which continually captures or recaptures the sense of discontent which motivates support for the organization.

Thus the association that is to help develop and sustain community integration should emerge as a result of dissatisfaction with existing conditions and should continue with deep sensitivity to this or other dissatisfactions. It is under such circumstances that associations are able to withstand inner conflicts, contemplate and initiate changes and fresh adjustments. This is not to suggest, as already implied, that other motivations are not valid, that they will not, indeed, accompany discontent, but it is to emphasize the appropriateness of stirring and testing discontent in the community as a basis for identifying areas of work and initiating the community organization process.

This does not imply that associations may not operate unless all members are motivated by discontent. Clearly this is not so. But many associations that continue without such motivation operate with casual interest and loyalty on the part of their members; their work is often that of an employed staff, in which members have little share and only marginal interest; and the operation is such that it can seldom withstand conflict or criticism. The association which emerges from discontent may actually have greater difficulty in finding agreed-upon methods of procedure, because there is deep feeling about the operation, but it has a vitality and a significance for its members that make it a dynamic force in the life of the community.

Many community chests, welfare councils, and welfare funds emerged from a common feeling of discontent with sporadic, uncoördinated, and inconsistent efforts in the welfare field. And most of these associations revealed great vitality in their early days. Many have, however, lost this feeling of discontent and have become mechanical means of raising money or of doing superficial planning. If they are to regain this vitality, they must regain some feeling about significant problems with which they might be concerned. There are scores of problems in the financing and operation of welfare services, any one of which might refire discontent in associations.[4]

It will be maintained by some that such is not possible in the community in which apathy and disinterest in community affairs predominate. But experience suggests that friendly discussion about the community and its problems, the encouragement of expressions about some of these problems, the exchange of experiences and knowledge about these problems, and the encouragement of the first faint hope that something can be done about such problems, result in a mobilization of discontent and a desire for action.

It will also be questioned whether any individual, group, or organization has the right to disturb people in this way (or is morally justified in doing so). We have already discussed this matter in Chapter 3, but it may be reiterated here, that what is being suggested is not a crusade against some specific community evil. Rather are we urging that a process be initiated which may lead a community to the desire to act in respect to some problem it conceives as requiring attention. As will be obvious from the concluding chapters, what is proposed is not a means of cajoling or coercing people to a certain state of mind; it is a process by which people are freed to talk, identify needs, associate with others in dealing with these needs. If discontent exists, it will emerge in this process; if it does not exist, the process will cease to operate, if it begins at all. This is not dissimilar to the "aggressive case work" program of the New York City Youth Board[5] in which workers deal patiently yet persistently with persons some of whom firmly reject recognition of a potential problem. If this latter does not exist for them, little can or will be done; but the Board insists on its right to open discussions with these people. The result is that some identify their need for help, and that help is provided. But there is not coercion

[4] Bradley Buell's study (*Community Planning for Human Services*, Columbia University Press, 1952) by itself provides a challenge which, if communities were sensitive to it, might stimulate profound discontent with the existing situation.

[5] Sylvan S. Furman (ed.), *Reaching the Unreached*, New York City Youth Board, 1952.

of recognition; there is facilitation of a process by which it *may* be recognized.

That which has been said above has been frequently used to justify protest movements of various kinds. The "Berkeley crisis" and the "March on Selma" are two such movements that have been used both to confirm and to deny the validity of the "discontent theory." It is true that at both Berkeley and Selma a great sense of community was achieved within the protest group, and this sense of community was initiated, nourished, and sustained by dramatizing and focusing discontents about "freedom." At the same time, however, these protest movements, by the nature of the means used to achieve their goals (i.e., developing highly charged and emotional appeals against "the authorities" or "the establishment"), prevented any possibility of developing a community in the wider sense of the term.

Much of what has been said here can be used to develop a sense of community in a functional community, a minority group, a protest movement. We recognize the validity of such movements on occasion. But the primary process with which we are concerned relates to developing a sense of identity in the wider community. Whatever may be said about the necessity of protest movements —and they have unquestionably led to considerable social advance—they do by their nature often prevent rational discussion between dissenting groups.

It is out of conflict of opinion and attitude that new conceptions of society often arise. Conflict has a usefulness, therefore, that cannot be denied. It is when conflict, as an instrument of social discovery and social development, is exploited that danger and damage may result. The exploitation of conflict is evident when leaders of protest groups become obsessed with "winning" at any cost. They do not seek compromise or a solution on any but the precise terms they have defined and, indeed, there are occasions when it is apparent that they would be unhappy to have acceptance of their terms by the "opposition." Conflict is not simply a means; it becomes an end in itself. One does not need to point out that such exploitation of conflict is not consistent with the community organization process as it is described here.

DISCONTENT MUST BE FOCUSED AND CHANNELED INTO ORGANIZATION, PLANNING, AND ACTION IN RESPECT TO SPECIFIC PROBLEMS

Discontent *per se* is of doubtful value. To provide motivation for action, discontent must be focused on something specific. In fact, unfocused discontent is often a major block to any kind of action. For discontent with "everything that goes on here," with "life in general," with "the whole town," which never becomes more specific than expressions of dissatisfaction with "all the graft" or "the way the big shots operate" or the "crummy attitude everyone has" inevitably leads to chronic dissatisfaction because "there is nothing you can do about it." Such discontent may not be a harmful point for beginning but it is only when it is focused and ordered that it is a healthy and suitable motive for action. Generalized discontent inevitably festers and becomes poisonous. It is not more healthy simply because it is focused clearly on the "condition of our streets," "the price of milk," the "lack of care for the aged," "the need for recreational programs." But when it has reached this stage, action about some of these discontents can be taken, and this action provides for release of some of the frustration which may accompany the discontent.

Therefore the discontent needs not only to be focused but to be channeled into a structure through which something may be done about the problem. In community organization, people who are aware of and disturbed about a problem need to come together, to begin discussions about the problem and its scope, to begin to plan how to deal with it, and in light of this to begin a program of action. Those who undertake the release, focusing, and channeling of feelings of discontent may do so with assurance of the value of the procedure. It is better from the standpoint of the health of the individual and the community for discontent to be specific rather than general; it is better that this discontent be explored than be left dormant; it is better that action be taken in respect to this discontent than it is just to talk about it. This process, experience suggests, is sound. But it is not without dangers. To encourage hope that unrealizable goals can be secured may simply increase frustration and create the condition of *anomie*. Exploration of discontent needs to be realistic and resolution must be focused on some achievable goals.

THE DISCONTENT WHICH INITIATES OR SUSTAINS COMMUNITY ORGANIZATION MUST BE WIDELY SHARED IN THE COMMUNITY

Discontent is an appropriate springboard for many different kinds of minority movements—political parties, religious sects, educational movements. But community organization is not a minority movement and cannot be initiated solely by reason of needs or discontents which appeal to only a very small group in the community. The discontent must therefore be recognized and understood by the major parts of the geographic or functional community. Some parts of the community will be more disturbed by the problem than others. Some parts of the community may at first be only casually interested. But the problem on which discontent is focused must be one which potentially many members of the community will recognize and wish to attack. Our previous description of community organization process makes this condition essential.

It is assumed here that there can be identified problems of "the common life," that these can be ordered or ranked by the community, and that in dealing with them all parts of the community can be involved in planning and taking action in respect to them. For, as indicated, we are concerned not simply with solving certain "community problems," important as they may be, but also with developing the capacity of the community to function in respect to these and other similar problems. It is essential, therefore, that the discontent focus on common problems. The process may lead to a "splitting off" and development of minority groups, but if community organization is to be initiated, it must be differentiated from these minority movements and be content to deal only with those problems about which there is or can be unanimous, or almost unanimous, agreement.

This may be achieved as discontent is being focused and ordered in group session. Many problems will be identified and discussed. In the process of ordering these, the group must be aware of the purpose they are seeking to achieve. If it is simply action, one group will outvote another on the ranking of the problem and the minority may resist with such conviction that they will withdraw. But if the group is aware of its need to find common ground, it will order or rank needs (certainly in the early stages of the association) in terms of those which appear to represent unanimous concern. As an association matures, it may well permit, if not encourage, action on problems about which only part of the community is deeply concerned, but which other parts support. But fundamentally, the strength of the association (for community organization purposes) rests on the common problems which concern the major groups in the community, the ability of the groups to identify these problems coöperatively, and to work coöperatively in resolving them. Thus while discontent needs to be stimulated and focused, it requires in community organization to be ordered in such a way as will provide problem areas or needs which are of concern to many and which provide a common framework for coöperative work by the community.

Thus in the welfare community, the welfare council seeks to have identified problems which are of deep concern to all its members. It is not content to operate on the basis of needs defined by a few of its agency members, but seeks to find the areas of deep discontent in the welfare community as a whole. Similarly, the neighborhood council attempts to discover the problems that are foremost in the thinking of its various block clubs. It does not devote itself exclusively to the concerns of one block club or one group of block clubs, but tries to find the problems about which all block clubs are disturbed. But once the council (welfare or neighborhood) identifies the problem on which it is to work, it seeks to sensitize reluctant members of the community to the nature of the problem, to share the discontent with others, with a view to mobilizing action on the part of the whole welfare community or the whole neighborhood. Obviously, one cannot always expect agreement by everyone in the community. Some agencies, some block clubs, or some individuals in each may oppose the action on the discontent which has been brought into focus. This is inevitable. But one must recognize here, however, that a large percentage of a welfare or neighborhood community may find common discontents about which they have deep feeling. Even if such widespread agreement is not always possible, it is likely that consistent effort to "spread the area of shared concern" in the community will result in greater capacity of all parts to find concerns which all share.

THE ASSOCIATION MUST INVOLVE LEADERS (BOTH FORMAL AND IN-FORMAL) IDENTIFIED WITH, AND ACCEPTED BY, MAJOR SUBGROUPS IN THE COMMUNITY

Community organization as it has been described here requires the participation of the people of a community.[6] This is the essence of the task. For what is to be united in common action is people.

---

[6] A question that may arise here is whether everyone is to be included through representation in the community association. We are suggesting that all the major groups, i.e., the street clubs, ethnic associations, secret lodges, should be represented in the neighborhood association, but not everyone in the neighborhood belongs to one of these associations and therefore not everyone is represented. Or as the association moves to define its purpose, those groups will be excluded who are not in sympathy with the association's purpose. Thus the K.K.K. or other anti-Negro groups, or a communist organization, will not be members. An argument can be made that in this situation the neighborhood association is a functional community, i.e., a group of units with a common interest in the geographic community. In a functional community like the welfare community, all agencies are presumably represented on the welfare council, but some agencies may choose not to belong, and therefore are not part of the formal welfare community. Our view is that all units which are in sympathy with the association's purpose should be represented in the association, and efforts should be made to include them, but this obviously is not always possible.

And what is to be changed is to be changed by people, who in this process themselves change and, it is to be hoped, grow in capacity.

Culture is mediated through persons, and . . . a culture, or a profession, or a level of administration, or a point of view, cannot be represented by a charter, a diagram, or a printed description, but only by living human beings who themselves embody the position which is to be taken into account.[7]

Obviously, however, everyone in the community (if it is of any considerable size) cannot be involved in face-to-face contact with all others in the community; a means must be devised for participation through representation. This requires, first, identification of those groupings of people in the community which have significance for the participants and, secondly, the identification of the leaders of these groups. These are the points, it may be said parenthetically, that most workers and associations in the community organization field are less knowledgeable about than they should be.

Identification of the major groupings requires some understanding of the social organization of the community in which the work is being initiated. In the geographic community there is a natural division of formal organizations like the church, the village (legal) council, the school board, and in larger cities the board of trade, the service clubs, the welfare agencies, etc. Far more difficult to identify, but quite as important, is the informal organization: the little friendship groups, the neighborhood social club, the ethnic group, the fraternity, the secret lodge. In North America, workers in community organization tend to proceed as if the formal (mostly voluntary) organizations caught up most of the people in the community. As most studies of participation in voluntary organizations show, this is not the case. There may be, in fact, as few as 50 percent of the people active in such formal organizations.[8] If,

[7] Margaret Mead (ed.), *Cultural Patterns and Technical Change*, UNESCO, Paris, 1953, p. 308. See also W. J. H. Sprott, *Human Groups*, Penguin Books, 1958, pp. 155–156.

[8] Hurley H. Doddy, "An Inquiry into Informal Groupings in a Metropolitan Area," *Autonomous Groups Bulletin*, VI (September 1951), 11. See also Ira

therefore, participation is to include groups which have as members most if not all the residents of a community, some of these informal groupings must be involved. In most North American cities such groups abound, and they often constitute the only meaningful group relationship for many people in the community. In one recent study of a small section of a metropolitan area there were identified "more than two hundred informal groups unknown to institutional authorities in the area studied." [9] It is clear then that in community organization in geographic communities, not merely the formal organizations but the multiplicity of informal groups, which include large numbers of people in most communities, must be involved. As already implied, the size of the community and the size of the community association will determine whether one deals with informal groups with ten members or whether one must group various subgroups so that one hundred or one thousand members are represented.

But of basic importance in both geographic and functional communities is identification of those formal and informal groups which hold the allegiance of the people. The association may wish to include Greeks and may invite participation of their church but neglect the Greek Athletic Club, for example. More careful study might show that the club is a large cohesive group with great meaning for its members and one with which all members identify strongly. Obviously, this latter group must be included if representation from the Greeks is needed, and other things being equal, it might have more significance in the lives of people for community organization purposes. Thus identification of groups for participation requires a sufficient knowledge of the community so that not only the groups, but their relative importance to people in the community, can be appraised.

Having discovered the major groupings in the community, the

De A. Reid and Emily L. Ehle, "Leadership Selection in Urban Locality Areas," in Daniel Katz *et al.* (eds.), *Public Opinion and Propaganda,* The Dryden Press, 1954, pp. 446–459.

[9] *Ibid.*

next question is how these groups can be brought into communication around some common problem. It is generally accepted that this can be done most effectively through group leaders. But it is of the greatest importance that these leaders be accepted by, and positively identified with, the subgroup they are to represent. As already indicated, a community association frequently selects the "well-educated young man" or similar persons because they appear to the association to be the "natural leaders" of a street club, a neighborhood association, or a welfare agency. Often this is far from the truth. Often these are persons who are seeking status in other groups or in the community at large; they are not positively identified with their own subgroup, and represent their subgroup inadequately. Even if the subgroup is asked to appoint a leader to represent them, they will often select someone like the "well-educated young man" who, they feel, is more like the "outsider," able to speak his language, and knowledgeable in his ways. For either of these or other reasons, then, many community associations tend to be made up of like-minded people who do not truly represent subgroups and who are not fully trusted by subgroup members.

If the community association is to be a forum where the real concerns and desires and needs of the people are to be identified, and if the association is to have a means of communication with the people in the community, it is likely that the accepted leaders (both formal and informal) of subgroups must be members of the association. These leaders know their people and in turn are known by their people. Such leaders can speak with confidence for their people, and with their people, for usually effective communication exists between them. When such leaders are part of the association, their people feel that they as a group belong for they identify closely with these leaders. This is as true for the Rotary Club or Chamber of Commerce in a large city as it is for a small group of Yemenites in an Israeli village.[10] Recently a Y.M.C.A. board was asked to appoint a member to a welfare planning council, and the

---

[10] This is based largely on Eisenstadt's work reported in Chapter 4, *supra*, pp. 123–124. See also Edward C. Banfield, *Political Influence*, The Free Press, 1961, p. 273.

matter was referred to the president for action. The president looked over the list of members of the board carefully and came upon what he considered a "natural"—a young school teacher named Franks. Now Franks was the youngest member on the board; he was there by virtue of the fact that the members of this Y.M.C.A. are allowed to have one member to represent them on the board, and Franks was selected, chiefly by the staff, because he could make a "good impression at board meetings." But not only was Franks not a good representative of the Y.M.C.A. members, few of whom knew him, but he was an exceedingly poor representative of the Y.M.C.A. leadership on a community committee. These latter were on the whole successful businessmen, tolerant, but not respectful, of men like Franks. Franks could not possibly represent the Y.M.C.A. board. He lived in a different world, spoke a different language, was unaware of the power factors that determined so much of what Y.M.C.A. board members did.[11] Welfare councils and other community organizations are full of people like Franks, pleasant people, "willing horses," men of good will. But unfortunately such people do not establish meaningful lines of communication in the community, nor do they involve in the affairs of the community the group they presumably represent.

The accepted and identified leaders when they come together will constitute quite a different picture from a group of "Franks." They are leaders not because they are pleasant, nor skillful at meetings, nor able to articulate with facility. Their leadership is based on a complexity of factors which may include, but is not dependent upon, getting on well with outside groups. Because they speak for a group, discussion may be a good deal more frank and honest, conflicts may appear more frequently, a common language may be more difficult to secure. But such a group of leaders is the com-

---

[11] One may question here whether any of these board members represented the Y.M.C.A. membership and whether, therefore, the welfare council should not seek other representatives from the Y.M.C.A. Such may be the case, but if the Y.M.C.A. is to coöperate, certainly its power group must be represented in some way.

munity in miniature; and the unity, within which diversity is to exist, is not easily achieved.

Formal leaders such as schoolteachers, ministers, priests, village administrators, etc. must be included in a community association as well. Some of these leaders are leaders in the sense that they "have a following," and some do not. But as a group they have a great deal of power, and without the interest and support of these formal leaders, many difficulties would confront community organization projects. Their participation is desirable because of their power, but also because they are able to communicate with individuals and groups in the formal social organization. Janowitz [12] has suggested that the formal leaders of a community tend to form an elite, and that there is considerable mutual confidence and trust among members in this group. Since not all formal leaders are, or can be, included in the association, it will be important to discover here the persons who are recognized leaders of the "leadership elite," for these would be the best representatives of the formal leadership.

As already implied, inclusion of the respected and trusted leaders with whom the major subgroups identify provides a major step in integrating the community and makes possible initiation of a process of communication which, if it becomes effective, will nourish and sustain the process of community organization.

THE ASSOCIATION MUST HAVE GOALS AND METHODS OF PROCEDURE OF HIGH ACCEPTABILITY

The association brings together diverse elements in the community, each with its own interests, attitudes, and behavior patterns. The task of welding these diverse leaders and the groups they represent into a group that can work comfortably together is a considerable one. There is, of course, no "one way" in which this

[12] Morris Janowitz, *The Community Press in an Urban Setting,* The Free Press, 1952. See also Robert Dahl, *op. cit.,* pp. 184–189.

is done, but establishment of common goals and agreed-upon procedures is an important step.

The discontents discussed earlier may provide for specific goals, and in moving towards these, the association may work out its manner of procedure. But if the association is to continue, it will require a statement of its general goals and methods of procedure. The tendency for most groups is to formulate these quickly, and the first task of an association is often to develop a constitution. But if the statement of purpose and methods of procedure is to be meaningful to all members, it cannot be developed quickly, but must emerge with practice, experience, and discussion. The reason why so many constitutions are formulated and then filed away and forgotten is that they do not represent a frame of reference for the association, but rather a mechanical and meaningless ritual which has little if any adhesive quality in the life of an association. The writer was surprised to find that in many of the collective farm settlements in Israel, some of which had been operating for twenty years or more, there was no constitution or bylaws. But everyone living in the settlement knew how the village operated, what were the procedures for achieving certain ends, what was permissible and what was taboo.

It is perhaps less important that the purposes and procedures be carefully written and filed than that they be known and accepted. For they represent "the common life" and the frame of reference for the association. These purposes and procedures provide a way of life for the association, a way of behaving in many situations, a way of carrying on the association's business. Such purposes and procedures need not only to be developed, but to be articulated frequently for new members and old members alike, and adhered to in practice. It is just such purposes and procedures which permit expressions of aggression and hostility within the association without severely damaging it.

What is peculiar is the usual practice of giving long hours to developing a constitution at early meetings of an association and then continuing to operate as if no such document had been developed. It may well be that it is enough to begin with a simple statement of purpose and to allow procedures to develop with experience. But once these have been developed through practice or put in written form, it seems important that they be used. For they constitute, as suggested, the common frame of reference. In periods of disagreement, disturbance, or conflict they can be referred to both as a means of discovering direction and as a means of illustrating the common purpose for which the group exists. Urbanization tends to segmentalize life, and most groups find it difficult not to be diverted in their efforts. Frequent reference to goals, to "what we agree on," to "our accepted way of doing this," to "our tradition," to "our form of organization," to "our established procedures," provides for security, stability, and consistent direction which is essential in an association made up of diverse groups in the community.

THE PROGRAM OF THE ASSOCIATION SHOULD INCLUDE SOME ACTIVITIES WITH EMOTIONAL CONTENT

We have already referred to the importance of emotional and cultural factors in the life of an individual or an association. Yet many of the latter operate as if life were exclusively rational and a sharing of intellectual interests were sufficient for a community association. This is far from the truth. To bind together diverse groups requires common ideas, feelings, and traditions. This is not something that can be done artificially nor can it be forced. Yet it may be encouraged and facilitated.

An association often develops strength and cohesion in ways similar to the family. There are friendship, mutual support, difficult tasks, gay times, hardship, conflict, celebrations. There are times for work, for laughter, for relaxation. Similarily in the association which brings the community together there is variety of activity—hard work, but time also for celebration and festive occasions. These latter are far more significant than is commonly recognized, for they build that community sentiment essential for community integration. Such activities of the association may provide rich emotional experiences which contribute tremendously to the binding mortar of common sentiment in the community. Far from confining its activities to serious discussions, the community association should encourage and sponsor community celebrations consistent with the nature of its community. This tends to be done more effectively on other continents than in North America, where folk festivals, celebrations, and even official days such as Thanksgiving, have lost their ceremonial meaning.[13]

Man needs not only a sense of common purpose with his fellows but constant dramatization of it. Part of this may come through ceremonies and observations that have emotional content and meaning for the individual. Rituals which symbolize the values for which the association stands are valuable not only because they reinforce loyalty to those goals but also because they unify the group around these goals. Erich Fromm stresses modern man's need to find rituals of meaning, when he writes:

What is the situation today as far as the ritualistic aspect of religions is concerned? The practicing religionist participates in the various rituals of his church and undoubtedly this very feature is one of the most significant reasons for church attendance. Because there is little opportunity for modern man to share actions of devotion with others, any form of ritual has a tremendous attraction even if it is cut off from the most significant feelings and strivings of one's everyday life.

The need for common rituals is thoroughly appreciated by the leaders of authoritarian political systems. They offer new forms of politically colored ceremonies which satisfy this need and bind the average citizen to the new political creed by means of it. Modern man in democratic cultures does not have many meaningful rituals. It is not surprising then that the need for ritualistic practice has taken all sorts of diversified forms. Elaborate rituals in lodges, rituals in connection with patriotic reverence for the state, rituals concerned with polite behavior, and many others are expressions of this need for shared action, yet often they exhibit only the impoverishment of devotional aim and separation from those ideals officially recognized by religion and ethics. The appeal of fraternal organizations, like the preoccupation with proper behavior expressed in

[13] This is especially relevant for welfare councils whose "big event" each year is an annual meeting which is frequently incredibly dull.

etiquette books, gives convincing proof of modern man's need for ritual and of the emptiness of those he performs.

The need for ritual is undeniable and vastly underestimated. It would seem that we are left with the alternatives of becoming religionists or indulging in meaningless ritualistic practices or living without any gratification of this need. If rituals could be easily devised new humanistic ones might be created. Such an attempt was made by the spokesmen for the religion of Reason in the eighteenth century. It has been made by the Quakers in their rational humanistic rituals and has been tried by small humanistic congregations. But rituals cannot be manufactured. They depend on the existence of genuinely shared common values, and only to the extent to which such values emerge and become part of human reality can we expect the emergence of meaningful, rational rituals.[14]

Anyone who has been in a small French village on the day of Confirmation for children, and sees the meaning and significance which this has for individuals and the community as a whole, will recognize the power of such a day in creating a feeling of community. There are countless such celebrations throughout the world, some of which have lost their meaning and many of which are identified with values which belong to a world that has passed. But an association in the community that is alert to the validity of individual and communal need for symbols, celebrations, and rituals that dramatize the common life of the community will be constantly seeking ways to develop such media.

THE ASSOCIATION SHOULD SEEK TO UTILIZE THE MANIFEST AND LATENT GOOD WILL WHICH EXISTS IN THE COMMUNITY[15]

In every community there are large numbers of people who are willing to contribute to, identify with, and participate in any constructive community effort. This is a fact frequently ignored by those who are convinced that only apathy and indifference exist.

The extent of this good will is seldom recognized and seldom utilized. A number of years ago one of the writer's classes did a study of a disorganized, heterogeneous neighborhood in a large city.

---

[14] Erich Fromm, *Psychoanalysis and Religion*, Yale University Press, 1950, pp. 110–111.

[15] See Charles P. Loomis and Zona K. Loomis, *Modern Social Theories*, D. Van Nostrand, 1961, p. 266.

On the "worst street" in this neighborhood, where it was known that people did not know their neighbors and were not interested in the neighborhood, mothers were canvassed to see if they would take care of a neighbor's children one period a week until the children's sick parents recovered. Everyone who was asked agreed to help! Apparently, there was considerable good will and willingness to help a neighbor when the problem was understood. When this same street was canvassed later for contributions to the Community Chest, however, the response was very poor. The Chest was an impersonal and complex organization that had little meaning in the lives of these people. The good will that existed could not be, or at least was not being, used by the Community Chest.

A police chief, addressing a group of community workers, detailed the work of his men and indicated the numerous areas in which the interests of the police force overlapped those of the social workers in the community. He concluded by saying, "I suppose none of you knows as much about the community as we do, none of you covers every section of the city twenty-four hours a day as we do, none of you is more anxious than we are to develop healthy community living, yet we struggle with the job alone and without very much skill. Why is it that we have never supplemented each other's work?" Why indeed? On the whole, workers in the community organization field have never recognized the potential good will and support which might come from the police force. In many cities, modern police officers are anxious to associate themselves with constructive community projects. This is but another illustration of a source of good will and support largely unexplored.

In Doddy's study, to which reference has already been made, many of the two hundred groups studied would be interested in associating themselves with community projects. But these groups on the whole are not even known to be in existence by the formal community associations.

Many of the groups might perhaps support selected institutional projects, but few have been approached *as a group* by institutional representatives. In the absence of contact with the institutions, they do not volunteer their services but pursue interests of their own. If by chance they learn of . . . [a] project . . . they are likely to lend support.[16]

All this is to suggest that there are probably extensive sources of good will and support in the community which remain to be mobilized in coöperative community endeavors. It is not utilized largely because (a) workers are unaware that such good will exists, or (b) recognizing that it exists, they are (like the Community Chest mentioned) unable to "tap," to release, or to utilize it—their concern is too complex or remote to interest these people. This latter is a question of some importance, since a continuing question for any association is how it can orient its work so that it will fit into the experiences and systems of belief of the people of the community, to the end that its work will be meaningful for, relevant to, and receive support from, these people.

No rules for this can be provided, since the way this is done must be related to the type of community and the tradition and patterns of belief in the community. Three general comments may be made at this point, however. One is that the subgroup leaders are likely to be the wisest people in knowing how to communicate with groups in the community, what level of work will appeal to groups, and how their support may be ensured. The association must depend for its life on the wisdom of the people and their leaders. The point at which the leaders need help is not the content of what shall be done, but the ways by which broader participation and support may be achieved.

Second, it seems fairly safe to generalize that more appeals to people for support should be on a personal basis. Likert and Lippitt recount the advice given to a P.T.A. group anxious to secure additional schools.

But he (a social psychologist adviser) emphasized, in talking with the P.T.A., that if they wished to motivate people to participate in voting, it would be very important to have each household called upon by a volunteer from the P.T.A. to encourage every eligible voter in the household to vote. Acting in a vigorous manner upon his advice, the P.T.A. organized an information program about the need for additional schools

[16] Doddy, *loc. cit.*

and the cost of these additions which was widely disseminated through the coöperation of the local mass media. Most important of all, however, the local P.T.A. organized a campaign in which every household throughout the city was called upon. In these personal calls on individual households, neighbors of the person called upon gave him facts about the situation and urged him to be sure to vote in the forthcoming election. The effect of this campaign with its house-to-house solicitation was a large vote in the election and one which was overwhelmingly in favor of the additional schools and of the bond issue to finance them.[17]

There are innumerable illustrations of the great value of such person-to-person contacts, not simply for "putting over" a campaign but for establishing neighborly contacts, sharing information, and strengthening the fiber of community life.

Third, people should be given the opportunity of participating and contributing at the level at which they can make their contributions comfortably and in a manner that has meaning for them. The Polish woman (or the British, or the Chinese, etc.) might be happy to set up a table serving a Polish meal at one of the Chest dinners but be unhappy about canvassing for the Chest in her church group. The former she would do well; it would be appreciated in a way she would understand; she would feel successful. The canvassing she might not do well; she might feel inadequate and would tend to withdraw. Many businessmen who will delight in the struggle to secure finances for a new community center will be uncomfortable in the planning group establishing the program of art classes or nursery schools for the center. Ethnic groups may find great happiness in participating in a folk festival, yet feel ill at ease at a formal dinner of various groups to raise money for a project. Awareness of the point at which groups are able to participate is especially important in the early stages of involvement. Later, as interest broadens and knowledge of the association grows, individuals and groups may extend the nature of their participation. In the beginning, if withdrawal is to be avoided, participation at a comfortable level is a prerequisite.

[17] Rensis Likert and Ronald Lippitt, "The Utilization of Social Science," in Leon Festinger and Daniel Katz (eds.), *Research Methods in the Behavioral Sciences,* The Dryden Press, 1953, p. 596.

7

Some Principles Relating
to Organization (continued)

IN THIS chapter we will continue a discussion of
those principles which, when applied, may facilitate development
of a community association that effectively nourishes the community
organization process. It needs only to be emphasized again that
these principles are not discrete units; they are, in fact, inseparable
and must be considered as a whole rather than as units capable of
separate application.

THE ASSOCIATION MUST DEVELOP ACTIVE AND EFFECTIVE LINES OF
COMMUNICATION BOTH WITHIN THE ASSOCIATION AND BETWEEN THE
ASSOCIATION AND THE COMMUNITY

The essence of community, as John Dewey suggested, is communication. For without communication there cannot be that interaction by which common meanings, common life, and common
values are established. This implies that communication involves a
good deal more than the mechanical process of receiving and transmitting messages. It posits a process by which the area of common
understanding and shared values is widened in the community.

Ideally, community organization provides a suitable means for developing "community" in this sense, for it brings together diverse groups in a common undertaking and sets in motion a process of interaction through which effective communication may be established. Unfortunately such a process does not often emerge and develop without difficulty. And some of the conditions of effective communication are in the process of discovery. Enough work has been done in this field to suggest some useful clues.

To begin with, effective communication within a group, or between groups, depends to a considerable extent on the quality of relationships between the people involved.[1] Where hostility, fear, aggression, distrust, disrespect predominate in these relationships, communication will be far less effective than where there are friendliness, mutual respect, and trust. This suggests the importance of the creation of a social climate which permits and facilitates communication. The hypothesis might be stated thus: communication in meetings will be more effective when people feel comfortable and secure; when there is freedom from fear and anxiety about others in the meeting; when people feel on equal-status terms; when contributions to discussion are not only welcomed but there is a subtle and persistent pull to ensure such contributions; and when contributions to the discussion are received with appreciation and understanding. If this hypothesis has validity, and there is some evidence to suggest it has, it emphasizes an essential task in the association devoted to community organization, namely, development of an atmosphere in which participants feel safe and able to express themselves freely. This does not mean that there will not be conflict or that interpersonal relations will necessarily be intimate, but it does imply that relations between the persons involved will be such that fear is a minor, and security a major, element.

---

[1] Elliot Jaques, *The Changing Culture of a Factory*, Tavistock Publications, 1951, p. 301; see also Harold H. Kelley, "Communication in Experimentally Created Hierarchies," in Dorwin Cartwright and Alvin Zander (eds.), *Group Dynamics*, Harper & Row, 1953, pp. 443–461. See also Peter M. Blau and W. Richard Scott, *Formal Organizations*, Chandler, 1962, pp. 116–139.

Second, the way in which communication is structured is also of importance. There are two aspects to this. One has to do with the arrangements of people and their relationships that are made to facilitate communication, and the other with the methods that are used to make interaction meaningful.

What is the best arrangement of people in an association? The traditional pattern in North America is the large board or central committee with perhaps forty or fifty members, with a variety of smaller subcommittees each working on a separate task. There is reason to doubt whether there is effective communication in a board group that is as large as indicated and that meets for less than two hours as infrequently as once a month. If this is so, it means that a subcommittee, which must report to the board or central committee, probably never communicates adequately the nature and result of its deliberations to the board or to other subcommittees. The question remains as to whether there are not more effective ways of organizing the work of an association so that communication may be facilitated. Two well-known pieces of research are suggestive at this point. All practitioners in the field of community organization have recognized the advantage of small groups, as opposed to large groups, if meaningful interaction between members is to take place. Hare's study [2] confirms and gives point to this impression. Not only is it likely that the small group of five members will achieve consensus more readily and will give its members more opportunity to speak than a larger group of twelve members, but the smaller group experience promises more satisfaction and more genuine community of feeling. Bavelas' work on leadership in small task-oriented groups is also of interest at this point. For while he found that leadership with "high centrality" produced more quickly and with fewer errors, the groups with such leadership tended to have lower morale and to achieve less insight than groups in which leadership was in a less central or dominant

[2] A. Paul Hare, "Interaction and Consensus in Different Sized Groups," in Dorwin Cartwright and Alvin Zander (eds.), *Group Dynamics*, Harper & Row, 1953, pp. 507–518.

position.[3] These tentative findings would suggest that communication would be most effective in small groups of five members, in which leadership functions were shared, and in which informal and intimate discussion of a problem was undertaken. Can such a hypothesis be tested or tried in a community association?

The tendency is to believe that the large board or central committee is essential for efficiency and legal purposes. It may be questioned how efficient such an operation is, however, if meaningful communication is one criterion of effectiveness. If the purpose of an association is not simply to "get things done," i.e., to pass resolutions, build schools, etc., but to establish effective communication, it may be asked if this particular committee structure does anything to further the purpose of the association. Since it is essential that a majority of the members participate in decisions that are binding on the association, a compromise to meet this requirement and to make for better communication might be experimented with. The regular two-hour meeting of the board or central committee might take a form somewhat like the following: (1) fifteen minutes to clear essential routine business; (2) half an hour for briefing on several major issues on which decisions must be made—the briefing being provided by a subcommittee or expert in the matter; (3) half an hour for discussion in small groups of five members to consider these issues; and (4) forty-five minutes during which the groups report their findings in general meeting and a decision on the issues is secured. There might be a variety of patterns useful here, and only experimentation will indicate which is feasible. It may be that such a structuring of a meeting will prove more time-consuming, that more awkward questions will be asked, that fewer resolutions will be passed, but if communication and building of common understandings are important, some sacrifice of the desire for quick action is required.

A second consideration which relates to the structuring of com-

[3] Alex Bavelas, "Communications Patterns in Task-oriented Groups," in Dorwin Cartwright and Alvin Zander (eds.), *op. cit.*, p. 505.

munication has to do with reliance on formal presentation in either written or verbal form as a means of establishing common understandings. But just as memory is selective, so is one's perception of what one sees and hears. Each individual sees and hears through a screen that each builds for himself. A message of any complexity transmitted from one person to another, without the second person having an opportunity to question or clarify the meaning of the message with the sender of the message, seldom has the same meaning for these two persons. Each tends to interpret the message in his own way. Anyone who has marked examination papers will recognize the variety of interpretations given to relatively simple and straightforward questions and statements. To listen to a variety of delegates report on the meaning and implications of the addresses presented at a conference will often cause one to ask if these people attended the same conference.

To rely on a simple exposition, either verbal or written, of complex matters is unrealistic. People need opportunity to understand, assimilate, and use new ideas and new information. The method suggested above, of small group discussion of essential matters, may facilitate such understanding. But this will require a more limited agenda than many associations are ready to consider. Yet it seems clear that if real understanding is to ensue in the community organization process, the content must be limited to a few manageable items, and sufficient time for interaction in respect to these must be provided.

It has been suggested, also, that communication systems can easily be overloaded. Messages can be sent out in such volume and number that they have little if any meaning. It is said that the German Intelligence knew the date of D-Day prior to its occurrence in World War II. But Allied Intelligence had secretly released information about so many other more likely dates for the invasion that the June 6th date was rejected by the German command. Overloading the communication system, as in this case, causes confusion and makes for ineffectiveness in transmitting messages. But lack of communication may lead to what has been called the "starvation phenomenon." Persons in an association or community who are not recipients of any messages, who are not informed, who are never consulted, will feel rejected and will find development of community attitudes difficult. Just as the child grows only through communication with others, so the individual will develop in the association and community only through communication with others in these settings. In communication, therefore, there must be neither "overloading" nor "starvation." These may both be viewed as points on a scale, and only careful study of a communication in a particular situation will permit one to find a point between these which will satisfy this particular requirement for effective communication.

Some studies of communication [4] suggest that messages move more effectively through accepted channels than through new channels. That is, a message about the association will be more widely distributed, and received with more understanding, if it is relayed through channels that are familiar to those for whom the message is intended. These channels will vary in all communities, and only study of local customs will reveal them. A message regarding government agriculture policy, for example, may be read and understood by more farmers if it appears in their regular farm journal than if it appears in a special pamphlet sent to them directly from a government office. On the whole, community groups will be more understanding if messages are transmitted to them by their own leaders instead of by an outsider or stranger. Again this is a point at which the wisdom of the local people themselves must be relied upon, for it is often these people who know what kind of communication is possible, and what media are most effective.

One of the most effective communication devices in less-developed countries is the pilot project, in which the problem is worked out on a small scale by the people who will later decide whether to expand the range and size of the project. The pilot project provides an opportunity to see and hear (perhaps to "feel") at first hand the nature of an idea, technique, or operation with which

[4] Eugene L. Hartley and Ruth L. Hartley, *Fundamentals of Social Psychology*, Knopf, 1952, p. 65.

there has previously been little experience and about which communication is extremely difficult. It provides for participation, demonstration, and understanding in a way that is difficult to match except in development of the full project itself.

All this indicates the complexity of the communication process. Yet the nature of the association which brings people together in face-to-face contacts holds the potentiality of overcoming many of the difficulties. Common errors are to develop one large committee, work on too many projects, "overload" a few people in the community, and to fail to utilize effectively existing media of communication. More effective work would, it is suggested, require one large central organization with a number of small task forces in which there was intimate sharing of ideas about the problems at hand; development of a feeling of responsibility and skill on the part of group leaders in serving as communicating "links" between the association and the community; processing of material so that there is emphasis on quality of communication rather than quantity; use of existing media (e.g., involvement of the neighborhood newspaper editor); identification of effective communicators (people who communicate well) and more adequate use of these skilled people in the association and the community.

THE ASSOCIATION SHOULD SEEK TO SUPPORT AND STRENGTHEN THE
GROUPS WHICH IT BRINGS TOGETHER IN COÖPERATIVE WORK

The association seeks to be an organization of the community. The community participates through the units or groups into which it has divided itself. These units come together through their leaders to achieve objectives all have defined as desirable. The association does not exist apart from these units—it represents the "common life" of these units.[5]

The association is no stronger than the sum of its parts—the groups which compose it. If the association is made up of groups which are themselves disorganized, torn by dissension, or apathetic,

[5] See Robert Morris, "Basic Factors in Planning for the Coordination of Health Services," *American Journal of Public Health*, LIII (March 1963), p. 471.

it has a narrow base of participation and support in the community, for weak groups are so withdrawn, or concerned with their own problems, that they have little capacity for coöperative activity. Therefore, while a leader of a weak group may participate in the association, he will find it difficult to involve his group in the planning and activities of the community association. A neighborhood council made up of block clubs inevitably finds that those clubs that are weak and ineffective provide the least support for the council's projects. A cleanup day in the neighborhood will find diligent work on the streets of the strong clubs, and indifferent, if not absence of, effort on the streets with weak clubs. Similarly at meetings and conferences, the strong clubs send representatives who speak with vigor, while the weak clubs are negligent in attendance and casual in participation.

If, therefore, the association is to be strong, the units which compose it must themselves be strong cohesive groups. The attitude of the association must be one which seeks to provide support, encouragement, and help to its member groups. It can do this by creating an atmosphere in which all groups feel accepted, free from criticism, and needed to help in achieving common goals. It can encourage development of weak groups by exchange of ideas among the various groups—of ways difficulties were overcome in successful groups. And it can provide direct services to the weak groups by studies, coaching of leadership, assistance by professional staff workers, etc. There must be consistent effort to help groups achieve cohesion and capacity to function independently. This may well mean applying the concept of community organization in the life of the weak group so that they become involved in identifying their problems and begin themselves to resolve these difficulties.

THE ASSOCIATION SHOULD BE FLEXIBLE IN ITS ORGANIZATIONAL PROCEDURES WITHOUT DISRUPTING ITS REGULAR DECISION-MAKING ROUTINES

We have emphasized the importance of accepted "rules of order" and methods of procedure which, as they become established, create a sense of security in the operation of association business.

To suggest flexibility is not to argue for disruption of these established procedures. These latter, especially in respect to decision making, must remain inflexible if active interest and participation are to be maintained. But within these established procedures there is opportunity for use of a variety of methods. At one point a specialist may be consulted; at another point a group of knowledgeable people from the community may be involved; at another point all the members of one of the participating groups may be invited to contribute because of their special interest in the problem under discussion; at several times the official meeting may adjourn to become a committee of the whole; on other occasions the association may authorize studies, make visits, appoint commissions; each spring the association may decide to move to a camp for a week-end meeting on some special problem. A great variety of patterns for acquiring data and consensus may be used without, at any point, taking responsibility away from the group charged with decision making.

THE ASSOCIATION SHOULD DEVELOP A PACE FOR ITS WORK RELATIVE TO EXISTING CONDITIONS IN THE COMMUNITY

The concept of pace has two connotations here. One refers to the pace which the association develops for its own work, and the second to the pace of life which exists in the community and which will condition the tempo of a community program.

As to the first, the association must acquire a pace for its own work. This develops as members learn to work together, as procedures are established, and as agreement comes as to accepted responsibilities. Some groups will meet weekly, others monthly; some will expect subcommittees to report at each meeting of the major association, others will be content with an annual report; some groups will expect members to assume heavy responsibilities, others will assign heavy duty to staff members and consider themselves mainly responsible for policy decisions. Whatever the tempo and responsibilities may be, they need to be understood throughout the association so that a pace for work becomes established. There requires to be a pulsation in the organization which all members feel and to which all adjust. Failing this, there will be disorder, if not chaos, with parts of a plan being carried forward without any conception of the whole, or with different parts of the plan emerging without coherence. Establishment of major objectives with minor objectives assigned, all with agreed-upon time schedules, may help to bring about a pace of work in the association to which all adjust.

There tends to be in many associations a pace which requires consistent and intensive work on one project following another. While the advantage of always having before it a project which catches and holds the interest of all members and groups is obvious, it may well be that the pattern of "withdrawal and return" would be more useful for many associations. That is, it may be desirable to accomplish one community project, to take time to celebrate this successful achievement, to relax, to meditate before continuing. Such a rhythm may be, in the long run, more productive, more meaningful, and closer to the needs of people than the steady (and heavy) pace of work which often becomes routine and monotonous.

It is the existing pace in the community, and the pace at which a community will involve itself in a community venture, that are perhaps most important. Many workers in the community field—technical experts, social workers, mental health experts—are what can only be termed "eager beavers." They are ambitious for their community, impatient for results, anxious to induce change. In case-work, the importance of adapting treatment procedures to the pace which the client finds comfortable and feasible is clearly recognized. The same principle applies in community organization. One begins at the point at which the client is at the present time and works at his pace. Rimrock and Homestead (see Chapter 4) are entirely different communities, and the worker in community organization who expects to begin at the same level, and to proceed at the same pace, in these two communities is entirely unrealistic.

Further, almost any community project, even though it implies a relatively simple development, requires adjustment not only to the obvious change but to the effects of the change on other aspects of the culture. A relatively simple change like introduction of a water system in a village requires decisions as to outlets for homes, gardens, and cattle, and each of these affects existing behavior patterns. A welfare council may wish unification of all the counseling services in the community, but this requires decisions regarding the professional staff of each service, the different fee policies of the various agencies, the clients who prefer one agency as against a central agency, the loyalty of committees to each single service, etc. To work out not merely the change, but the implications of the change, requires a good deal of time in any situation, but the time period needed will depend on the disposition and capacity of the people making the change. To press for change, or a series of changes, may be simply to overload or overwhelm those expected to make the changes, and may result in frustration, withdrawal, or active resistance on the part of those affected.

If these changes are to be worked through, the community must be thoroughly involved. The degree to which this latter is possible and the pace at which it occurs depend on prior relations between groups, attitudes towards the community, the strength of the association, and its leadership. Pace must be adjusted to these realities. But even when these factors are all favorable, more time is required than is ordinarily expected. For what is involved in the community organization process is change in the whole culture—people and their ways of behaving must change—and if this is to be worked through so that the experience of change is a constructive growing experience for the participants, a good deal of time is required, and this time must be determined indigenously rather than by some external agent.

The structure of the association in which leaders of various groups are involved in determining what project shall be worked upon, in what way, and at what speed, provides for realism in respect to pace. On the whole, such leaders will select projects that have meaning and will establish a pace that is consistent with that of the community and comfortable for it. Yet people involved in identifying and planning for action in respect to community problems often develop a readiness for action that is not shared by those who are less deeply involved in the planning process. At such points adjustments must be made, the association must slow down, must help the community develop a similar readiness for action. Times of crisis, of conflict, of stress may of course be times when the pace may be stepped up, when speedy action is required and demanded. But here again, the knowledge of members of what is traditional, what is acceptable, what pace is feasible in particular situations is the most effective guide as to what can be done.

The implication of a good deal of the above is that movement is slow, and particularly so if people in the community are to participate and develop a project that is to facilitate community integration. All this is true. Yet people like to have immediate satisfaction; there are fewer today who are content with a "wait and see" philosophy, most want to "live today." [6] Thus there is likely to be a good deal of dissatisfaction with long-term projects, projects which require a good deal of work, but the results of which will not be seen for some time. Months of planning, negotiating, referring matters back to subgroups becomes wearisome, and there is little achievement to sustain morale. Here it seems important for someone (probably the professional worker) to act as interpreter, to emphasize foresight of consequences, to picture that which may eventually be accomplished. Further, the program of an association might well be developed as a novelist develops the major and minor themes in his book. There is one major theme that sustains interest throughout, yet each chapter has some unique development which is of interest in itself. Similarly the organization may have a long-term objective which will take a year to achieve, and the group will work toward this end; but meetings may be more satisfying if, in addition to discussion of progress in respect to this major objective, there are other smaller projects or interesting developments which provide

[6] Robert S. Lynd, *Knowledge for What?* Princeton University Press, 1948, p. 91.

some sense of immediate achievement. Short- and long-term targets, clearly differentiated, may constitute a useful strategy for the work of a community association.

THE ASSOCIATION SHOULD SEEK TO DEVELOP EFFECTIVE LEADERS

Primarily, we are concerned here with development of those kinds of leaders who will facilitate the community organization process, who will help the central association to be productive, and who will contribute to development of morale both in the association and in the community.[7]

If there is one common fact that is being discovered about leadership, it is that it is a complex role with a multiplicity of functions, and with many changing and interacting forces determining what is appropriate behavior in this role. In fact, it may be useful to ask whether there is ever *one* leader in a group, or whether it is not more accurate to suggest that while there may be one *central figure*, there are actually many persons contributing to the leadership of the group. Bales [8] has shown, for example, that in most small work groups there need to be both a "popular leader" and a "task leader." The latter presses to keep the group engaged in its work, but his consistent pressure for decision and work on the part of the group tends to provoke irritation and to injure the unity of the group. The "popular leader" or the "best-liked person" helps to maintain and to restore group unity and to keep the members of the group happy. Two such leadership functions, Bales suggests, are seldom found in one person. But where these two types of leaders recognize and accept each other's role and work together for group ends, they constitute a strong leadership team. It may well be, as research proceeds in this field, that it will be found that there are many leadership functions, which must usually be assumed by someone

[7] For an excellent discussion of this topic, see Cecil A. Gibb, "Leadership," in Gardner Lindzey (ed.), *Handbook of Social Psychology*, Addison-Wesley, 1954, pp. 877–921.

[8] R. F. Bales, *Quarterly Report*, Carnegie Corporation, New York, October 1953, p. 1.

other than the "central figure" in the group. Some group members may assume leadership functions in matters of content or special kinds of content; others may assume leadership functions in matters of process or special aspects of process; some may perform special leadership functions in respect to special aspects of both content and process. This does not do away with the value and functions of a central figure in the group, but it suggests that he does not perform all the leadership functions, and indeed, that the leadership functions he does perform depend also upon the leadership capacities of members of the group of which he is the chairman or central figure.

It seems clear, though, that however much the leadership functions are distributed in the group, the central figure or chairman or formal leader will facilitate group productivity when he is accepted and supported by members of the group. We have already referred to Eisenstadt's research and the importance it seems to place on the positively identified leader in terms of group cohesion (see Chapter 4). Another small study, which tested for some differences in thirteen groups in which formal leaders were accepted and supported, and in which formal leaders were not supported, showed:

On every criterion of effective group functioning as measured by the participant observers' ratings, the mean ranks of the strong formal leadership groups were higher than weak formal leadership groups. The mean ranks of the former were at least two positions higher in volume of participation, usefulness of suggestions, extent of participation, degree of coöperation, and assumption of responsibility.[9]

It may well be that effective groups contribute to the development of "strong leaders," but in any case, it seems clear that there is an association between cohesion and productiveness in group life and leaders that are accepted and supported.

The central figures who recognize the varied nature of the leader-

[9] Neal Gross, William E. Martin, and John G. Darley, "Studies of Group Behavior: Leadership Structures in Small Organized Groups," *The Journal of Abnormal and Social Psychology*, XLVIII (July 1953), 431.

ship role and ensure that it is decentralized so that many persons in the group assume various aspects of this role apparently secure consistently better results in terms of group productiveness and cohesion. Cartwright and Zander, in summarizing a number of studies in this area, write:

All of the leaders in these experiments were externally imposed upon the group, but even so those leaders who tended to distribute the functions of leadership more widely obtained group performances generally regarded as "better" in our society. When production was measured, it was higher. When interpersonal affect was measured, it was more friendly. And when cohesiveness was measured, it was stronger.[10]

Similarly it is reported that leaders who encourage participation, who do not impose their ideas, enjoy better results than supervising leaders who manage the production of group discussions.

The results indicate that the participatory style of leadership was more effective than the supervisory style in creating changes in attitudes. Members of groups with participatory leadership were also more satisfied with the meetings, more interested in the task, found the groups more friendly and enjoyable, and were more productive.[11]

On the surface, the evidence here seems to be complete and definitive. Yet it must be emphasized that productive work does not depend solely on the central figure and the way he performs. The character of the group is a factor of equal importance. Just as every leader affects the group, so does every member affect the group and the leader. One rather intensive study of sixteen groups in which membership was rotated so that each member worked in five different groups at a variety of tasks concludes:

Relationships were found, indicating that individual members significantly affect the characteristics of small groups. In general it was found that effective group functioning was facilitated by coöperativeness, efficiency, and insight, while behavior which we have called "striving for

10 Cartwright and Zander (eds.), *op. cit.*, p. 544.
11 *Ibid.*, p. 548.

individual prominence" reduced group cohesiveness and friendliness
. . . mature, accepting persons facilitate while suspicious nonaccepting
persons depress group characteristics indicative of smooth functioning.[12]

Thus each individual member of the group affects group productiveness and cohesion. And one might logically expect that distribution of leadership functions throughout the group would increase
the influence of the individual member on these group characteristics. It may well be, therefore, that in community organization
what is required is less training of individuals in the community and
more training of groups to the end that all members of the groups
will coöperatively define their roles, learn to coördinate these with
others, and implement them with skill.

Some support for this suggestion comes from another study which
raises serious questions as to whether all groups everywhere will
function more effectively with permissive, or sharing of, leadership.
This study, of seventy-two small decision-making conferences in
business, industry, and government, summarizes its findings as
follows:

(1) There is a general expectation in the present population of
groups maintaining that the socially designated leader, the chairman,
should be the sole major behavioral leader. . . . (a) Leadership sharing
by members other than the designated leader tends to be related to a
decrease in group cohesiveness and satisfaction with the meeting over
the entire sample of groups, and in groups with more and less permissive
leaders. (b) These results also hold in groups contrasted on whether
the leadership sharing is generally supporting or less supporting of the
chairman.[13]

Thus it may be that the customs and expectations of the group
may determine how many and what kind of leadership functions

[12] William Haythorne, "The Influence of Individual Members on the Characteristics of Small Groups," *The Journal of Abnormal and Social Psychology*,
XLVIII (April 1953), 284.
[13] Leonard Berkowitz, "Sharing Leadership in Small Decision-making
Groups," *The Journal of Abnormal and Social Psychology*, XLVIII (April
1953), 238.

the central figure or chairman should assume. And if change in the direction of more or less sharing of leadership functions is to be made, it should be made with all members of the group actively participating. Such a process of group training may, as suggested, be the most realistic and effective means of leadership training.

The implications of these data and speculations for the association seeking to develop coöperative work in the community are manifold. First, because of their importance as communication links, and as status figures in the community, it is essential that the positively identified leaders (both formal and informal) of the various groupings of people in the community be involved in the association. The importance of involvement of these strategic figures in community organization has already been emphasized. By the same token, it is important that subgroup leaders who constitute members of the association should have as their chairman or central figure someone whom they will accept and with whom they can identify. The question of which way the group will distribute its leadership functions is usually one of great delicacy. For here we have a group of "recognized leaders," each with his own conception of leadership, each from a somewhat different background, each with rather different expectations of how the chairman should perform. As with other procedures, this must be worked out by "trial and error," but probably at the conscious level. This implies conscious awareness of the "leadership problem," articulation of methods used to deal with it, sharing in the evaluation of results, searching for agreement of the "most effective way to operate." This will be, in effect, "leadership training," but leadership training at the group level, where all participate and where the processes of identifying and assigning leadership functions may increase leadership skills and strengthen group cohesion. Various new techniques such as the use of the observer, "feedback" procedures, use of sound recorders, and other devices, may greatly facilitate the development, and have as yet hardly been used in this, the most complex group relationship in the community.

THE ASSOCIATION MUST DEVELOP STRENGTH, STABILITY, AND PRESTIGE IN THE COMMUNITY

Community organization is a process which moves toward increasing coöperation among community groups as the latter deal with common community projects. At best this is an intricate, and at times vague, concept. It requires to be made more meaningful to the community, and this can be accomplished in part at least by the successful achievements of the association, by persistent and consistent interpretation, and by the high prestige of the association, be it a council, committee, or board. The association can become a symbol of community coöperation. The people in the association, and the way the association functions, can represent the actuality of the idea for many people in the community. If it is to do this effectively, the association must have strength both in terms of its involvement of accepted group leaders and in terms of its ability to work through difficult community problems. Such an association will win the participation and support of the people, and will be a symbol which stands for, and induces community coöperation.

Needless to say, there are many difficulties that confront such an achievement. To paraphrase Myrdal, it can be said that the psychological impediments to overcome in making community coöperation more effective are all concerned with how to get leaders, and behind them their groups, and ultimately all the peoples, to experience allegiance to the common cause, and to do this when, in fact, community coöperation is so weak. For while, on the one hand, the main means of fostering this larger allegiance is the actual experience of coöperation, coöperation cannot develop except with allegiance as a basis. This is the eternal problem of man and his institutions. The institutions preserve human attitudes fitting them, but such attitudes develop only in response to living in the institutions themselves. This is the basic sociological difficulty in community coöperation.[14]

[14] Gunnar Myrdal, "Psychological Impediments to Effective International

This is to say, the association will be a symbol for loyalty only when it has enough loyalty to make it a worthy symbol. But these are not separate achievements; they grow and emerge together. The association begins with a minimum of security and loyalty; as it proceeds and distrust diminishes and self-confidence develops, loyalty and allegiance increase, which feed into the association, leading to more impressive achievements, which in turn lead to increased status, which in turn makes it a more worthy object for loyalty, etc. This is the history of many such institutions. But the achievement of status as a worthy symbol comes slowly and only as people learn to work together, taste the satisfaction of coöperative endeavor, enjoy success, find common values and rituals to express these values, begin to achieve insight into the process in which they are participating.

One of the fundamental aspects of this development is the relationship between the association and the groups whose leaders constitute its members. If the association becomes a competitor of, or takes over projects or activities that traditionally belong to, groups in the community, the opportunities for coöperative work are greatly reduced. People in a free society do not coöperate when they are threatened. And an association which threatens in any way the existence of certain traditional groups becomes not an object for loyalty but an object of suspicion. Ways must be found, therefore, to clarify this relationship; the association exists to carry on planning only in those areas which members agree represent common concern and suitable fields for coöperative work. If this is understood, if the atmosphere of the association meetings is accepting and noncritical, and if support is provided for the activities of subgroups, the chances for coöperative work are thereby improved.

As in all associations, but perhaps to a greater extent in community groups because of their heterogeneous membership, the association established for coöperative work must be prepared for outbursts of hostility, scapegoating, threats of withdrawal and reprisals, and failures. Jaques' admonition here is that these incidents cannot be avoided; that they must usually be worked through, since to attempt to avoid them merely postpones their eventual disposition; and that only through self-understanding will a group be able to achieve cohesion and productiveness. Reluctance to deal frankly with such problems is being overcome at Glacier Metal Works by:

. . . first, the growing recognition that problems which are not tackled directly are expressed indirectly and cause even more trouble and disruption; second, the experience that difficulties in group relationships can be successfully tackled and worked through. . . .[15]

The result is that:

Once a group has developed insight and skill in recognizing forces related to status, prestige, security, authority, suspicion, hostility, and memory of past events, these forces no longer color subsequent discussion nor impede progress to the same extent as before. Dealing with them accounts for a smaller part of the group's activities, absorbs less of its energies, and allows it to handle more effectively those issues which are on the written agenda.[16]

If, therefore, the association can undertake a process which leads to some degree of self-understanding, it can anticipate a great release of creative effort in its work. But such a process cannot be recommended without reservation to community groups. It would be an unusual community group that would not require highly skilled professional help in this process. In other words, what Jaques is describing is a technical process which can (we believe) be engaged in only with competent professional help. With this help it can undoubtedly lead, as it did at Glacier, to significant results. Without this help many associations must learn to withstand the storms and stresses of operation by the strength of the bonds which hold them together. The individual with sufficient ego strength can withstand many shattering experiences without therapy and without understanding their nature, cause, or effect. Similarly an organi-

---

[15] Jaques, *op. cit.*, p. 296.
[16] *Ibid.*, pp. 307–308.

zation can develop sufficient strength through conviction about its purpose, mutual friendship and respect among its members, confidence in its capacity to fulfill its purpose, to be able to endure many difficulties. To face internal and external expressions of fear and hostility with full understanding is undoubtedly preferable, but to engage upon a search for such understanding prematurely and without skill may be a completely shattering experience. The association without highly skilled professional help should seek, therefore, to build those bonds of friendship, respect, acceptance, and conviction of purpose which will permit it to endure and overcome attacks from within or outside the organization.

An example of this strength is the reaction of the Y.M.C.A.'s in North America to the criticisms of their work with the armed services in the first world war. These criticisms were extensive, found both outside and inside the Y.M.C.A., and were extremely damaging in nature. Those not near the center of the Y.M.C.A. could hardly realize how devastating were these attacks or how close they came to stimulating panic. Yet the Y.M.C.A. survived, and with remarkably little difficulty in light of the severity of the attacks. And it survived without ever clearly understanding what had happened, what caused the focusing of hostility on the Y.M.C.A., why some members within the organization suddenly turned upon the organization. But it was able to survive because of simple but remarkable strengths. The Y.M.C.A. was almost completely decentralized in Canada and the United States. Thus one might criticize the Y.M.C.A., but the fifty men responsible for the Y.M.C.A. in Sydney or Akron, or Regina or Boston could see no justification for the criticism in light of their own work, and rose to support what they had themselves built. The Y.M.C.A. also specialized in "fellowship" (a term now in disrepute) which emphasized warm, intimate, friendly relations in Y.M.C.A. work, and this led to strong personal bonds within the organization. Third was the conviction about, and loyalty to, the purpose of the organization. There were other factors but these were perhaps primary. And while the Y.M.C.A. never understood the nature of the attack, or made anything more than fumbling efforts to meet it, the organization had sufficient strength to withstand the difficulties. For the most part it accepted the attack with indifference and "Christian charity" and went on with its postwar work.[17]

Many organizations "live through" such experiences just as families endure periods of stress. It is undoubtedly true that this could be done more effectively with insight into the sources of stress. But insight is not a substitute for existing strengths in an organization, bonds of friendship and affection, feeling of responsibility, conviction about purpose. Perhaps, therefore, the community association must begin by seeking to build upon its common purpose, its shared feeling about community problems, its conviction that the community can work together, its vision of the future. These are fundamental bonds of strength. From this foundation the association moves into a process of self-education in which it learns to develop procedures, its members begin to understand and accept one another, it has success and failure and it seeks to understand each, it takes on additional responsibilities and grows in doing so, its leaders and its members become more knowledgeable about the community, themselves, and how to work together. The result of this process is a gradually maturing association and community. With skilled professional help, members may begin to understand why certain items on the agenda always seem difficult, why there is always heated discussion around Mr. M's report, why a few leaders never seem to become part of the association. As the association goes through this process, creative energies are released, the association moves with new freedom and confidence.

[17] This theme is developed in my book *The Y.M.C.A. in Canada*, Ryerson Press, 1951, pp. 291–294.

8

The Role of the
Professional Worker

IN THIS chapter we will attempt to develop a conception of the worker's role, and we will do this by elaborating a point of view about the role as a whole which should guide all that the professional worker does. If this *gestalt* is understood, the worker's function in any situation will be clear. There may remain the question of how he should perform a particular function, but if our conception of the worker's role is adequately conveyed, there should be no question about his role or function in any situation.

In the sections that follow we will discuss the role of the professional worker (a) as a guide, (b) as an enabler, (c) as an expert, and (d) as a therapist.[1]

THE ROLE OF GUIDE

PRIMARY ROLE

The primary role of the professional worker in community organization is that of a guide who helps the community [2] establish, and

---

[1] See Irwin T. Sanders, "Professional Roles in Planned Change," in Robert Morris (ed.), *Centrally Planned Change: Prospects and Concepts* (N.A.S.W., 1964), pp. 102–124.

[2] We assume, when we use a phrase such as this, that the worker is

find means of achieving, its own goals. The role of a guide connotes here a person devoted to helping the community move effectively in the direction it chooses to move. The guide has some responsibility to help the community choose this direction intelligently, with due consideration of many factors of which he (the guide) may be aware because of his expert knowledge. But the choice of direction and method of movement must be that of the community. This means that the professional worker does not under any circumstances use the community for his own ends, manipulate people, or coerce action.

Yet the professional worker does not operate without biases of what should be done and how it should be done in and by the community. He may well be convinced that a certain project is essential for community development, he may stimulate a feeling of need in respect to this project, he may encourage discussion of the project, and he may suggest the advantages of action on such a project. But the professional worker is aware of his bias, controls it, and moves only when and to the degree the people in the community are ready for such action. His preference for certain projects or for certain lines of action in the community is always placed behind his primary goal of helping the community function effectively in respect to its needs. And these latter, he recognizes, must be defined by the community. He is aware that the process by

dealing with the community when he is working with the leaders of the major subgroups in a particular community. Thus we do not imply the possibility, or the need, for the technical expert to work with every person in an Indian village, for example. Neither does the welfare council secretary need to deal with every member of every agency in the welfare community. Rather do we suggest that the technical expert regards the village as a whole, and that he works with this whole as he works with a council composed of the formal and informal leaders of the village. Similarly, the welfare council secretary deals with his community as he is able to view the welfare community as a whole, and as he is able to work with the leaders of the various welfare groups in a particular locality. We assume, as has been pointed out before, that when leaders who truly represent the feelings and attitudes of the major groups in a community come together, the primary and principal forces in the life of the community are represented in this association.

which these needs are identified is an essential aspect of the process by which a community may gradually develop capacity to recognize and deal with its problems.

A British Colonial officer provided the writer with an illustration that is useful at this point. This officer was sent to a village by a senior administrative officer to help and encourage the people there to introduce a new crop, which it was felt would provide the villagers with a higher crop yield and financial income. He began to work with the villagers in a manner somewhat like that suggested here, i.e., by exploring with the villagers their conception of their need. The problem that arose was that, as the people expressed their views, it became evident that what they wanted first was a new water system and that they felt no need or wish to change the nature of their crops. The officer was convinced that the present water supply was adequate, that the new crop was essential, and perhaps most important that his superior officer would not be happy with anything less than the change in crops advocated. In this conflict between what seemed like a good principle and a required course of action, he ventured to adhere to the principle. He encouraged the people to organize and deal with the problem of water supply, which they did with enthusiasm and success. The following year, with his help, a group of villagers traveled some distance to another village where the recommended crop was growing. So impressed were they with this crop that they returned and produced the new crop with great success in their own village. The fact that over the years this village developed great capacity for change and dealing with its own problems is only partly relevant at this point. The question is whether the officer should have insisted (as he had the legal authority to do) on what he knew was "right" or whether he should have followed the principle of accepting the judgment of the people on what they considered important. Our view is that the professional worker helps the community to explore its discontents; the worker has the right, if not the obligation, to indicate his own conception of what are legitimate and reasonable discontents or objectives; but he has not the right (nor should he wish) to impose his conception of need or objective, or to ask that it be explored to any greater extent than that of any problem, discontent, or objective suggested by any other individual in the community.

There will be those who will suggest that the above does not take adequate account of communities that are not able accurately to identify their needs, or of communities that identify needs or objectives that the "expert" knows are invalid. The officer in the illustration above felt he was "right" in recommending the new crop, but in the final analysis what was "right" in this case was a matter of judgment, and often the people's judgment is more adequate than that of the experts. There are cases, the realists point out, where "right" is not a matter of judgment. For example, a study of Crete [3] showed that nine-tenths of the farmers felt their primary problem was securing an adequate supply of a particular kind of fertilizer in which there was a high proportion of potassium. The experts, who had tested the soil and found quantities of potassium in it, were agreed that the use of such fertilizer would actually endanger the productivity of the soil. Is this not a case in which the worker should insist that his expert knowledge be followed? To the professional worker such a question is as unrealistic as the people's desire for harmful fertilizer. For the worker is not simply concerned with the growth of crops but with the growth of a sensitivity, of responsibility, of feelings of confidence that "we can do something about this," of capacity to function coöperatively on common problems. With such concerns in mind the worker does not "insist" on any course of action, for he recognizes that such insistence destroys the very seeds of growth he seeks to nourish. He will undoubtedly seek to point out the facts of the situation, and even if they are less obvious than those in respect to agriculture in Crete, he will have confidence in the ability of the people to make reasonable decisions. But even if they do not accept the facts as he portrays them, he recognizes that growth in

[3] Leland Allbaugh, *Crete, A Study of an Underdeveloped Area*, Princeton University Press, 1953, p. 18.

community capacity may involve errors and poor judgment as necessary aspects of such growth.

The professional worker is committed to a program which respects the rights, traditions, and desires of the community. He cannot be the crusading evangelist, the inspired communist, the advocate of technology, or any person whose ends are defined in terms of a specific project. The professional worker's objectives are stated in terms of a particular process in which direction, tempo, and character of relationships are determined not by the worker, but by the community.

The professional worker is not averse to encouraging discussion, asking leading questions, focusing thought, etc. on problems he believes important. He does not operate completely in terms of impartial interest and objectivity, but he is controlled by his primary goals of helping the community itself to become aware of its own needs and to find the means of working coöperatively at these needs. His control over his disposition to establish direction and pace in the community is, of course, a matter of degree. At times he may unconsciously interfere, use undue influence, or take over the direction of a project. At other times he may deliberately take a "calculated risk" and intercede because he recognizes certain danger signs, or the need for emergency action, of which no one else in the community is aware. But his basic assumptions in respect to his work force him to recognize that in the degree to which he accepts responsibility for content, pace, or action in the community, in that degree he may be defeating his own purposes. Thus his work is always being regulated by awareness that at the point at which he takes responsibility away from the community, the possibility of learning and growth in the community is thereby reduced.

INITIATIVE

The role of guide is not one of laissez-faire. Traditionally, the physician or psychiatrist deals only with people who come for help (or who are sent for help by law). The professional worker in community organization may not only take the initiative in approaching a community that has not asked for help, but he may take the initiative at a number of points in working with any kind of community. His role of guide, as a person who encourages local initiative, does not mean that he operates simply as a passive follower.

Perhaps the worker's most difficult task is with communities which appear apathetic, disorganized, degenerate. Here the worker faces the difficult task of stimulating a sense of need for a more adequate life. Many such communities are content with the *status quo*. Not only do they not wish to change, but they resist the possibility of change with a strong and rigid defense structure. Here the community worker takes the initiative. The initiative takes the form not of offering help, but of stimulating a sense of need, of discontent, of "pain" about existing conditions, and of suggesting other alternative conditions which may prove to be more rewarding. Contrary to popular belief, the creation of awareness of the sources of frustration, the stimulation of need or discontent, the stirring of feeling of desire for changed conditions in the community is not necessarily disruptive in long terms. True it creates tension and some unstability, but these are aspects of movement from a state of lethargy or apathy. In fact the stirring of consciousness of such frustration or blockages may often be justly regarded as beneficial. For it forces the community to reëxamine the situation, to consider alternative ways of community life, and stimulates the community to find some means of dealing with its problems. It is quite conceivable that this stirring of feeling in the community may provide the stimulus and impetus that lead to significant growth. Certainly in many communities, only such a method will overcome existing apathy.   •

In some situations, then, the professional worker may take the initiative in stirring discontent. But he does so only with some knowledge of the culture of a people, with awareness of their potentialities, and with some conception of what the future might be if the present state of lethargy could be overcome. He recognizes that the community as a whole will not develop and that the vast resources of the world, available in some degree to all, will not be used unless the community itself begins to strive, to move, to achieve. Therefore he takes the initiative in creating those conditions which will stimulate indigenous striving. And, as implied so frequently here, a profound sense of discontent may lead more effectively than any other feeling state to this initial desire to struggle. Therefore the worker seeks to encourage awareness of problems which may well lie latent, to bring these into the open, to permit negative expressions of feeling as a necessary prerequisite to more positive hopes, to encourage the first positive hopes, and to stimulate organization to channel and focus desires for action. In all this he may take the initiative. But, as implied, if he is to adhere to the objectives of his profession, he will not impose his own views of what specific discontents must be worked upon. He seeks to stir consciousness of existing conditions, to encourage initiative, to begin a process.

Even in the "healthy" community, the worker may be required to take the initiative in respect to these matters. For not only will he need to stir discontent among the complacent, but he may need to point out conditions to which the community has become so accustomed that it does not recognize these conditions as inconsistent, unhealthy, or weakening. The Colonial officer previously referred to in this chapter accepted the judgment of the people in the community, but he did not cease to urge their consideration of a problem that they may have lived with for so many generations that they were neither aware of it as a problem nor had they any desire to recognize it as a problem. In such matters the worker may take the initiative, but he does not insist on his interpretation, his understanding, his method. He interrogates, exchanges views, explains his position, introduces his facts. He initiates a process of decision making but recognizes that this process may not always eventuate in the acceptance of his views.

OBJECTIVITY

The professional worker tries to be objective about conditions in the community. In this respect he is similar to the psychiatrist, who recognizes symptoms for what they are—expressions of deep-seated difficulties—and is more interested in causal factors and the treatment of these than in approving or disapproving certain symptomatic behavior. Without being content with existing conditions, the worker can accept the situation as it is. He does not criticize, make comparisons that cast the community in an unfortunate light, or act in ways which suggest he himself is from a superior community or group. He understands that ignorance, vested interests, rigid beliefs and customs, aggression and hostility, inconsistent behavior, are found in every community. These are all part of his field. He accepts these as inevitable aspects of community life, and as forces with which he will have to deal in himself as well as in the community. They are factors that add both to the complexity and to the interest of his task.

As implied, the professional worker, certainly in the initial phases of his work in a community, expresses no feeling about conditions in the community. He neither praises nor blames. For to do either may be to strike at sensitive spots in community life and to destroy his usefulness. But as he proceeds in the community, as he comes to understand its nature, and to know its people, he may begin to identify for his own use (1) aspects of the community which he must simply accept and not in the foreseeable future even raise as topics for discussion, e.g., a deep-rooted religious controversy in which a working pact has been secured before his arrival in the community; (2) areas of community life which are both "weak spots" and "blind spots," and which, as he himself becomes accepted, he can afford to raise as topics for discussion—e.g., traditional use of certain fields which are always used for the same crop, a practice which is ruining these fields; concentration of leadership roles in a few people; "starvation" of one or more ethnic groups by excluding them from the social life and organization of the community; (3) characteristics of community life which he can and should praise—e.g., successful coöperative projects in the past; indications of good will and willingness to coöperate with other groups; strivings to define or come to grips with community problems; efforts to achieve self-understanding in the community association, etc.; (4) groups or efforts in the community which require his support—e.g., the small ethnic group struggling for recognition and acceptance; the deliberate efforts of the community association to find agreement and a *modus operandi*.

This is to imply, that while the worker in community organization may accept the community as it is, he works consistently towards his objective of involving members of the community in a process of working on their conception of community problems. He is, in the beginning, reluctant to express feelings of commendation or disapproval of any aspects of community life, but as his understanding of the community grows, he identifies problems which he feels may be raised for discussion and areas of life in the community to which encouragement and support may be given. But even in this latter he is careful to recognize the importance of timing—that some items must not be mentioned for many months, while other items may be raised for discussion in the near future.

IDENTIFICATION WITH COMMUNITY

Consistent with the above, the professional worker in community organization identifies (i.e., associates) with the community as a whole rather than with any one part of it, or group in it. Thus the worker resists being "captured" or used by one group or class in the community. He seeks to understand and establish good relations with groups that are suspicious of him or tend to reject him. He tries not to be part of a "left wing" or "right wing," of a higher or lower class, with advocates of socialized medicine or advocates of private enterprise in the health field. He identifies himself with the community, with democratic methods of discussion, with problems and projects which the community association has agreed upon.

His role does not lead him to support the advocates of new high-ways as opposed to those who wish a new swimming pool. His function does not require him to recommend this project as against that, or to support one group against another. His primary task is that of helping people discover and use processes by which co-öperative decisions are made. He may present factual data, experiences from other communities which have had similar problems, he may provide other kinds of resource material, but he does not insist on a particular course of action. His special expertness is in bringing diverse groups together, in clarifying issues, enlarging the area of common concern in the community, in establishing processes and procedures by which a community can make a collective decision. If he is to function effectively in this role, he cannot be a partisan of one group, or one project, or one organization. He is an advocate of certain community processes, certain methods of community work, a certain type of community association. With these procedures and the outcome of these procedures he identifies himself, and this involves identification with the community as a unit.

ACCEPTANCE OF ROLE

The professional worker in community organization must learn to accept, and be comfortable in, his role. A great deal of discipline is required to operate in this role; and it may be added, the worker who does not function comfortably in this role, with its strict limitations, should learn to do so or not continue in this field. There is seldom an hour in which the professional is at work in the community that he is not tempted to forsake this role. At a meeting he will be asked, "What would be the best project for us this year?" "What is the most important thing for us to do now?" The temptation is to pass judgment, to set the group on the course the worker is certain is right, to provide the answers. But to do so is to forsake the role of the professional worker. He may provide data upon which a judgment can be made, he may summarize and clarify various arguments and points of view, he may point out the implications of different courses of action, he may even suggest alternatives which have not previously been considered—but he does not himself recommend or urge a particular course of action. These latter are decisions with which the community itself must struggle. By providing a solution, the worker denies the validity of the process which assumes that communities grow in capacity as they strive to achieve consensus.

Again, an occasion may arise in which the community association decides to approach a higher government body for help, and the professional worker is asked to lead a delegation from the community. Again this is tempting. But under ordinary circumstances, the professional worker will refuse. He may appear with the delegation, he may help them to prepare, he may support them in other ways. But his function is to help the community accept and undertake responsibility. His role does not involve taking the major aspect of this responsibility away from the community. The professional worker who yields to the temptation presented by these situations, who yearns to be the "recognized leader," who wants to "run the show," who craves recognition for "his part" in the work, does not belong in this field and cannot succeed in terms of the objectives outlined here.

INTERPRETATION OF ROLE

The professional worker must learn to interpret his role so that it is understood in the community. This he has to do, persistently and consistently, in a great variety of situations. It will be only after a considerable period of time, during which the people of the community will attempt to change his role many times, that his role will be understood and accepted—and then only if the professional person has interpreted and performed consistently and well. In the illustrations provided above, the professional worker has excellent opportunities to interpret to the persons present what precisely is his role. In explaining why he cannot be "the leader" or make the decision, or recommend the "right" course of action, the worker can, without being pedantic, indicate the importance of the community's assuming responsibility for its decisions and actions, and the peculiar role of the worker in assisting the community in its tasks. There will be many such opportunities which the alert worker will use to suggest what he conceives his responsibility to be. But here, as in psychiatry, in research, in various kinds of consultative roles, there appears to be a testing process initiated by those being served. They wish a different function performed. This is their real need. They are unhappy about the kind of help they are getting, etc. But if the professional worker continues accepting this discontent, is not affected by hostility directed at him, remains firm as to the areas in which he can help, there will gradually be developed a frame of reference within which he and the community can work comfortably together.

THE ENABLER ROLE

In general terms, the role of the enabler is simply to facilitate the community organization process. But this role is as varied and complex as each situation with which the worker deals. The following generalizations, however, may illuminate this role somewhat.

FOCUSING DISCONTENT

The professional worker helps or enables, by awakening and focusing discontent about community conditions. Most people have such discontents, although for many they may be deeply submerged, and for others they may be projected on a scapegoat of some kind. The task of the worker is to help people verbalize their discontents. For some, these discontents are so deeply buried that a good deal of skill and patience is required to facilitate expression, for others verbalization of discontent will bring a flood of hostility directed at some minority group, for others the problems revealed will be those which generally come under the heading of "personal problems." The worker must be skilled in dealing with the withdrawn, he must permit the flood of negative and hostile expressions of feeling (which is often a prerequisite to more positive expressions); he must be able to help individuals and groups see that many of their "personal" problems are "social" problems (i.e., if there is only one working mother in the community who has a problem of caring for her child while she works, this is a personal problem, but if there are twenty such mothers, there may well be a community or social problem). The worker must proceed on the assumption that constructive forces of good will and cooperation exist and that it is his task to release them. Primarily, as implied, he does this by encouraging verbalization, by patient listening, by skillful interrogation. Gradually he seeks to focus thought on problems which seem to be shared in the community. At first he acts as a communication link, e.g., "There are some people who feel if we could only secure playgrounds for children in this part of the city, we'd be doing something important. Do you think this might be so?" Gradually as some problems become focused, he attempts to bring diverse groups together for discussion of these matters.

The worker's role at this point is that of a catalytic agent. He is not a salesman who sells the people a plan and a way of attaining a plan. He is a person who helps people look at themselves, to look below the surface and probe their deepest feelings about community life. He encourages verbalization of these feelings, he helps people see the commonality of their feelings, he nourishes the hope that something can be done collectively about these. As feelings and consciousness of common problems begin to crystallize, the worker functions in a way that will support efforts to come together, to organize, to deal with these problems.

One serious and frequent error of professional workers is to encourage undue optimism about the quick and easy success a community can achieve. Part of his task as an enabler is to help people see the nature of their discontents, the deep roots of many of these discontents, their interrelationship, and the difficult blocks to overcoming some community problems. While the worker encourages and supports efforts to organize and to deal with community discontents, he recognizes that unless people view the problems realistically they are likely to be quickly disappointed with results.

ENCOURAGING ORGANIZATION

In many communities it is not easy to move toward organization. Apathy is a socially patterned defect in many urban communities, and passivity is often the norm. Thus the worker must be prepared to recognize the community organization process as one which is often painfully slow. If he is not to "sell," or to lead with unrealizable dreams of what might be achieved, but rather to help people feel and identify the problem for themselves, he must be prepared to move slowly in most situations. But he relies on the assumption that the process by which the people in the community gradually come to recognize for themselves that they have common problems, which can be dealt with only coöperatively, is an essential foundation for development and growth. Further, he recognizes, as we have emphasized before, that time taken to discover problems and discontents which are deeply felt and widely shared will provide that motivation which may make it possible to work through many of the difficulties that lie ahead. The first essential task of the enabler, then, is to initiate and facilitate the process by which discontents about which most people in the community feel keenly are identified. From this basis he seeks to establish meaningful communication about these discontents so that various parts of the community may come together to rank these discontents and to begin to organize to deal with them.

But even when the way has thus been well prepared, some communities falter at the point of organization. Individuals or groups lack confidence, some fear being related to other individuals or groups, some feel the new plan or association threatens an established way of life. Individuals and groups will move only if the

new situation holds promise of being more comfortable and pleasant than the present and/or if they are strongly motivated to
proceed with what they conceive to be a desirable movement. The
degree of readiness at this point will depend on the degree to
which the worker (and others) have prepared people for movement. This latter will depend, as implied, on the extent of discussion
(individual and group), the depth of feeling of discontent expressed in these discussions, and the spread of conviction that
"something must be done about this." Even if all these conditions
exist, the professional must provide a good deal of reassurance for
those who come to the point of organization and then falter. Here
it may be necessary to review previous discussion, to raise original
questions, to encourage verbalization about all the points previously
discussed, to recapture the feelings that led to the conception of
the idea of action, and to support the faintest feelings of confidence
that what appear to be overwhelming difficulties can be overcome.
It is, of course, fatal for the worker to push, to accelerate the pace,
to minimize difficulties at this or at any other point. The approach
is less "Don't worry, everything will be all right" than it is "How
do you feel about the problem we want to work at?" and "How
much are we willing to sacrifice to overcome this problem?" The
worker supports, in the sense that he approves the idea of striving,
believes in the worth of the struggle, feels confident that the community can achieve its ends, and indicates willingness to work with
the group through the problem. But he does not push or coax or
urge action. To move a community before it is ready to organize
and act is often to increase withdrawal and lack of confidence. The
role of enabler requires judgment, therefore, as to how much
encouragement can be given, how much anxiety relieved, how
much support provided. But it is clear that responsibility for action
must lie with the community through its association, it must
recognize the possibility of failure, it must accept responsibility for
this eventuality if it occurs.

NOURISHING GOOD INTERPERSONAL RELATIONS

The professional worker seeks also to increase the amount of satisfaction in interpersonal relations and in coöperative work. He is a warming congenial influence in group and community meetings. This implies a warm, friendly person, sensitive to the deeper feelings of people, and interested in the "little things" that are important in the lives of individuals and communities. He is concerned with meetings in which people feel comfortable, enjoy themselves, and feel free to verbalize. To this end he is alert not only to the physical and psychological conditions which make for such comfort, but seeks to create these conditions and uses his own self to facilitate these. This means he is adept not only in room arrangements, introductions, casual conversation, but that he is sensitive to the process of interaction which goes on in a group and knows when and how to ask that question which will catch and focus the interest of the group, when to interpret what is being attempted, when to praise. People can enjoy working together when they begin to know one another and sense what they can do coöperatively. Part of the worker's role is to assure such satisfaction for the group.

In the initial stages of work in the community, the worker is often the only link between different groups in the area. He is often the influence that brings these groups together. If the professional worker is accepted, liked, and trusted, persons identify with him, will attend meetings he feels are worth while, will accept other people whom he accepts, will coöperate with others because he approves of such coöperation. This implies a use of self which some will find unprofessional or unethical. This should not be so. What the worker is attempting is not manipulative. He is using his own well-established contacts as a bridge by means of which different groups can meet, and because of their confidence in him can meet in relative security. This is not essentially different from the *rapport* which the caseworker or psychiatrist attempts to establish with a client so that the latter will feel comfortable and able to talk. What the worker in the community is seeking is the use of himself not only to arrange a physical meeting but a meeting in which people are relatively free to meet one another without fear or suspicion. Of course, the worker must recognize that the community must not depend on him permanently to perform such a role, and that he must gradually shift this responsibility as the people in the community develop the skill to carry it themselves.

The professional worker in the community field helps to remove or to circumvent "blocks" to coöperative work. As part of his work he will seek to understand those intergroup tensions and conflicts, those vested interests, those class differences which stand in the way of, or prevent, coöperative work. His method of dealing with these difficulties depends a good deal on the level at which he is capable of working. If he operates as a social therapist (and this role will be discussed later), he will approach the problem at a level rather different from a professional worker in community organization without therapeutic skill. The average worker must rely on more indirect, and in a sense more superficial, methods for dealing with such blocks: (1) he attempts to emphasize the common goals, the binding nature of the task confronting the community, the common values to which all are dedicated; (2) he seeks to calm some storms, by clarifying the issues about which violent disagreement arises, by interpreting varying points of view so that they are understood by all, by being objective and serene in crises, by calling upon the reasoned and best judgment of all; (3) he works directly on some blocks to coöperative work, e.g., he asks for the support of a high-prestige figure in dealing with a lower-prestige figure whose neurotic and authoritarian behavior is expressed in an attack on some groups or individuals or the process itself; he discusses at length some problems of organization, or of process, or of feeling, with individuals separately, attempting to find common ground for an approaching meeting; he encourages the participation of the withdrawn nonverbal member; he approaches a talkative person about the need to encourage others to participate in a meeting that is to be held soon; he helps to calm the impatient, to speed up the slow, etc. In some situations, depending upon his own competence and the strength of the group, he may interpret to the association some of the aspects of community life which seem to him to prevent or block community work so that the association may understand and deal with the individual and social pressures which create tension and separateness. All of these things he may do as an enabler. As a participant-observer he is aware of the strains and stresses which may wreck the work in which the association is involved. Without taking responsibility away from the association for its central task, he seeks to help the process by calmness and objectivity; by focusing on common goals; by analysis and treatment of the causes of tension to the degree that he and the group are able to handle them.

EMPHASIZING COMMON OBJECTIVES

The professional worker seeks to help so that in the process consistency is maintained with the objectives of developing both effective planning and community capacity. He does this usually by asking relevant questions. "Is it possible to get facts on this point about which we disagree?" "What will be the effect on City Hall if we adopt this plan—how will this in turn affect our plan?" "Is there any place for young people in the planning and development of this recreation program?" "What will be the result of making a decision if the representatives of M___ group are not here? Should we wait to consult this group?" "What is the relation of this idea to what we are really trying to do?" And so on. Questions may simply be of this nature—attempts to remind the group of the need to be thorough and consistent in its work. This is a technique which may seem simple but is of great difficulty and requires great skill. People in a community association tend to get so involved in a particular task that they lose perspective, although none of their enthusiasm. The professional worker must maintain his objectivity, must remind the group of long-term goals, must be willing to raise questions of timing, relationships, content. He must be aware of the whole community, the whole project, the whole process. He must see the point in the process where the group now operates and be able to raise those questions which help the group to gain perspective, sense of movement, and fresh concern with long-term objectives. And this he must do without dampening enthusiasm, offending, or making the task seem unduly complicated.

As an enabler the worker's role is consistently directed at freeing the community (through its leaders) to realize its potentialities and strengths in coöperative work. Primarily (although not entirely) it is oriented in the direction of helping people (mainly in groups) to express their concerns about social (as distinct from personal) problems, to find "common ground" with their fellows in the community, and to achieve satisfaction in coöperative work. As an enabler the worker seeks to facilitate the community process through listening and questioning; through identifying with, and in turn being the object of identification for, group leaders in the community; and by giving consistent encouragement and support to indigenous striving with common problems. He does not lead; he facilitates local efforts. He does not provide answers; he has questions which stimulate insight. He does not carry the burden of responsibility for organization and action in the community; he provides encouragement and support for those who do.

THE EXPERT ROLE

As an expert, the worker's role is to provide data and direct advice in a number of areas about which he may speak with authority. This does not conflict with his role as an enabler, which is primarily one of facilitating community process. As an expert, he provides research data, technical experience, resource material, advice on methods, which the association may need and require in its operation. Here he speaks directly, offers content material, makes direct contributions to the deliberations of the association. What are provided, however, are facts and resources. There is no recommendation about what the community or its association should do; there is development and presentation of material which should help the association make a decision more intelligently. This distinction is not unlike the variation in the role of the psychiatrist who consistently seeks to help his patient engage in a process of identifying, understanding, and overcoming his own problems. In this process the psychiatrist may play a supporting, helping, facilitating role. But he may also play the role of an expert, e.g., relieving fears by providing facts about homosexuality, brain tumors, criteria of psychosis, etc. Similarly in community organization the worker as an enabler plays a "supporting role" but as an expert he may directly confront the group with facts and concepts which may be reassuring and helpful to it. There need be no conflict in these roles, for they should supplement and support rather than compete with each other. In some respects, the role of enabler is more subtle, more demanding, and more important. But the role of expert is useful, and without expert help the community may stumble unnecessarily.

The kinds of functions performed by the expert may illuminate somewhat the distinction in roles:

COMMUNITY DIAGNOSIS

The worker may serve as an "expert" in community analysis and diagnosis. Most communities have little understanding of their own structure or organization. The worker may be asked about, or may wish to point out, certain characteristics of the community, neglect of attention to which may seriously impede the work of the association. For example, the informal social organization of the community, the nature of the forces which separate certain groups in the community, the significance of certain rituals in the lives of particular ethnic groups, etc., may all need to be understood if coöperative work is to be secured in the community.

RESEARCH SKILL

The worker should also be skilled in research methods, able to carry on studies on his own, and to formulate research policy. Frequently a community will find some need for minor research projects which the worker may pursue. Or a problem may be faced which requires to be formulated in research terms. The worker should be able, at least, to make an initial formulation of the problem, to indicate the scope and nature of the research undertaking, and if necessary, to work closely with those who may be engaged to carry out the research project. In sophisticated communities the worker may not be the most knowledgeable person in the research field, but it is an area in which he should be able to speak with confidence, if informed opinion from him is requested.

INFORMATION ABOUT OTHER COMMUNITIES

In addition, the worker should be informed about research, studies, and experimental work in other communities. He should be able to acquaint the community with projects developed elsewhere and with useful principles derived from these. While the community must struggle with its own problems, it can learn from others, use data from experimental work, avoid mistakes made in other community projects. The worker has some obligation at appropriate times to feed material derived from other experiences and from his knowledge in the field.

ADVICE ON METHODS

The worker may also have expert knowledge of methods of organization and procedure. Local custom will govern practices at this point to a considerable degree, but the worker can provide a good deal of useful advice, e.g., making certain all the major subgroups are represented in the initial stages of organization, taking time to identify the real leaders of informal groups in the community, etc.

TECHNICAL INFORMATION

The worker should also be well informed and able to provide resource material on technical plans. That is, he should know where and how to get material on any project being contemplated, be it a library, school, health service, roads, or agriculture. This implies that he knows the resources of government departments, private agencies, international organizations, and ways of securing available help in specialized fields. The number and variety of such resources is, of course, considerable, and the help which can be provided to a local group on a project of almost any kind may save a good deal of time and effort, if the source of this help is known and can be used. The worker should be able to bridge the gap between the resources available and the community's need for such resources.

EVALUATION

The worker must also be able to provide some evaluation or interpretation of the process of coöperative work which is being carried on. The professional worker must be able not only to understand with objectivity the content of discussion, but also the process of interaction and the effect of this on individuals and groups. He should be able to interpret these to the community without damage and in a way which will increase people's understanding and ability to operate as a group in the community.

In all these areas the worker may function as an expert, providing data and resources useful to the group. These are given to the group to use; they are not offered as final solutions. The worker as an expert does not insist on acceptance of his "expert knowledge." This is offered for consideration and discussion, to be used as effectively as the community is able to adapt it.

THE SOCIAL THERAPY ROLE

Some professional workers in the community function as social therapists. This is a specialized function illustrated by the work of the Tavistock Institute of Human Relations and by some major industrial projects in this field. What is involved here is therapy at the community level. It implies diagnosis and treatment of the community as a whole. Obviously such treatment must be carried on through representative groups or leaders, but it may require these leaders, with the help of the professional worker, to face many of the underlying forces, the taboo ideas, the traditional attitudes, which create tension and which separate groups in the community. If the community is able to recognize these deep-rooted ideas and practices, verbalize about them, and begin to cope with them, it may develop a capacity (just as the individual or group) to function more effectively as an integrated unit. The professional, working at the community level in this way has, of course, a wider field for diagnosis. He must know the origin and history of the community as a whole and in its separate parts, he must understand the social roots of many of the present beliefs and customs, the association of beliefs and practices, the power structure of the community, the roles and relationships between roles established in the community. His diagnosis must provide the community with some understanding of its nature and character. His treatment must involve the community in a process in which self-understanding relieves tension and removes blocks to coöperative work. The difference in method of the therapist and the average worker in the field is the depth and thoroughness of the analysis and treatment. The social therapist deals with those deep-lying and often unconscious forces which are constantly (and often in hidden form) threatening to disrupt the community organization process.

One brief example of work attempted at this level was the writer's work with an Israeli Kibbutz.[4] While this work was hampered by lack of time, some of the essential considerations for diagnosis and treatment of the community as a whole were present.

The Kibbutz (pl. Kibbutzim) is a collective agriculture settlement in which all members work for the community, possess few

[4] Murray G. Ross, "Social Structure and Social Tension in the Kibbutz," report prepared for UNESCO, 1954.

personal goods, receive food, clothing, housing, and health services, according to their needs and the resources of the community. All work is planned by the members, tasks are assigned by elected officials, profits are used for those goods judged most needed for the community by members in meeting. Housing is, in most cases, comfortable two-room apartments for married couples, rooms or dormitories for single persons. All adults eat in the community dining hall. Children are raised from infancy in children's houses and are cared for by members assigned to this task. The children live in small groups, play together, receive their education in their group, and when old enough (approximately 12 years of age) work a few hours daily at useful community tasks. They spend several hours daily with parents during week days and longer periods on Fridays and Saturdays. All services such as laundry, health, dining hall, recreation, education, etc. are organized, administered, and in most cases staffed by members of the community. A general assembly is held every Saturday night at which committees report and policy is discussed and decided upon.

Tension in a few Kibbutzim was overt at the particular time the writer visited them (spring and summer of 1953) and an exploration of the causes of this tension was undertaken. The number and complexity of causal factors cannot be fully reported here but a brief summary of some of the factors which were not generally recognized should suffice to indicate the nature of the diagnosis.

The ideology of the Kibbutz demands great personal sacrifice and discipline and permits little flexibility. The basic objective of the Kibbutz is associated with the Zionist idea of "opening the land for the exiles." This can only be done, people in the Kibbutz believe, by pioneering on the land, hard work, and a collective (or socialist) form of community. Development of farms on sand and swamp is, indeed, a task to try men's souls. To achieve such an objective requires complete dedication to a specific ideal of the greatest importance. Associated with this ideal, and symbolic of it, are certain accepted practices in the Kibbutz. Such practices as communal raising of children, the community dining hall, rejection of money as a value, heavy manual labor, acceptance of the rugged hard life, self-labor, etc., are identified with Kibbutz ideology and all have therefore a halo quality. Any change, or threat of change, in practices appears to threaten the whole ideal of the Kibbutz and to suggest that the sacrifice was (or is) less important and necessary than it once appeared to be. If the sacrifices required are to be meaningful, the object of sacrifice must not be blurred or distorted. Change, or threat of change, of "halo practices" thus represents not merely a change in means; it has the appearance of destroying the very foundation upon which one has established one's life.

The status of the Kibbutz is changing. In a society as dynamic as Israel, change is inevitable. One such change is in the status of the Kibbutz itself. "The opening of the land" was of the greatest importance some years back, and the pioneers (the Kibbutzers) were the elite of the Jewish community in Palestine. Now Israel must industrialize to survive. The Kibbutz is a less significant factor; it has lost much of its prestige, and city folk often refer to "the odd people" who live in a Kibbutz. This blow to the status of the Kibbutz is an especially bitter one. Sacrifice is acceptable when one is sure of the supreme importance of the task at hand, has reassurance of this from the nation, or is sure of praise in any case. But when questions as to the importance of the task arise outside, and begin to penetrate the community, loyalty and discipline begin to waver, morale to be weakened.

There is little social space in the Kibbutz. Kibbutzim range in size from 80 to 2000 persons, but the majority are small communities, the median being probably around 300. Within the Kibbutz individuals live, eat, work, and play with the same people day after day. There is little room for privacy or private living. It is not only difficult to be alone; one is constantly surrounded by the same people. The writer was impressed in many dining halls with the lack of conversation at mealtimes. Perhaps all topics of conversation become exhausted after a period; more likely individuals build psychological walls around themselves to the end that they may have some privacy. It is well known that tension develops among "ten men in a life-boat," and the lack of social space in a Kibbutz is undoubtedly a tension-producing factor.

There is a relatively low ceiling for the expression of feelings. Pioneering life in the Kibbutz is recognized as rugged and difficult. One is expected to suffer or enjoy with little overt expression of feeling. Many mothers, for example, have been raised in western countries and have been accustomed to home life with parents and children living together. For some of these, it is a strain to have their own children separated from them to the extent that is usual in the Kibbutz. Yet one hears few complaints about the difficulty of such separation; on the contrary, the practice is vigorously defended, even by those likely to find such practice a hardship. A concert artist who played at a number of Kibbutzim reported that she found it difficult to communicate with the people in the audience as they appeared quite unresponsive and applauded sparsely, if at all. Yet it is well known that there is a high appreciation of classical music in the Kibbutz. The writer sat with two members of a Kibbutz through one of Hollywood's poorest productions. They laughed frequently and it appeared they enjoyed the movie thoroughly. On the way home they denied this fact and protested vigorously when it was suggested that the movie had some funny scenes. Since, in many Kibbutzim, there are no religious services (although religious holidays and celebrations are observed), one gets the impression that there is little outlet for emotion; less overt expression of sadness, laughter, aggression, hostility, etc., than one would find in other parts of Israel or in western communities; and that tradition suggests rigorous repression of such feelings.

The social system tends to become rigid. Theoretically the Kibbutz is flexible, with new committees being appointed and key positions being filled annually on the vote of members. While there is undoubtedly turnover in some of these positions, there is a tendency for persons to become skilled in one area of operation, to get advanced training in this field, and to become accepted leaders in their areas of specialization. Similarly, workers get accustomed to the routine of their particular jobs and dislike change from it.

At the same time, while there is interaction in the community as a whole, one does make special friends, and small cliques are not unusual. Thus, in spite of the supposed flexibility, occupational and social roles tend to become fixed and rigid. The role of the mother, for example, is strictly limited. The main responsibility for child care rests with the community and the mother has little to say about the diet, sleeping habits, or education of her own child— although, through the education committee, she may influence the care of all children in the village. As long as these roles are acceptable, they do not, *per se*, create friction. But if one is unhappy about one's role, unable to express one's feelings about this situation, and forced to accept the inevitability of this particular structure of roles and role relationships, there may well be a welling of hostility which will break out at some point.

These are but a few illustrations of some of the factors which seem to underlie tension in three of the Kibbutzim studied. It seems to be a relatively safe assumption that these and other factors, in various combinations, lie behind some of the tension that comes rapidly into focus when certain routine matters come before the weekly meeting of the community. We are here less concerned with pressing this diagnosis further than in suggesting the kinds of factors which must be examined in a diagnosis. The social organization, structuring of roles and role relationships, the position of the community in historical and current milieux, the relationship of belief and practice, etc., are all matters for consideration. Careful examination of such factors not only suggests the source of much that emerges in disruptive forms of behavior, but also a cause-effect relationship of which members of the community are not consciously aware.

It is, however, one task to make such a diagnosis and quite another to provide treatment. Here it is quite clear that treatment cannot be provided unless the community is suffering to the extent that it urgently desires and asks for help. The writer experimented in one Kibbutz in which there was a good deal of tension which was rigidly controlled. In informal discussion with groups of members, indications of tension would often be revealed. When, however, the writer would raise questions consistent with the previous diagnosis, these would be vigorously rejected. Even such an apparently obvious matter as the changed status of the Kibbutzim in Israel was not only rejected, but strong counter and irrational arguments were presented. As with an individual, a community may create a defence structure which resists any consideration of the problems which threaten its integration. And unless the problem becomes so severe that these defence structures no longer seem adequate, the community (as the individual) will resist consideration of the problem and possible changed behavior.[5]

In one Kibbutz in which there was far more consciousness of the tension and in which an open division in the community was threatened, the writer was asked informally to suggest methods of coping with the problem. Again, in a series of informal meetings and through an interpreter, there began a long exploration of some of the causal factors reported above. These were discussed, pursued to minute points of detail, considered, rejected, and reconsidered. Gradually a conception of the problem was formulated and some plans were made for dealing with it. Of considerable importance here is that the focus of concern in the community was shifted from an issue which was disruptive, tension-creating, and for the moment unsolvable, to more fundamental issues which all could identify and which all could consider with some degree of objectivity. This shift in focus meant that new "common ground" was provided and a new frame of reference was supplied in which all factions could meet to discuss a common problem. Further, it meant the beginning of restructuring some aspects of communal life, and this in itself served as a cohesive force in the community.

As implied, the difference in method of the worker in community organization and the social therapist is one of degree, the latter dealing at a deeper level, often with unconscious forces, and often with subtle and fundamental patterns of interpersonal relationships. The difference is not unlike that of the caseworker and the psychi-

[5] For a conceptual approach to the phenomenon of community controversy, see James S. Coleman, *Community Conflict*, The Free Press, 1957.

atrist. The average worker in the community hesitates to move into the diagnostic and treatment field because here he will deal with anxieties and tension both within the community and in himself with which he has not been trained to deal. But the advanced worker in the community organization field may well begin such experimental work as implied above with some justification, although a collaborative experience with persons trained in psychiatry or group psychotherapy would perhaps be a more adequate way to begin. The problem is that the average psychiatrist or group psychotherapist has not been trained in community diagnosis and he is as ill-equipped to deal with some factors of community life as the community worker is with aspects of treatment. Each may undertake relatively simple experimental work on his own, but if progress is to be made here, collaborative work such as that undertaken at the Tavistock Institute of Human Relations seems the most appropriate approach.

We have attempted in this chapter to identify various aspects of the professional worker's role in community organization. Social therapy we suggest as an addendum, a role not yet recognized nor perhaps to be accepted by the community worker, but one in which a few advanced workers may experiment with the help of practitioners of other disciplines. The function of the worker in community organization is to facilitate the community organization process and this he does by helping the community struggle to achieve some degree of integration as it attacks some of its problems.

Part Four

Principles and Practice

9

Integrating Principles
and Practice

INTRODUCTION

The oft-heard complaint voiced by many community organization workers that principles and concepts are more easily pro-
claimed than performed is not without foundation. For one thing,
theory moves in an orderly manner. It lacks the quality of tension
which is an inescapable aspect of the world of practice. Theory,
before it has entered the body of practice, is like a drug on the
chemist's shelf—a visible, independent entity—but once theory is
dissolved, as it were, into life situations it loses its visibility.

In practice, theory becomes diffused throughout the social system;
its progression, when viewed as a phenomenon apart, gives way.
The concepts and principles are subject to disarray when meshed
with problem-solving that the community organization worker and
his lay leaders perform in the course of discharging day-to-day
responsibilities.

Granted that integrating theory and practice is no simple task, to
evade the challenge is to engage in a form of community organization work that devolves into "planless empiricism" wherein action
may be triggered largely by the worker's intuition.

In this section an effort will be made to approximate life situations in which some of the principles set forth in this book will be put to work as three records are examined. The analysis will be concerned primarily with identifying the concepts rather than evaluating the performance of the practitioner cited in the various cases. The selected case material reflects three widely differing communities. "Hanwella" constitutes a geographic entity, "Merton Center" deals with a natural local area, and "Branstown" represents what has been defined as a functional community (pp. 41–45 *supra*).

These differences have been explicitly noted because there is a tendency on the part of many workers to view the communities in which they practice as so unique that comparison and contrast are all too often regarded as pointless. Such a view is basically incompatible with a professional method of practice, in that it permits little or no carry-over of acquired knowledge, experience, and skill from one setting to another. Community organization is conceived as a helping method that cuts across various types of communities. Thus, despite individual differences, we shall attempt to identify common elements as a basis for a generic approach to the three varying social systems described in the cases.

The records from which the case material was derived are, in each instance, far from complete. This is a weakness characteristic of much case material. It is especially true of community organization, partly, no doubt, because of the multiplicity of causal factors at work in shaping community situations. Where necessary facts or details are absent, interpretations will be based on assumptions as to the nature of situations, which may make some observations seem arbitrary or oversimplified. Under the circumstances, this is unavoidable.

Within the confines of this section it will be possible to examine a limited number of problems and issues. Consequently, the analysis of the cases is by no means exhaustive; rather it is illustrative of the way in which principles and practice in community organization may be integrated. Hopefully, the discussions which follow each record will help the reader to venture on his own search, extending points which have been raised and identifying others that remain to be examined.

HANWELLA

Flood waters carried by overflowing rivers recurrently plague many towns and villages in Ceylon. Thus the Kelany River would, when driven by monsoon winds, invariably bring havoc to Hanwella, one of the villages on its banks with a population of about 3000. But as soon as the waters receded the inhabitants of Hanwella would rebuild their mud huts and resume their day-to-day existence. Many of the villagers were relative newcomers to Hanwella. In contrast to the recent settlers were the pottery makers, whose forebears constituted one of the village's founding groups.

Although of low caste, the pottery makers were looked to for leadership in communal matters because they were so deeply rooted in Hanwella. When Piyadasa Seneviratne, the representative of the Rural Development Society (R.D.S.), first showed up in the village, he soon learned that it was the pottery makers to whom he must turn if he were to make any progress in his efforts to interest the inhabitants in coming to grips with the flood problem.

After the swollen waters of the Kelany had washed away many of the mud huts, he went about helping families to rebuild. As he helped he talked to the inhabitants. What was the sense, he asked, in going on year after year building huts that were sure to be destroyed by the next flood? Why keep facing the disease and privations the Kelany River ceaselessly brought them? The people listened, agreed he was right, and shrugged their shoulders; it was the fate that generations before them had faced and they in their lifetime would also have to resign themselves to the same fate, they would reply.

But the representative from the R.D.S. did not accept their bland fatalism. Had they ever given serious thought to an alternative, Piyadasa Seneviratne would counter, whenever he was confronted with villagers who were prepared to accept the havoc as part and parcel of their life. Some would speak vaguely of notions they harbored about changing conditions, but the representative told them frankly that daydreaming about improving the situation in Hanwella would accomplish nothing. He suggested that they consider coming together to discuss ways and means of launching some action that would lead to an improvement in their village.

As a result of this prodding people began to meet informally to discuss various problems connected with the floods. After the latest flood, medical aid had been slow in arriving and the death of two children could, the villagers claimed, be traced directly to the length of time it had taken to bring a doctor to their community. Others mentioned that they had heard of building materials that could withstand the flood waters of the river and wondered what the cost would be in rebuilding their homes with these stronger materials. The R.D.S. representative told them that he would do all in his power to see that after the floods medical aid was brought more quickly to Hanwella. To those who were asking about the stronger housing materials he admitted that he did not know much about the subject but offered to bring an expert who would talk to them about it once agreement on the matter had been reached in the village.

About 180 people concerned primarily with the problem of medical aid came together to consider this matter and also the question of housing materials. In the informal discussions which led to this large meeting, the pottery makers were naturally quite active, and the individual who was looked to for leadership was Badal Gedara Kira, a member of the pottery makers' group. In another part of the village an even larger group, numbering some 255 people, met to discuss the same problem. The man who was instrumental in convening this group was Badal Gedara Sirisena. He, too, was a pottery maker. A man in his middle fifties, Badal Gedara Sirisena was the most beloved leader in Hanwella. He was known for his wisdom and kindness, and his advice was frequently sought by many of the villagers in times of adversity. Badal Gedara

Kira, about ten years younger than Badal Gedara Sirisena, was an aggressive man who was much admired for his resourcefulness in mustering help for the village in time of need.

Shortly after the formation of the two groups the R.D.S. representative met with the two leaders. He informed them that because of an emergency in another part of the area he was being called away for several weeks. He nevertheless looked forward to coming back to Hanwella and he expressed the hope that the meetings on the flood problem would go on in his absence. He assured them that the government was interested in helping. Moreover he pointed out that the military, which owned a tract of land close to the village, would be moving in shortly to build army depots. He was rather hopeful that the Army might turn out to be coöperative in dealing with the floods and assured the two leaders that he would speak to the military authorities at the earliest opportunity to determine what help, if any, they might be able to give.

In his absence the two leaders continued calling meetings but each group developed distinctive plans of its own. The group under Badal Gedara Sirisena was in favor of a project that called for raising the land to a height above the level to which the Kelany waters rose during flood time. This group felt that the village could supply the necessary working force provided the government would undertake to pay the wages. Moreover, they felt that the government would have to take the responsibility for bringing in the heavy equipment that would be necessary for moving the loads of earth to raise the level of the land.

The group meeting under Badal Gedara Kira produced another plan which called for the transfer of the whole village to higher land. As it happened, this land belonged to the military and had been designated as the area for army depots. Like their leader, this group had become very militant in insisting that it was easier for the army to move than for a village to raise river banks. They were in favor of the other groups joining them in sending a delegation to Colombo with this proposal. Badal Gedara Sirisena suggested that they hold off sending deputations until Piyadasa Seneviratne returned. He also pointed out that the two plans need not be regarded as irrevocably in conflict; rather they should be seen as alternative solutions to their very difficult problem. The advantage of the proposal that was made by his group, Badal Gedara Sirisena pointed out, was that it allowed the villagers to remain in their familiar surroundings and, moreover, the project offered employment opportunities for a good many members of Hanwella for about two years. This was the time span that the inhabitants of Hanwella reckoned it would take to raise the land bordering on the Kelany River. However, one disadvantage was that it would entail long, hard, and sustained labor to complete the job and might interfere with the pottery making which was the cottage industry that provided the main source of income to the village. He said that it might also interfere with paddy (unpolished rice) cultivation which the inhabitants undertook in their spare time and which provided a major means of food supply. Reviewing the proposal made by the other group, Badal Gedara Sirisena pointed out that it also had certain advantages: it would spare Hanwella the work required in raising the river banks. At the same time, there was a disadvantage in that the entire population in the village would be uprooted; the move to a new environment might produce difficulties which were not now foreseen. Badal Gedara Kira argued that the village was uprooted regularly when the Kelany flood struck, so that moving to a new location should not prove to be such a difficult experience. After discussion of the pros and cons Badal Gedara Sirisena's suggestion that a final decision be deferred until the R.D.S. representative returned was adopted.

When Piyadasa Seneviratne returned he was informed of the two proposals which had been framed in his absence. He reported that he, too, had a proposition to make on behalf of the government authorities in Colombo. He told the two leaders that for a long time the government had been concerned over the amount of money that had been going out of the country for importing white polished ceramic ware. While the brown pottery produced in such villages as Hanwella was serving the needs of the kitchens in the homes of Ceylon, the demand at the dining-room table was for imported polished ceramics. In order to change the adverse effect on the economy caused by the importation of these utensils, the government was determined to set up a number of factories which would produce polished ceramics. One of the first factories planned was to be situated in a nearby area which could draw on the inhabitants of a number of villages on the banks of the Kelany River.

Both leaders felt that this new development should be reported to the people directly. At the meeting convened by them, Piyadasa Seneviratne repeated what he had told the two leaders, adding that the people on the whole would be able to increase their income by working in the new factory. Moreover, the factory would provide them with working conditions that would be a drastic improvement over their present crude kilns. The inhabitants of Hanwella, who had grown up with the idea that pottery making was exclusively a cottage industry, were clearly caught unawares by the report of the representative. The latter, realizing this, suggested that it might prove most valuable if the rest of the meeting were devoted to asking questions which he would try to answer. After the question period they might want to talk things over in smaller groups. He also suggested that they might want to send one of their own people to discuss the matter with the authorities in Colombo. This was something to which they readily agreed.

There was some hesitation in choosing between Badal Gedara Sirisena and Badal Gedara Kira. In order to tide the meeting over the embarrassing situation which had developed around the choice of a representative, Badal Gedara Sirisena said that there were a good many others to choose from and that they might consider some of the younger people, any one of whom would make an excellent representative at Colombo. At this, Bedal Gedara Kira quickly rose and moved that Badal Gedara Sirisena be sent to Colombo. Everyone seemed relieved at this suggestion and Sirisena good-naturedly yielded to the pressure, although he said that it was time others assumed responsibility in communal affairs. Badal Gedara Kira insisted that it was not the time to bring in new leadership when negotiations on such an important matter were involved, and Badal Gedara Sirisena agreed to make the trip the very next day.

Badal Gedara Sirisena returned to the village enthusiastic about the new factory. He declared at a public meeting that the government was, in any event, going ahead with the plan to build the factory since it was in the interests of Ceylon's national economy. Thus the village had no real choice in the matter. He urged the village to take full advantage of this new factory going up, citing the rise in wages and the higher standard of living which would certainly follow. After Badal Gedara Sirisena presented his case, Badal Gedara Kira rose and urged caution. He stressed that the men's leaving their homes to go to the factory would have a disturbing effect on paddy cultivation. With the breadwinners away from their homes, the older children leaving the village for work in the larger towns, and the younger ones attending compulsory school, who would be available to attend to the crop, he demanded. Then, surprisingly, he said that the suggestion previously put forth about raising the land in Hanwella was, after all, not a bad one. On his own initiative he had been in touch with the army during the absence of the R.D.S. representative. He had found the leadership of the army most coöperative and understanding of Hanwella's plight. Though the army would not be able to reimburse the citizens of Hanwella for their labor in raising the land, the military could, in return for the work, transfer to the village a piece of land on which a school could be built.

The information which Badal Gedara Kira brought to the meeting raised the spirits of all those in attendance. The people were pleased at the possibility of a school's being built in their midst, since it meant that their children would not have to go to the next village to attend classes. So much enthusiasm was aroused by the report that Badal Gedara Sirisena had to remind them that they had come primarily to discuss the factory proposal. It was with some effort that they shifted attention to this matter. A handful of those present agreed with Badal Gedara Sirisena that the higher wages would be of crucial importance in improving the lot of the people of Hanwella. This small group joined him in approving the idea, but the overwhelming majority were in favor of holding back on the decision regarding participation in the factory until they had more definite news about the plan the army had in relation to Hanwella.

Badal Gedara Sirisena went back to Colombo and reported on the meager results he had achieved at the meeting. The authorities, however, were not disappointed. They felt that Badal Gedara Sirisena would get better results by recruiting workers on an individual basis or in smaller groups than by addressing them from the platform at a large meeting. They also told him that he was a man whose reputation had reached them in Colombo and they felt that he was the most appropriate person to assume the job of supervisor of personnel for the new factory. Badal Gedara Sirisena was immensely flattered by the offer and agreed to accept it.

When he returned to Hanwella he began his round of visits in an effort to interest people in the new factory. Whatever interest he managed to arouse quickly dried up when the military arrived to take over the adjacent land. As Badal Gedara Kira had indicated, the army proved to be most coöperative and the soldiers working side by side with the villagers literally wrought a miracle. A job that had been calculated to take up to two years was completed in seven months. As the project moved ahead the villagers seemed to enjoy being on this project with the army. And for the duration of the project the village literally hummed with activity. True to its word the army began to build a school as soon as the land around Hanwella had been raised.

Throughout that time Badal Gedara Sirisena kept talking to the people but he succeeded in interesting only the younger folk. This in some measure irritated the parents, since they were generally not in favor of seeing their young people leave home to take jobs at the factory. Badal Gedara Sirisena became so busy with his new job as supervisor of personnel in the factory that he stopped going around the village to enlist prospective workers. Badal Gedara

Kira, who became indispensable as a liaison between the village and the army, was approached by the villagers to head a committee to secure teachers for the new school.

One evening the R.D.S. representative was leaving the first meeting of the committee appointed to deal with education in the new school when he happened to see Badal Gedara Sirisena coming home rather late from work. He stopped to talk to him and noticed how tired he looked, to the point of being ill. Piyadasa Seneviratne asked Badal Gedara Sirisena whether he had ever given thought to the idea of moving closer to his place of work so that he would not be under such strain in going to and from the factory. The latter answered that he had given some consideration to the possibility of moving, but then he looked about and said that Hanwella had, after all, been his home and that he hated to leave the village. He conveyed this feeling with a real measure of sadness. Shortly thereafter Badal Gedara Sirisena became ill and was unable to work. When he was hospitalized with a stomach disorder, the superintendent of the factory quickly assured him that his job was waiting his return and that he need have no worry while he was recuperating. On his release from hospital Badal Gedara Sirisena went back to work and several weeks thereafter moved from Hanwella to a location much closer to his place of work.

RELEASING DISCONTENT

Hanwella is confronted with a stark situation. It is at the mercy of a rampaging river that brings in its wake destruction and loss of life. To the outside observer the question naturally occurs: Why has such a situation been permitted to go on from generation to generation? Why have the inhabitants endured their appalling lot for such a long time?

The reasons why Hanwella has been so docile in accepting its fate are not discussed in the record. It is obvious, however, that Piyadasa Seneviratne, the representative from the Rural Development Society, sees from the very outset that before the people of

Hanwella can mobilize themselves to tackle the flood waters of the Kelany River, their traditional attitudes and responses to this problem will have to undergo drastic change. Fatalism and apathy will have to give way to a high degree of discontent (pp. 158–169 *supra*).

But how does a worker, unknown in the community, go about building up discontent in order that it may be utilized as a jumping-off point for creating much-needed change? In the first place, he must become involved in the day-to-day life of Hanwella and thus learn to understand first-hand how deeply entrenched the apathy is and what strengths in the community might be marshalled to overcome this attitude. Thus the worker begins by going from family to family helping them to rebuild their destroyed huts.

THE ROLE OF GUIDE

In the course of these rounds, he gets to know the community. He forms relationships with the people of Hanwella and in due time he is able to challenge their fatalism, although it is clear from his readiness to pitch in and help that he is in full sympathy with them in their adversity. At this stage the worker has assumed the role of guide (pp. 204–215 *supra*); he is stirring up discontent where apathy has existed. But he has done more than that: he has not allowed the discontent to remain a fragmented concern carried about separately as individual problems by the people with whom he has met and worked. By encouraging informal group meetings he is instrumental in raising the concern created by the floods to the point of a shared community issue.

ENABLER AND EXPERT

For the worker to have aroused community-wide dissatisfaction without channelling this feeling in a positive direction might have resulted in no more than a village full of stirred-up, frustrated inhabitants. Thus the role of guide gives way to that of enabler (pp. 215–222 *supra*), in which the representative of the Rural Development Society keeps the informal groups related to such tangible problems as medical aid and building materials. Hence the energy released by their newly found discontent finds focus in two specific concerns or needs, both identified by the people of Hanwella themselves.

Furthermore, the large casual meetings take on a more formal character as two natural leaders, with different degrees of status and differing outlooks, assume stewardship over the two constituent elements of the village population. As the groups become more formalized structures, the worker assumes the role of expert in the matter of providing resources in relation to the two needs which have been established. At this point the worker begins to move to a more indirect contact with the village as a whole, and to a more direct relationship with the Hanwella leaders. This is inevitable, since the on-going job of making decisions on local issues will eventually have to be located within some type of community surrogate or intergroup committee or council.

SPECIFIC CONTENT APPROACH

Throughout these developments the worker helps keep the interest of the villagers riveted to the crisis created by the flooding Kelany River. As a result, two plans are produced which aim at solving the problem. Although the proposals are different in nature, both are based on the specific content approach (pp. 18–20 *supra*), since they are designed to cope with the same urgent question.

THE PROBLEM REASSESSED

Up to a point, Hanwella proceeds as though it were fully in control of its own destiny, but then the R.D.S. representative returns to the village with the news that the national government of Ceylon has decided to establish a ceramics factory and that Hanwella is invited to avail itself of the opportunity to participate in the development of what is in effect a new industry. The government is determined to correct the adverse effect on the country's economy resulting from the importation of white ceramics. This goal can be achieved by transforming Hanwella's cottage type of industry, geared to producing the cruder, brown utensils, into a modern factory system capable of putting out white, mass-produced ceramics.

The factory offers Hanwella new opportunities in employment, improved working conditions, and higher wages which eventually will help to raise the community's standard of living. One would expect the inhabitants of the village to leap at the proposal offered by the national government, but these rewards are not without their price. The mass production of ceramics will undoubtedly disrupt traditional manufacture in Hanwella, as well as the family life that has been ordered around its cottage industry. With families being broken up to supply factory help, it will become very difficult, if not impossible, to cultivate rice. Finally the new labor force located in the factory will, undoubtedly, serve to undermine the social position that the pottery makers as a group have secured over the course of time. It is hardly surprising, therefore, that the people of the village balk at the idea of giving up their traditional way of life for the opportunities held out by the factory.

COMMUNITY PLANNING AND INTEGRATION

While they resist the factory proposal the villagers move with immense vigor to meet the challenge presented by the Kelany River, a crisis in the face of which they seemed so helpless a short time ago. Indeed, as they proceed to raise the river banks, Hanwella gives evidence of real growth, as may be defined in community organization terms (p. 40 *supra*): the inhabitants identify and give shape to their objective; they develop the will, confidence, and resources to take action with respect to it; and in the process they develop coöperative and collaborative attitudes and practices. Based on the high morale with which the people tackle the job of raising the river banks, it can be said that Hanwella has transcended what started out as community planning and has achieved community integration (pp. 51–60 *supra*).

SOCIAL THERAPY

Hanwella has met the challenge offered by the floods and in the process has been successful in securing a new school. However, the problem presented by the new factory remains unresolved. Much has already happened to indicate that the village will yet have to come to grips with this development. Some of the younger people have already forsaken the cottage industry for the factory. More significant, Badal Gedara Sirisena, once Hanwella's most respected leader, has, after much anguish (which may have brought on his sickness), separated himself from his people and decided to pursue a career at the ceramics factory.

He strikes a sad figure indeed in his meeting with the R.D.S. worker, caught as he is between his commitment to the factory and his deep attachment to Hanwella. It is interesting to speculate why the worker should have counselled him to leave Hanwella. Should he have advised him instead to remain in the village? What would have been accomplished by such advice? Badal Gedara Kira has achieved dominance as Hanwella's leader; the community has shown in unmistakable terms that it was not prepared to become involved with the ceramics factory; Badal Gedara Sirisena had gone a long way in his association with the government representatives in Ceylon; for him to have remained in Hanwella would have meant continued exposure to rejection by his own people. Moreover, advising him to remain would also have unmistakably indicated that the worker was challenging the community in its decision to shift its confidence from Badal Gedara Sirisena to Badal Gedara Kira. On the other hand, moving closer to the factory offered Badal Gedara Sirisena the opportunity of adjusting to a location in which his status was high and his ability greatly respected. Note that the worker does not go into details with Badal Gedara

Sirisena about his community leadership. The former does not reveal that he may very well have a deep understanding of what is happening to the latter. This may not be the time for such a decision. Ill and unhappy as Badal Gedara is, he may not be in a position to deal with his feelings at this time, and the worker delving into them in the course of a casual street encounter might only add to his difficulties. Thus the worker keeps his understanding of the problem to himself. Indeed, he is aware of other developments that he may not be able to discuss as easily with the people as he did when he first arrived in Hanwella. For example, it may well be that the extraordinary demonstration of enthusiasm the village has shown for raising the river banks stems from an unconscious determination on the part of the inhabitants to keep to their traditional ways in the face of the factory development. The worker when confronted with such latent attitudes would have to relinquish the prodding role of guide for that of social therapist (pp. 225–232 *supra*).

PROCESS OBJECTIVE

In dealing with these subtle and, at times, hidden attitudes the worker's timing (pp. 29 and 34 *supra*) will be essential. One can respect and sympathize with Hanwella's desire to spare itself the disorganization and pain that industrialization threatens to bring. At the same time it is inevitable that the factory, with its beckoning inducements of higher wages and modern conditions, will ultimately have the very effect that the people of Hanwella sense and fear. The specific content objective which worked so well in dealing with the flood waters may have to give way to a process approach (pp. 22–24 *supra*) as the community is helped to gain the strength and courage to make its peace with the industrial age which the national government is, in effect, bringing to this small village. Perhaps the gains which the community has made from the collective effort it expended in raising the river banks will serve Hanwella in good stead as it faces this next problem.

MERTON CENTER

Mr. Newton, Chairman of the Management Committee, had just delivered his report to the Board of Merton Center (a settlement house), and one of the members commented on the fact that the interest groups had shown a remarkable increase of 72 percent over the past two years while the club groups had declined by 35 percent over the same period. This meant that Merton Center had better be prepared for an onslaught on its various program offerings, the member cautioned. Another member asked why the club groups had decreased, but no one was able to provide an answer. Members were uniformly pleased at the way the new residents in the area had taken to the services offered by Merton Center, but before approving expansion of programs and the cost that this step would involve, they felt that some sort of survey should be carried out to provide a more precise picture of trends developing in the neighborhood.

Donald Simpson, Secretary to the Board and Executive Director of Merton Center, suggested that perhaps the Management Committee might undertake such a study. Mr. Newton, obviously pleased with the impact which his report had made on the members of the Board, agreed to recommend the project to his committee.

At the Management Committee's next meeting approval was given for the survey and a special committee of four was appointed to carry it out. A time limit of two months was given the two businessmen, a lawyer, and a housewife, who composed the new committee. Mr. Newton pointed out that the committee would have to have a chairman. There was a long pause during which none of the four individuals volunteered. Finally Mrs. Lloyd, the housewife, reluctantly offered to act as chairman if, she stressed, it would be all right with the other three. The three gave their approval readily and Mrs. Lloyd became chairman of the survey committee.

Mr. Newton then asked Stan Morris to act as consultant to the special committee. Stan Morris was Secretary to the Management

Committee but his primary role at Merton Center was that of head of the club group section.

Mr. Cooper, one of the businessmen acting on the survey committee, said that it would be a good idea for the group to get together briefly immediately after the Management Committee meeting to work out preliminary plans.

"After all," he pointed out, "we have a time limit and we might as well get started tonight."

Thus, late that evening, Mrs. Lloyd took the chair somewhat hesitantly. She said, "Now where do we go from here?"

"Well," offered Mr. Lawson, the older of the two businessmen, "let's think of what we want to ask the people."

"Or what we want to find out," added Stan, smiling.

"All right, let's discuss what we want to find out," Mr. Lawson amended, somewhat impatient with Stan.

Mr. Cooper raised his hand, and Mrs. Lloyd seemed relieved to call on him. Mr. Cooper said, "The Board wants some practical answers to practical problems and I think we can provide them quickly if we don't get lost in a lot of theory about opinion polling and the like. What we are being asked is to establish some trend, right?" After a nodding approval from the other three, he continued, "The first thing we do is find out what's in store for that area."

Mr. Lawson said that this information could be secured easily enough from the City Planning Department and he volunteered to do so. Stan suggested that perhaps one of the people from the Planning Department might be asked to come to a meeting. Mr. Lawson thought that the idea was a good one and he agreed to try to get a representative from the department to meet with them.

"The next step, it seems to me," Mr. Cooper said, "is to ask the people in the area what services they are using, how they like them, and what else they would like to see Merton Center provide in the way of community programs. Between the information from the Planning Board and from the people who live in the district, we should be able to get the full story."

Stan said that he was in agreement with the suggestion made by

Mr. Cooper, and then added, "At the risk of seeming technical I want to pick up the point about asking the people in the area. Getting the answers you need from this neighborhood may prove to be a bit tricky. For example, to the south we have a whole new group of Portuguese immigrants who have replaced the Jewish and Italian families who lived in that part for many years. Very few of them speak English, but they will have to be asked. The north end, or Merton Markets (as the area was commonly called), has had to give up a lot of land to large apartment blocks. The families moving into these apartments are the ones who are showing up at Merton Center in increasing numbers. They, too, have to be asked. There are the business owners at the new Plaza over near the apartments; then there are the old-time Merton Markets shopkeepers. All of these people will have to be asked. How are you going to approach these different groups of people?"

"You're right, at that," Mr. Lawson said quickly, as though atoning for the impatience he had shown with Stan earlier. "I am over on Merton Street, I do a fair trade with the Portuguese; in fact my clerk is a Portuguese young man. I don't know the language but I can get him to talk to his people and find out. As for the remaining old-time Jewish and Italian residents, I know them well. I could speak to them myself." Then he added laughingly, "But don't ask me to talk to my competitors on Merton Street. They'll think I've got something up my sleeve. They wouldn't even tell me the time."

Mrs. Lloyd said that she could interview the people in the apartments. "In order to make it representative," she conjectured out loud, "how would it be if I rang every tenth door bell in my own apartment house and the same for the two adjoining ones? Since there are a hundred suites to each apartment building, that would give me a total of thirty replies."

Mr. Shepherd, the lawyer, who was much younger than the two businessmen, felt that his time had come to speak. "As you know," he said, "I have my office over one of the stores at the Plaza. I'll be darned if I can tell one customer from the next. But the other businessmen at the Plaza are greatly interested in Merton Center. In fact, I am their representative on the Management Committee and I'll be glad to get their reaction."

Stan summed up, saying, "I think we've got the job pretty nicely divided and, if the committee is agreeable, I'm prepared to talk to the shopkeepers on Merton Street."

Mr. Cooper then spoke, "You're right Stan, we have got the job pretty nicely divided, especially since I'm left with very little to do."

Everyone laughed at his comment; then he added, "But I may be able to carry my weight in preparing the report. I wish I could help with the interviewing but like so many of the others active in this organization I'm not a resident in the area and don't know many of the people. If Stan could draw up a few questions that might serve as a guide to the three of you, you could get down to the interviewing without delay."

Stan said he would be glad to do it together with Mrs. Lloyd, the chairman, provided the committee would spend a little time outlining what they felt should be asked. Mrs. Lloyd replied that Mr. Cooper had already outlined what was needed, namely, a few simple questions indicating whether the people were using the services; what kind of services they were using most; what else they would like Merton Center to provide to the neighborhood. The committee then fixed six weeks as the time limit for getting the answers and the two remaining weeks for preparing the report for the Management Committee. They asked Mr. Lawson to try to secure a representative from the Planning Department for the next meeting, which was scheduled for two weeks away.

Five days later Mr. Lawson called Stan, agreeably surprised that the Planning Department had readily agreed to provide a representative who would attend the meeting of the survey committee. At this meeting Mr. Lawson introduced Mr. Gordon, the representative of the Planning Department, who expressed appreciation at being invited and produced a number of beautifully drawn sketches depicting plans in store for Merton Markets. He pointed out that the population in Merton Markets would, as a result of further building activity, increase threefold, or in other words from some 10,000 to 30,000 residents. This would, of course, call for additional shopping facilities and increased parking space, as well as greater recreational resources. He went on to point out that the south would be left alone. "Merton Markets," he stressed, "is a landmark. The city doesn't want to lose an area whose character has taken generations to build. We want to clean up the area and beautify it. We want Merton Markets to remain with its open stalls and quaint marketing facilities which have lasted for over sixty years. It's a kind of shoppers' Bohemia and the people definitely want it with its clutter and all." He also said that the streets adjoining Merton Markets would be left alone, since the housing there was in pretty good condition. Moreover, the successive waves of immigrants seemingly had found there a comfortable niche. Then Mr. Gordon added, "When we first drew these plans up we had a meeting with the Merton Shopkeepers Association. They were very enthusiastic. Some of them even offered to provide paint and to start a clean-up program among the residents. However, nothing seems to have come of these plans. In fact, we aren't getting anywhere with the residents of the area. Most of them don't speak English. On two occasions we've tried to approach them but each time we drew a blank."

Mr. Lawson joined in and said with a good measure of feeling, "These people may shy away from the representatives of the Planning Department but they certainly are not so shy with us. We've done our best but all we get is resentment and often opposition. In fact, one Monday morning we even found a terrible spectacle when some of us arrived at our stores. Dead rats had been flung in the doorways of many of the shops."

Mrs. Lloyd shuddered at Mr. Lawson's last remark. He apologized to her for having raised the point, but felt that the story had to be told. Stan informed the group that the incident had come to his attention; in fact a number of Portuguese had led a kind of protest move. They got together at their small church where they aired their grievances. The priest had come over to Merton Center in an effort to get help with the situation. The Portuguese were bitter, charging that the businessmen were anxious to provide paint for them to beautify their homes but were doing nothing to clean up the garbage and refuse at the back of their own stores. This indifference, the Portuguese claimed, was threatening the values of the homes which some of them had just bought. Stan also reported that the older immigrants in the area felt stranded. They were only there waiting until they could sell their homes at a good price and get out as fast as they could. The Portuguese felt that in addition to facing the hardship of a new life in a new community they were being asked to beautify the area without the coöperation of the shopkeepers or the old-time residents.

Mr. Gordon was amazed to hear this and said, "How come this has never come to our attention?"

Stan said he would be ready to meet with Mr. Gordon to see if Merton Center could be of any help in reducing the tension that had developed around the problem.

Mr. Cooper was of the conviction that as long as people lived together they would fight together; these things could not be helped.

Mrs. Lloyd thanked Mr. Gordon for coming to the meeting, and the latter in turn expressed appreciation for having had the opportunity of meeting with the committee. Turning to Stan, he said he would be coming around to Merton Center to pursue some of the matters he had just learned about.

Several days after the meeting Mrs. Lloyd telephoned Stan to tell him that she had begun her interviewing. She seemed rather distressed at the answers she was getting. Nearly all the people she had interviewed were using the services of Merton Center. They were emphatic in their complaints at the poor quality of the programs. Criticisms levelled at the children's programs were perhaps strongest. Mothers complained that the person conducting ballet classes was a rank amateur and that the same held true for the art classes. In the absence of anything better, the parents indicated, they had no choice but to use Merton Center services.

Mr. Lawson telephoned with a similar tale of woe about the Portuguese families. To both Stan replied that there was little to do but reveal the situation at the meeting of the survey committee.

When the committee was convened, Mrs. Lloyd reported that she had interviewed 30 families of whom no less than 24 were using the services of Merton Center. She pretty well repeated the story that she had given to Stan some time earlier and said that the parents wanted to form a committee to approach the municipality in order to establish the recreational facilities that had been promised for the area. They felt that a settlement house was not geared to the program activities and quality of service they were seeking.

Mr. Lawson said that his report would not relieve the gloom. Together with his clerk some 42 people had been spoken to. The clerk had talked to 32 Portuguese, and of these some 12 knew that their children were going to Merton Center. They could not say what they were doing in the settlement house, nor did they seem much interested. The others were indifferent, some even hostile, avowing that they restrained their children from going there. Two Jewish youngsters and two Italian children were using the services of Merton Center; the parents to whom Mr. Lawson spoke were not sure exactly what their children were doing there. Although at one time these people had been fairly close to Merton Center, in recent years they had not given much thought to the settlement house.

Mr. Shepherd said that he had spoken to the shopkeepers at a meeting which was attended by all 21 businessmen who rented stores in the Plaza. There, too, there was dissatisfaction. The businessmen had given a grant of $1,000 annually to Merton Center over the past two years. Although this had been written up in the neighborhood newspaper as a good-will gesture, what the storekeepers were actually interested in was that Merton Center should act as a kind of magnet to attract the teenagers who were hanging around the Plaza. The businessmen felt that this job had not been done. On the contrary, more and more teenagers were loitering about, disturbing customers, and generally creating an unpleasant atmosphere at the Plaza. Stan said that he happened to know that a good many of these teenagers, who incidentally came from the apartments, were using the Merton Center facilities for sports activities. However, very few of them were interested in club groups.

After these reports had been delivered, Mrs. Lloyd laughed wearily. She asked, "Well, what kind of trend does this give us?"

Mr. Cooper observed, "What worries me is how are we going to bring this report to the Management Committee? After all, that committee deals with concrete things, such as recommending the purchase of sports equipment, art supplies, designating use of property, authorizing repairs, and the like. They need to know how the neighborhood is going to use Merton Center in order to prepare their plans. All we've got is a lot of complaints, and how's that going to help the Management Committee? Maybe what we ought to do is summarize the stuff the representative from the Planning Department gave us. Then the Management Committee can come up with estimates about equipment and so forth."

Stan said that what was being reflected in the reports seemed important. Mr. Cooper replied that that might be so, but the Management Committee was not equipped to deal with these complaints. Mr. Shepherd felt that perhaps an exception might be made in this case in view of the importance of the complaints being conveyed in the report. It was finally decided that factual material of the kind supplied by the representative from the Planning Department should be presented in summary by Mr. Cooper, and that Mrs. Lloyd, with the help of Stan, should prepare a summary dealing with the various opinions expressed by the people interviewed.

At the end of the stipulated two-month period, the committee was ready to make its report to the Management Committee. The report was the last of twelve agenda items which the committee was to process between 9:00 and 11:00 P.M. Mr. Simpson, the Executive Director, had assured Stan that the eleven items preceding the report were very short and routine in nature; at most they would require no more than an hour, and the report to be

delivered by the survey committee would be given 50 percent of
the meeting time. Stan relayed this assurance to Mrs. Lloyd when
she became upset at the length of the agenda.

As the Director had promised, the eleven points dealing with
such things as the purchase of two volleyball nets, approval of
cost for window blinds in the gymnasium, the fixing of a maximum
price for sweaters to be purchased for the basketball team, and so
forth, were first on the agenda. Although the chairman steered
these matters through quickly and efficiently, the members of the
Management Committee were becoming restless. Two of them had
left the meeting at 10:00, leaving twelve of the fourteen members
to hear the report of the survey committee. Mr. Newton introduced
Mr. Cooper, who delivered a very thorough report in his precise
manner. On the basis of Mr. Gordon's statistics he drew a picture
of the area as it would be in ten years, projecting the increase in
users as well as in the cost of providing the program activities
currently being offered by Merton Center. He pointed out that in
view of attitudes expressed by people interviewed, Merton Center
might well have to consider changes in its programs. However,
Mrs. Lloyd would be dealing with that aspect of the situation;
he was limiting himself to facts and figures.

Mr. Cooper's report was most interesting and Mr. Newton
thanked him for its thoroughness and the precision with which it
was delivered. He then introduced Mrs. Lloyd, who, he pointed
out, had secured some critical comments in respect to the services
being offered by Merton Center. Before Mrs. Lloyd could speak,
three more members had left the room. She became so nervous that
she delivered her comments, read from a sheet, very quickly. Indeed, it was difficult to follow her. During the course of the report
she was interrupted by one member who excused himself, saying
that he had to leave. By the time the report had been finished, Mr.
Newton seemed somewhat helpless; he said that Mrs. Lloyd's
comments were interesting but that they should be conveyed
directly to the Board, which was empowered to act on these prob-

lems. He closed the meeting on a high note of appreciation to the survey committee for its good work.

Mrs. Lloyd seemed somewhat crushed by the experience and looked to Stan for some reaction. Stan came over to her and said, "I guess Mr. Cooper was right about this committee. You can't teach an old dog new tricks. Our work actually begins at the next meeting of the Board of Merton Center, where your report will get the attention it deserves."

Mrs. Lloyd looked up at Stan and said with some uncertainty, "I hope you're right, Stan." Stan said that they would be getting together in plenty of time before the next Board meeting. He bade Mrs. Lloyd good evening, and went over to the Director. "I think we ought to have a good look at this whole situation," Stan said to the Director.

"You're right," said the Director, and they made a note to discuss the matter at their next regular conference which was coming up in two days.

PRACTITIONER ROLES

From the very outset the differences in role structure are apparent as between Piyadasa Seneviratne in Hanwella and those of Donald Simpson, Executive Director of Merton Center, and Stan Morris, head of the agency's club group section. Piyadasa Seneviratne comes to Hanwella as a representative of the Rural Development Society. His professional role is legitimated by a source external to Hanwella's own power structure. This role structure has important implications. With an outside source such as the R.D.S. placing the stamp of authority on the worker, he is able to maintain role mastery in relation to the client community. Thus the relationship between Hanwella and the worker is somewhat akin to the doctor-patient or caseworker-client relationship. This means that the worker in Hanwella is able to face conflict, power, and other emotional content with a considerable measure of emotional neutrality. It also means reduced stress, leaving the worker more freedom in timing his moves. This is evident as Piyadasa Seneviratne assumes different roles at different stages in his work with Hanwella, or as he moves from his close relationship with the community at the broad base to a more direct tie with the leadership.

By contrast, the role of the workers in the Merton case is not legitimated by an external source. The members of the Board of Merton Center serve simultaneously as the employers of Donald Simpson and Stan Morris and as the representatives of the client community surrounding the settlement house. This immediately presents difficulties to the workers in that the client-worker relationship is not as clearly structured as it is in the case of Hanwella. In Merton Center the workers must deal with board members as the legitimaters of their professional role as well as the recipients of their help. This ambiguity in role structure has an important bearing on the actions of, and the relationship between, the workers and the leaders of Merton Center.

RESEARCH AND COMMUNITY DIAGNOSIS

In the case of Hanwella the worker is involved with a compact village society whose sub-groups are stable and readily visible. He has only to go from family to family to determine the degree of apathy that exists in the community. With the knowledge that he gains of the community he is able to develop a strategy to deal with the crisis presented by the river floods. For the Merton Center workers, however, such intimate relationships with the community surrounding the settlement house are virtually impossible. The urban neighborhood is far larger and encompasses many more people than does the village of Hanwella. But more important, the area has undergone drastic change in a few short years. The sub-groups are hardly aware of each other, and the Merton Center leadership is out of touch with the people it is supposed to represent.

Furthermore, in Hanwella little of the worker's time was taken up with formal committee structure; by contrast, committee structure in Merton Center is so complex that it requires much of the workers' time and energy in serving and maintaining it. This inevitably cuts into the time available to the workers for developing informal relationships within the community at the broad base. Yet, information as a basis for action is no less important to the workers and leaders of Merton Center than it was in the Hanwella situation. Fact-finding is a prerequisite to diagnosis and action, no less for the community than for the individual client.

What the Board members want are a few simple facts to help them plan a program that will be acceptable to the neighborhood. What the study reveals is quite something else. A new group of middle-class apartment dwellers has located in the area who are not prepared to accept the folk-art type of program that used to be so well received by the earlier Italian and Jewish residents. These program offerings are not adequate in the eyes of middle-class apartment dwellers, who may be searching for programs and corresponding teaching skills of the type provided by conservatories and ballet schools. The apartment dwellers are so dissatisfied with the services of Merton Center that they are prepared to go to the city in the hope of securing the types of program they want.

The Portuguese immigrants are also distressed and disillusioned with Merton Center. They see the agency as catering to the wishes of the middle-class apartment dwellers and to the businessmen in the area. As for the Plaza shopkeepers, they seem to have very little intrinsic interest in the Center itself; the $1,000 grant that they allocate annually to Merton Center is for the sole purpose of attracting the teenagers to the settlement house and away from their stores. Finally, the Merton Markets merchants are prepared to beautify the fronts of the houses but show very little consideration for the backyards of their neighbors, the new Portuguese homeowners.

Instead of the desired facts and figures, the study has revealed a high degree of discontent with the agency's services as well as a good deal of conflict among the various sub-groups in the immediate neighborhood. Indeed, research in community organization must do more than provide facts; it must reveal to the leaders the relationship between the facts and their emotional connotations for the community (pp. 143–145, 223–225 *supra*) as a basis for realistic action.

GENERAL CONTENT APPROACH

In Hanwella the worker mingles with the village people. In the process he acquires an understanding of the community, helping it to release discontent and overcome apathy. The discontent in turn is focused on a specific content goal, namely, the project to deal with the flood waters of the Kelany River. In the Merton Center situation the study also constitutes a first step in awakening discontent. It is difficult to say from the record whether this was Donald Simpson's purpose in suggesting the study, but it does seem that Stan Morris had discontent in mind when he sought to redirect the Management Committee's interest from merely asking questions to finding out what the community around Merton Center was really like.

Nor does the record tell us in what direction the discontent is to be channelled. But we might profitably consider the type of goal which Stan Morris and Donald Simpson may conceivably discuss in their forthcoming conference. The community is not confronted with a type of physical danger, such as faced Hanwella, to which a specific content objective is the answer. Nor is the community ripe for a process objective such as Hanwella is approaching; there is as yet no beginning of neighborhood solidarity, the sub-groups are too distant from each other, and the leadership is virtually out of touch with its constituent elements. Such a development may come at a later stage, as it did in Hanwella, but the immediate goal may very well be one of general content (pp. 20–22 *supra*). What is at stake in the area is the orderly development and initiation of new services by Merton Center. The goal here is not a single reform but a more general objective of effective planning and operation of a special group of services in the community (p. 20 *supra*). It is the Board's explicit general interest in the provision of services to the neighborhood which has led to the study's being undertaken by the Management Committee.

LEADERSHIP

The approach to leadership in Merton Center is the very opposite of that taken in Hanwella. Whereas the worker in Hanwella starts with the community at large and gradually moves toward a relationship with the leaders, in Merton Center the workers commence with the leaders and through the study move into the community. Furthermore, in Hanwella there is a direct link between community and the leadership. By contrast, in Merton Center we have a Board that has lost touch with the community, and what in effect is now required is new leadership which is positively identified (pp. 120–124 *supra*) with the sub-groups who have in recent years moved into the neighborhood.

The Board members of Merton Center see themselves as a group of patrons ready to endow a community, which they view as disadvantaged, with a variety of services. This is unfortunately typical of many settlement houses where, by virtue of a kind of ecological arrangement, the high status decision-makers and what they perceive as the lower status users of services coexist in the same organization with very little confrontation between the two groups. Because of the role problem discussed earlier, workers often feel intimidated by such boards, and opportunities to recruit new leadership are left unexploited. If the neighborhood surrounding Merton Center is to be properly served, what is needed is participation of representatives who not only know the extent of conflict that exists, but are also aware of the reservoirs of manifest and latent good will which are present in the area.

This does not mean, of course, that the incumbent group of board members must be removed forthwith or resign in a body.

To initiate such an unrealistic and foolish move would create a vacuum which would endanger the entire agency. What present leadership needs is help in understanding that it must provide opportunities for indigenous leadership to begin participating at various levels in the committee structure, and thus create effective communication between Merton Center and constituent groups in the area.

PRINCIPLES OF ORGANIZATION

Actually, an indirect step toward the introduction of new leadership has been taken with the decision to do the study, although it has been faulty in its execution. The fault may be traced back to a Board which attempts to arrive at decisions on the basis of factual content, largely ignoring emotional factors (p. 176 *supra*). A purely statistical approach to the problems confronting Merton Center will produce unrealistic decisions. Yet the Board perpetuates this bias when it refers the study to the Management Committee. The result is that the Management Committee, in turn, virtually repudiates the emotional content revealed by the survey. Mr. Cooper, who is representative of the current leadership active in Merton Center, presents a statistical report which is highly acceptable to the Management Committee, while Mrs. Lloyd's presentation is given short shrift. Even if the committee were in a position to consider Mrs. Lloyd's report, coming as it did at the end of such a long agenda, it was bound to suffer, in that the members were by this time quite tired of deliberating.

Mrs. Lloyd, judging from the survey results, seems to have good contact with the apartment dwellers and might, in time, make an effective representative of that group. However, as a result of her experience at the Management Committee meeting, she has suffered a setback in her confidence as a beginning volunteer. She will need help if she is to regain security, and Stan Morris is prepared to assist in this respect. In the relationship with Mrs. Lloyd around this situation the worker is concerned with failure, not only as a personal problem but as a challenge to community leadership. Desirable as Mrs. Lloyd's regained self-confidence may be for her own personal well-being, Stan Morris must help her to gain a measure of authority when she appears before the Board, since she will be introducing the type of emotional content from which this leadership group has been shielding itself. While Morris is working with Mrs. Lloyd in preparation for the Board meeting he (and/or Simpson) will also have to prepare the members for the type of material Mrs. Lloyd will be presenting. This means individual discussions with the Board members prior to the meeting. Throughout this process the relationship between worker and volunteer is crucial to the change in attitude which the Board members must undergo.

BRANSTOWN COMMUNITY CHEST

The committee which met to fix the goal of the Branstown Federation campaign for the ensuing year noted that four of the casework agencies had, in the previous year, spent a combined amount of $380,000 in supplementation to clients receiving public assistance. The members of the committee wondered why the practice of supplementary assistance had been allowed to go unquestioned during budgetary reviews. They felt that the $380,000 constituted a burden that should not again be shouldered by Branstown's forthcoming annual drive. They argued that public assistance was a government responsibility; if rates fell short of meeting client needs, it was the responsibility of the government to raise public assistance levels. They were adamant that voluntary agencies should not be called upon to make up the difference between public assistance grants and basic requirements.

The matter was subsequently taken up at the Board meeting of the Branstown Federation. The members reversed the decisions of the budget committee and upheld the view of the goal committee. The matter was then referred by the Branstown Federation to the Branstown Health and Welfare Council, a beneficiary agency of the former.

The Federation, of course, conveyed its decision directly to the agencies, but what it sought additionally from the Council was a measure of interpretation to the agencies so that the essential point of the Federation's new policy would be understood and accepted. The Council therefore met with the agencies. The representatives of the latter pointed out that they had no quarrel with the policy adopted by the Federation and by the Health and Welfare Council of Branstown (which was in agreement with the Federation); the question at issue was the time limit. The agency representatives (both lay leaders and professional workers) felt that they could not be put in a position where the government might not raise its rates while simultaneously the Federation proceeded to cut its supplementary assistance allocations. The agency representatives held to the position that the rates had to be raised before the Federation could continue supplementary assistance.

In order to strengthen their case, each of the agencies presented to the Council facts and figures showing how inadequate were the public assistance rates and how clients trying to cope with these grants alone would have been in grave difficulties. Basing their argument on this material, the Executive Director and the President of the Council met with the Federation to present the position the casework agencies had taken. The Federation, however, held to its stand and firmly insisted, indeed demanded, that the Council take the necessary steps to see that government assistance rates were increased.

When advised by the Executive Director of the Council that the Federation remained firm in its stand, the agency representatives felt that in the interests of their clients they would have to go to the community at large, arguing that public opinion would force the government's hand quickly on this matter. The Executive Director cautioned against this step; publicity at this point, he argued, would make it virtually impossible to carry on free discussion and negotiation. Nevertheless, the agency representatives convened at a news conference and informed the four Branstown newspapers of the policy which the Federation had adopted and the likely effect it would have on agency clients unless public assistance rates were raised immediately by the government. The reaction of the newspapers was different from what the agencies had expected. No pressure was applied to government; instead, three of the four dailies published editorials to the effect that the forthcoming campaign would suffer if the Federation adopted its proposed policy. In general, the editorial statements agreed that the Federation was right in pointing the finger of responsibility at the government but that there was, nevertheless, an absence of compassion in the abrupt way in which the supplementary grants were being cut off. The newspaper comment created a great deal of ill-feeling within the Federation's campaign cabinet members toward the agencies.

The Branstown Health and Welfare Council was also put in a difficult position. Since it was anxious to have the active participation of the local Department of Public Welfare, it was loath to involve itself in the kind of militant social action which the agencies were pressing for in connection with increased public assistance rates. What the Health and Welfare Council did was to form a committee of twenty-five community leaders who were members of the Council. This group, armed with the material which the family agencies had made available, petitioned the governor of the state for an increase in public assistance rates. The committee was received cordially by the governor. He indicated that action would have to be based on a thorough study of the situation. This inconclusive response left the agencies in an insecure position, with the Federation's time limit still hanging over their heads. They therefore insisted that the Council continue its pressure on both the Federation and the government: on the former to postpone the deadline on its adopted policy, and on the latter to increase rates in order that the agencies would not be caught with insufficient funds should the Federation go through with its decision.

The Federation was also anxious that the Council continue pressing the government on the question of financial assistance, since it felt that yielding on its part to the agencies would be a bad precedent. A positive response from the government would, the Federation felt, bring the entire problem to a favorable end, public opinion could be dealt with on the basis of an increase in public assistance, and the Federation could maintain its policy without seeming callous to agency clients. The Federation was deeply concerned about the matter because it was anxious to launch the forthcoming campaign in the customary spirit of public good will, particularly since in the previous two years the campaign had fallen short of its goal. The campaign cabinet felt that by cutting away the burden of supplementary assistance, Branstown would, for the first time in three years, have a goal that could be successfully reached.

As a result of the sustained pressure from these two sources, the Council leadership, adopting the suggestion put forth by the Executive Director, decided to convene a public meeting to which the local and state officials (both elected and appointed) were to be invited, in order to meet with the representatives of the casework agencies on the question of supplementation. The underlying idea was to provide a platform on which there would be a kind of confrontation between both elements, with the community at large invited to sit in judgment, as it were, on the entire issue. The conference was arranged in a large public auditorium, which was filled on the night of the meeting. Representatives of the agencies as well as of the state legislature took their places on the platform. A good many individuals who had met previously with the governor were also on the platform, and the same man who had led the committee of twenty-five acted as chairman. Representatives from the local Department of Public Welfare were present but preferred not to sit on the platform.

Following the chairman's introductory remarks a representative of the Branstown Department of Public Welfare rose and with a good deal of feeling questioned the authenticity of the brief which had been presented by the committee of twenty-five. He pointed out that the contents of the brief were based on facts compiled by the voluntary social agencies. The caseworkers who had compiled the information about local public assistance had gone purely on the say-so of their clients and had not checked for accuracy with the Branstown Department of Public Welfare. At this point several caseworkers heatedly challenged the official to deny the accuracy of the information they had supplied to the committee.

The mounting argument between the representatives of the local Department of Public Welfare and the private agencies was quickly creating a furor. Some of the leaders on the platform tried to play the role of mediators. Finally the Director of Public Welfare for the state restored calm. He said that although it was impossible to give a commitment to the meeting, he could assure those present that if increased public assistance rates were indicated, the government would take the necessary action to effect such a raise. Furthermore, as an immediate first step, the government had agreed to increase current per capita grants to the municipalities. Although communities were free to use these funds for any purpose they deemed advisable, the Director stated that all municipalities would be advised that the grants were being raised explicitly to help the communities to apply a greater proportion of funds to public assistance without having to hold off such action pending the decision from the state government as to increasing the assistance grants.

On this conciliatory note the meeting was concluded. In order to ward off any further unfavorable publicity which might have come as a result of the public meeting, the Federation subsequently came out with a face-saving statement to the effect that it was satisfied that the state government was serious about raising financial assistance rates. Consequently, supplementation of the agencies would, in the meantime, continue.

The agency representatives felt that they had achieved a real victory. They had not only been successful in forcing the Federation to retract its time limit for cutting off supplementary assistance allocations, but had also compelled the government to make some additional funds immediately available to the municipalities. In the light of the publicity that had been given to this issue they felt that the public authorities in Branstown would have no choice but to divert the increase to public assistance. The whole matter of higher rates would now be aired at the state level as an aftermath of the public meeting; increases seemed only a matter of time.

Despite the sense of triumph on the part of the family agency representatives and their conviction that social action was used effectively on this occasion, the Health and Welfare Council of Branstown faced some serious consequences. The members of the committee of twenty-five who had carried the issue felt let down because their submission to the government appeared a good deal less than authoritative. As a result, some of the leaders began to waver in their support of, and participation in, the Council. Moreover, the local Department of Public Welfare had been alienated and there was concern within the Council over the effect this would have on a pilot project dealing with hardcore families which the Council had initiated. This project involved the Department of Public Welfare and the four agencies with which it had been locked in dispute at the public meeting.

Evaluating these developments at a Council staff meeting, the Executive Director commented philosophically that every achievement had a price. There was no doubt that results had been achieved at the public meeting, but he wondered about the price that had been paid.

STRUCTURE

Each of the three case records discussed here constitutes a setting for community organization practice, but there is a marked difference in structure between the village of Hanwella, on the one hand, and Merton Center and the Branstown Council, on the other.

The individual is born into a community such as Hanwella, but not into a Merton Center or a Health and Welfare Council of Branstown. The former provides the conditions for what Park has termed as biotic or functional interdependence, molar or group identification, and spatial or distinctive location.[1] The latter con-

[1] Maurice R. Stein, *The Eclipse of Community*, Harper & Row, 1964, p. 111.

stitute secondary resources whose aim is to enhance individual and group life when the community's natural avenues for self-expression have been weakened or are threatened with breakdown. In Hanwella the population as a whole is involved and acts through its indigenous leadership, while in the Branstown Council the concern is with a specific group of users of agencies' services who require public assistance. These individuals are represented not by their natural leaders but by professional workers and volunteers acting on agency boards.

The basis of a functional community such as the Branstown Health and Welfare Council is, in effect, the social problem which draws together kindred social agencies seeking its solution. The geographic community has its locus, of course, in a particular area in which may be found a great variety of groupings and institutions, both formal and informal, varying greatly in their interests and outlook. An example of such a community is the neighborhood surrounding Merton Center.

Yet the assumptions which the worker carries into his relationships hold true for the three situations described in the records. These assumptions are based on the faith that the community, through its representatives, has the inherent capacity to identify and resolve its problems, that people should have the opportunity to participate in the shaping of their own destiny, and that the community, as a social system, is based on the democratic principle of self-regulation (pp. 77–100 supra).

ASPECTS OF PLANNING

Rational planning invariably entails a series of discrete sequences (pp. 139–154 supra). The first stage is, of course, the development of a clear definition of the problem. Although self-evident, this step is frequently neglected because the many factors that may combine to produce a community problem often obscure causality.

The web of competing interests may be plainly seen in the neighborhood surrounding Merton Center. Similarly, the Branstown case culminates in a public meeting that is virtually split by conflicting equities. Such action as is taken by the Branstown Health and Welfare Council does not issue from a clear perception of the problem but from what would appear to be a desire to keep the peace or maintain equilibrium among the warring constituents.

The Federation has taken the position that public assistance is a government responsibility and should not be supplemented by philanthropy. The validity of this stand is not the issue; it is the undue hurry with which the Federation has decided to discontinue supplementary assistance to the four agencies. At the basis of this haste may be the keen desire of the Federation to be rid of the $380,000 burden which supplementary assistance represents. Since the removal of this considerable sum from the campaign goal will give the Federation a reachable objective for the first time in three years, the urgency is understandable.

On the other hand, such an abrupt move will cause great hardship to the families who depend on this money and, possibly, chaos in the community. If the underlying function of the Council is the general content purpose (pp. 20–22 supra), i.e., coördination and orderly development of services, then the Federation must be made aware of the likely consequences that may result from the precipitous course it plans to follow. However, the Council does not pursue a general content goal but, instead, becomes a medium for the exchange of irreconcilable views. One of the underlying reasons for the Council's failure to confront the Federation may be due to its status as a beneficiary agency of the latter. This situation may have a built-in coercive effect, with the result that the Council's authority may be chronically impaired in its relationship with the Federation. We get a glimpse of this problem at the meeting, where the Federation makes demands of a passive Council which does not counter with a position of its own.

Since the Council may be unable to bring the issue to the Federation, its capacity to represent the four agencies in the situation is also impaired. In a sense the position of the Branstown Health and Welfare Council is quite opposite that of Merton Center; the latter is much too detached from its community while the Branstown Council seems to be at the mercy of its member groups.

Had there been a more accurate assessment of the problem and of the social planning role, a number of principles relating to sound organization (pp. 188–199 *supra*) might have followed which would have given strength and support to its member groups and added stability and prestige to the Council. Instead, the agency representatives, feeling the weakness of the Council, decide to approach the press in an effort to ward off the action threatened by the Federation. What the Council has failed to do, the newspapers accomplish with the editorials which are directed at the Federation.

By this time the problem has been dropped into the lap of the community at large and is out of the hands of the leadership of the Council. As a result, the capacity for timing its moves, perhaps the key to sound organization (p. 190 *supra*), is badly disrupted within the Council, and the planned pace, which is much more evident in Hanwella, is lacking in Branstown. Had the Council retained its mastery in the matter of timing, it might have been in a position to prepare its own data for the committee of twenty-five in their meeting with the governer. Instead, the Council was forced to rely on secondary material provided by the agencies, and this resulted in the alienation of the Branstown Department of Public Welfare and in sparking the uproar which was created at the public meeting.

Indeed, the public meeting is indicative of a desire on the part of the Council to remain in control of the situation after the problem has become one for the community at large. The meeting could have been a sound planning tactic if it had not been devised as a means of escaping pressures which the Council found relentless. Even the most effective organizational structure cannot, at times, prevent member groups from entering into insoluble conflicts. In such circumstances the public meeting can be a sound move in which the position of the central planning body in no way suffers a defeat. Organizations have learned to come to the community at annual meeting time to revise constitutional procedures, to induct new leadership, and to secure approval for new services and programs. Similarly, in times of crisis when problem-solving through committee process has been exhausted, it should be possible to come directly to the community to resolve such dilemmas. This is akin to plebiscite action taken by governmental bodies when they are unable to reach a decision within their legislative confines.

What was required in this instance was a full understanding on the part of the four agencies, the Federation, and the other member groups as to the need for the meeting and their active participation in planning it. But with the Council fearful of its constituents, it seems that the various organizations remain uninvolved in the meeting plans. The approach to the gathering is one of apprehension rather than a sense of accountability because of a conviction that it is an elementary matter of democratic practice for the community to intervene at this juncture.

Nevertheless, the meeting was instrumental in accomplishing a good deal, as the record indicates, but this achievement has come through the interplay of random forces at the meeting proper rather than through premeditated intervention on the part of the Branstown Health and Welfare Council. What could not be prevented in the process was the loss of prestige to the Council and the wavering of the Council's leadership structure as a result of the incident.

WORKER'S NEXT STEP

The Executive Director's observation at the conclusion of the record conveys a sense of helplessness as to the Council's future direction. Professionally, his position is similar to that of Donald Simpson in relation to the Merton Center Board. Both are confronted with leaderships which simultaneously represent the client community and act as sources of professional role legitimation. Neither worker has the well-defined status of the community organization practitioner from the Rural Development Society in Hanwella. Frequently, where the professional role is not too clear, the worker may feel compelled to give emphasis to administrative tasks that the lay leadership may perceive most readily as comprising the community organization worker's role. However, the administrative aspect is only part of the worker's responsibility and it can serve as a useful start from which the practitioner can broaden his professional mandate to include the role characteristics exhibited by the worker in Hanwella.

Following the meeting, the Executive Director is at a point where he can retreat into day-to-day organizational routines or he can initiate a process to help the Council regain the ground it has lost. One step in that direction would be a thorough evaluation of the entire process which led to the meeting. Understandably, the Executive Director may be apprehensive about involving his leadership in a post-mortem that may open up old wounds. But if carefully planned, such an analysis can provide a valuable learning experience for future action. It can provide the leaders with a new sense of commitment and courage gained from a deepened insight into an unsuccessful activity. Moreover, such an evaluation, if effectively carried out, can be productive of growth in the relationship between worker and leadership, with the former moving from the mere position of executive assistant to the role of enabler in the eyes of his board.

Another thing that the Council must start immediately is the process of restoring the deteriorated lines of communication which now exist among its various member groups. This means more than vague good-will exchange; what is required is a meeting of minds around fundamental issues. As a starting point in this direction, the status of the multi-problem family project might be reviewed. There is the concern that the Branstown Department of Public Welfare may now refuse to coöperate with the four social agencies in this project as an aftermath of the public meeting. What needs to be established is that this venture does not rest within the preserve of any agency but ultimately belongs to the community as a whole. Presumably, it was undertaken because it is essential to the society's welfare. One way of restoring agency perspective in relation to this project is by stimulating renewed public interest in it, perhaps through effective use of the public media and/or community meetings. The principle underlying this approach is that the Council must seek to bring the agency's values and aspirations into alignment with those of the larger community it serves (pp. 117–120 *supra*).

These are simply two ways of conjecturing as to what steps the Branstown Council might take to begin the process of restoring its status. However, it should be borne in mind that despite the setback from the incident described in the record, the Branstown Health and Welfare Council, as an organization, is involved in a variety of programs and activities which undoubtedly serve to maintain its firm place as a social planning body in Branstown.

SUMMARY

In reviewing the roles of the community workers depicted in the three case records, it is evident that they differ from those of the therapist who works with the individual, family, or small group, in that the latter encounters the client as a totality. By contrast, the workers dealing with Hanwella, Merton Center, or Branstown cannot for obvious reasons relate to these communities in their entirety; the communities must be approached through microscopic representations commonly known as intergroups or councils or community surrogates.

Although the direct relationship is with these small social structures, in all three cases the workers are also required to be intimately acquainted with the various aspects of life in the community as a whole; this is indispensable if the surrogates are to function as true reflections of their larger societies. Morever, although the goals may be those of the entire society, paradoxically they are arrived at by leaders interacting in a small community representation. Hence the worker serving a Hanwella, or a Merton, or a Branstown, in addition to understanding the broad community needs and resources, must have an insight into personality structure and small group processes if he is to establish a genuine relationship with community leaders. Thus, the involvement of the workers acting in the three communities under discussion moves at all times on two levels—the community as a whole, and its small representation through which its affairs are transacted.

Questions for Further Discussion

1. Should the worker attempt to interest Hanwella in industrialization when the village wants to keep to its traditional way of life? Does this constitute professional behavior or is it actually a form of coercion?

2. What role will be left to the current leadership in Merton Center if and when the indigenous leaders from the neighborhood surrounding the settlement house begin to participate in the Center?

3. Is it safe to trust Mrs. Lloyd with the job of giving the report to the Merton Center Board, considering her weak performance at the Management Committee?

4. Distinctions have been made between the professional role of the worker in Hanwella and the two senior workers in Merton Center and in the Branstown Council, respectively. Would you say that these differences also hold true as between the Rural Development Society representative and Stan Morris?

5. How does the community organization worker deal with the political implications that surround the situation which has developed in Branstown?

6. Does the professional agency executive who represents his agency on a central body such as the Branstown Health and Welfare Council perform the role of a layman or that of a community organization practitioner?

7. Which would you say reflected a greater degree of prestige and power in Branstown, the Federation, or the casework agencies?

8. Why is it that the Branstown Council should have felt more intimidated as a beneficiary of the Federation than did the four social agencies? How can a beneficiary agency maintain a position of authority and autonomy in its relationships with the financing body?

Bibliography

Adorno, T. W., *et al.*, *The Authoritarian Personality*, Harper & Row, 1950.

Alexander, Chauncey A., and Charles McCann, "The Concept of Representativeness in Community Organization," *Social Work*, I (January 1956).

Allbaugh, Leland, *Crete, A Study of an Underdeveloped Area*, Princeton University Press, 1953.

Alinsky, Saul D., *Reveille for Radicals*, University of Chicago Press, 1946.

Angell, Robert C., "The Moral Integration of American Cities," *American Journal of Sociology*, LVII, Part 2 (July 1951).

Bales, R. F., *Quarterly Report*, The Carnegie Corporation, New York, October 1953.

Banfield, Edward C., *Political Influence*, The Free Press, 1961

Barry, Mildred C., "Current Concepts in Community Organization," in *Group Work and Community Organization, 1956*. Papers presented at the 83rd Annual Forum of the National Conference of Social Work, St. Louis, Mo., May 1956, Columbia University Press, 1956.

Bavelas, Alex, "Communication Patterns in Task-oriented Groups," in Dorwin Cartwright, and Alvin Zander (eds.), *Group Dynamics*, Harper & Row, 1953.

Becker, Carl, *Progress and Power*, Stanford University Press, 1936.

Bendix, Richard, "Social Theory and Social Action in the Sociology of Louis Wirth," *American Journal of Sociology*, LIX (May 1954).

Berkowitz, Leonard, "Sharing Leadership in Small Decision-making Groups," *The Journal of Abnormal and Social Psychology*, XLVIII (April 1953).

Bettelheim, Bruno, and Morris Janowitz, *The Dynamics of Prejudice*, Harper & Row, 1950.

Biddle, William W., *The Cultivation of Community Leaders*, Harper & Row, 1953.

Biddle, William W., and Loureide J. Biddle, *The Community Development Process: The Rediscovery of Local Initiative*, Holt, Rinehart & Winston, 1965.

Blau, Peter M., and W. Richard Scott, *Formal Organizations: A Comparative Approach*, Chandler, 1962.

Boehm, Werner W., "The Nature of Social Work," *Social Work*, III (April 1958).

Brinton, Crane, *The Anatomy of Revolution*, W. W. Norton, 1938.

Brownell, Baker, *The Human Community*, Harper & Row, 1950.

Buell, Bradley, and associates, *Community Planning for Human Services*, Columbia University Press, 1952.

Butts, R. Freeman, *A Cultural History of Education*, McGraw-Hill, 1947.

Carter, Genevieve W., "Practice Theory in Community Organization," *Social Work*, III (April 1958).

Cartwright, Dorwin, and Alvin Zander (eds.), *Group Dynamics: Research and Theory*, Harper & Row, 1953.

Clark, Kenneth B., "Some Implications for a Theory of Social Change," *The Journal of Social Issues*, IX (1953).

Cohen, Nathan E., *Social Work in the American Tradition*, The Dryden Press, 1958.

Coleman, James S., *Community Conflict*, The Free Press, 1957.

Coser, Lewis, *The Functions of Social Conflict*, The Free Press, 1956.

Cyr, John, "Analysis of Committee Member Behavior in Four Cultures," *Human Relations*, IV (1951).

Dahl, Robert A., *Who Governs?*, Yale University Press, 1963.

Doddy, Hurley H., "An Inquiry into Informal Groupings in a Metropolitan Area," *Autonomous Groups Bulletin*, VI (September 1951).

Dunham, Arthur, "The Outlook for Community Development—An International Symposium," *International Review of Community Development*, V (1960).

Dunham, Arthur, *Community Welfare Organization: Principles and Practice*, Thomas Y. Crowell, 1958.

Eisenstadt, S. N., "Reference Group Behavior and Social Integration," *American Sociological Review*, XIX (April 1954).

Eisenstadt, S. N., "Social Mobility, Group Cohesion and Solidarity," unpublished paper, Jerusalem, 1954.

Eisenstadt, S. N., "The Process of Absorption of New Immigrants in Israel," *Human Relations*, V (1952).

Festinger, Leon, and Daniel Katz (eds.), *Research Methods in the Behavioral Sciences*, The Dryden Press, 1953.

Festinger, Leon, Stanley Schachter, and Kurt Black, *Social Processes in Informal Groups*, Harper & Row, 1950.

Follett, Mary Parker, *The New State*, Longmans, Green, 1918.

Foss, Daniel, "The World View of Talcott Parsons," in Maurice Stein and Arthur Vidich (eds.), *Sociology on Trial*, Prentice-Hall, 1963.

Frank, Lawrence K., *Society as the Patient*, Rutgers University Press, 1948.

Frankel, S. Herbert, *The Economic Impact on Under-Developed Societies*, Harvard University Press, 1953.

Fromm, Erich, *Psychoanalysis and Religion*, Yale University Press, 1950.

Fromm, Erich, *Man for Himself*, Holt, Rinehart & Winston, 1947.

Fromm, Erich, *Escape from Freedom*, Holt, Rinehart & Winston, 1941.

Furman, Sylvan S. (ed.), *Reaching the Unreached*, New York City Youth Board, 1952.

Gans, Herbert J., *The Urban Villagers*, The Free Press, 1962.

Gerard, Harold B., "The Effect of Different Dimensions of Disagreement on the Communication Process in Small Groups," *Human Relations*, VI (1953).

Gibb, Cecil A., "Leadership," in Gardner Lindsey (ed.), *Handbook of Social Psychology*, Addison-Wesley, 1954.

Gouldner, Alvin W. (ed.), *Studies in Leadership*, Harper & Row, 1950.

Green, Helen D., *Social Work Practice in Community Organization*, William Morrow, 1954.

Gross, Neal, William E. Martin, and John G. Darley, "Studies of Group Behavior: Leadership Structures in Small Organized Groups," *The Journal of Abnormal and Social Psychology*, XLVIII (July 1953).

Handasyde, Elizabeth, *City or Community*, The National Council of Social Service, London, 1949.

Hare, A. Paul, "Interaction and Consensus in Different Sized Groups," in Dorwin Cartwright, and Alvin Zander (eds.), *Group Dynamics*, Harper & Row, 1953.

Harding, John, and Russell Hogrefe, "Attitudes of White Department Store Employees toward Negro Co-workers," *The Journal of Social Issues*, VIII (1952).

Harper, Ernest B., and Arthur Dunham (eds.), *Community Organization in Action*, Association Press, 1959.

Hartley, Eugene L., and Ruth L. Hartley, *Fundamentals of Social Psychology*, Knopf, 1952.

Hayes, Samuel P., Jr., "Personality and Culture Problems of Point IV," in B. F. Hoselitz (ed.), *The Progress of Underdeveloped Areas*, University of Chicago Press, 1952.

Hayes, Wayland J., *The Small Community Looks Ahead*, Harcourt, Brace & World, 1947.

Haythorne, William. "The Influence of Individual Members on the Characteristics of Small Groups," *The Journal of Abnormal and Social Psychology*, XLVIII (April 1953).

Heath, Monna, and Arthur Dunham, *Trends in Community Organization*, Social Service Monographs, 2nd series, The School of Social Service Administration, University of Chicago, 1963.

Hendry, Charles E., "Community Development," in *Encyclopedia of Social Work*, 15th issue, National Association of Social Workers, New York, 1965.

Hendry, Charles E., "Implications for Social Work Education in Community Planning, Community Development and Community Organization," in *Community Organization, Community Planning and Community Development*. Papers presented at 9th Annual Program Meeting, Council on Social Work Education, Montreal, February 1–4, 1961 Council on Social Work Education, New York, 1961.

Hendry, Charles E., and Margaret T. Svendsen, *Between Spires and Stacks*, Welfare Federation of Cleveland, 1936.

Hicks, Granville, *Small Town*, Macmillan, 1947.

Hillman, Arthur, *Community Organization and Planning*, Macmillan, 1950.

Hoeven, Dr. P. J. A., ter., *Attitude Change: A Dynamic Process*, Ministry for Social Work, The Hague, 1964.

Hollingshead, August De B., *Elmtown's Youth*, John Wiley & Sons, 1949.

Homans, George C., *The Human Group*, Harcourt, Brace & World, 1950.

Horney, Karen, *Our Inner Conflicts*, W. W. Norton, 1945.

Horney, Karen, *The Neurotic Personality of Our Time*, W. W. Norton, 1937.

Hoselitz, B. F. (ed.), *The Progress of Underdeveloped Areas*, University of Chicago Press, 1952.

Hughes, Everett C., *French Canada in Transition,* University of Chicago Press, 1943.

Hunter, Floyd, *Community Power Structure: A Study of Decision Makers,* University of North Carolina Press, 1953.

Hunter, Floyd, Ruth Connor Schaffer, and Cecil G. Sheps, *Community Organization: Action and Inaction,* University of North Carolina Press, 1956.

International Federation of Community Settlements and Neighbourhood Centres, "Community Organization: Theories and Values," *International Review of Community Development,* No. 5 (1960).

Jahoda, Marie, "Towards a Social Psychology of Mental Health," Research Clinic for Human Problems, New York University, 1950.

Jahoda, Marie, "Some Socio-Psychological Problems of Factory Life," *British Journal of Psychology* (January 1942).

Janowitz, Morris, *The Community Press in an Urban Setting,* The Free Press, 1952.

Jaques, Elliott, *The Changing Culture of a Factory,* Tavistock Publications, 1951.

Johns, Roy, *Confronting Organizational Change,* Association Press, 1963.

Johns, Roy, and D. F. Demarche, *Community Organization and Agency Responsibility,* Association Press, 1951.

Katz, Daniel, Dorwin Cartwright, Samuel Eldersveld, and Alfred McClung Lee (eds.), *Public Opinion and Propaganda,* The Dryden Press, 1954.

Kelley, Harold H., "Communication in Experimentally Created Hierarchies," in Dorwin Cartwright, and Alvin Zander (eds.), *Group Dynamics,* Harper & Row, 1953.

Ketchum, David, Annual Address, Canadian Psychological Association, *Canadian Journal of Psychology,* 1951.

Kinneman, John A., *The Community in American Society,* Appleton-Century-Crofts, 1947.

Kleinberg, Otto, *Tensions Affecting International Understanding,* Social Science Research Council, New York, 1950.

Konopka, Gisela, *Social Group Work,* Prentice-Hall, 1963.

Krech, David, and Richard S. Crutchfield, *Theory and Problems of Social Psychology,* McGraw-Hill, 1948.

Lappin, Ben, *The Redeemed Children: The Story of the Rescue of War Orphans by the Jewish Community of Canada,* University of Toronto Press, 1963.

Lebowitz, Milton, *The Process of Planned Community Change: A Comparative Analysis of Five Community Welfare Council Change Projects,*

D.S.W. dissertation, New York School of Social Work, Columbia University, University Microfilms, Ann Arbor, Michigan.

Leighton, Alexander H., *My Name Is Legion*, Basic Books, 1959.

Leighton, Alexander H., *Human Relations in a Changing World*, E. P. Dutton, 1949.

Leighton, Alexander H., *The Governing of Men*, Princeton University Press, 1945.

Lewin, Kurt, "Group Decision and Social Change," in T. M. Newcomb, and E. L. Hartley (eds.), *Readings in Social Psychology*, Holt, Rinehart & Winston, 1947.

Lewin, Kurt, *Resolving Social Conflict*, Gertrud Weiss Lewin (ed.), Harper & Row, 1948.

Likert, Rensis, and Ronald Lippitt, "The Utilization of Social Science," in Leon Festinger, and Daniel Lippitt, (eds.), *Research Methods in the Behavioral Sciences*, The Dryden Press, 1953.

Lilienthal, David E., *T.V.A.—Democracy on the March*, Pocket Books.

Lindzey, Gardner (ed.), *Handbook of Social Psychology*, Addison-Wesley, 1954.

Linton, Ralph. "Cultural and Personality Factors Affecting Economic Growth," in B. F. Hoselitz (ed.), *The Progress of Underdeveloped Areas*, University of Chicago Press, 1952.

Lippitt, Ronald, Jeanne Watson, and Bruce Westley, *The Dynamics of Planned Change*, Harcourt, Brace & World, 1958.

Loomis, Charles P., and Zona K. Loomis, *Modern Social Theories*, D. Van Nostrand, 1961.

Loring, William C., Jr., Frank L. Sweetser, and Charles F. Ernst, *Community Organization for Citizen Participation in Urban Renewal*. Prepared by Housing Association of Metropolitan Boston, Massachusetts Department of Commerce, Boston, 1957.

Lund, Robert, *Hour of Glory*, George G. Harrap & Co., 1951.

Lurie, Harry L., *The Community Organization Method in Social Work Education*, Vol. II of *The Curriculum Study*, Council on Social Work Education, New York, 1959.

Lynd, Helen Merrell, *On Shame and the Search for Identity*, Science Editions, 1961.

Lynd, Robert S., *Knowledge for What?* Princeton University Press, 1948.

Lynd, Robert S., *Middletown in Transition*, Harcourt, Brace & World, 1937.

Lynton, Harriet Ronken, Rolf P. Lynton, *et al.*, *Asican Cases: Teaching Cases from the Aloka Experience*, Aloka Centre for Advanced Study and Training, World Assembly of Youth, Yelwal, Mysore, India, 1960.

MacIver, R. M., *Society: Its Structure and Changes,* R. Long and R. R. Smith, 1933.

MacIver, R. N., *Community: A Sociological Study,* Macmillan, 1920.

McMillen, Wayne, *Community Organization for Social Welfare,* University of Chicago Press, 1945.

McNeil, C. F., "Community Organization for Social Welfare," in *Social Work Year Book,* American Association of Social Workers, New York, 1951.

Mead, Margaret (ed.), *Cultural Patterns and Technical Change,* UNESCO, Paris, 1953.

Merton, Robert K., *Social Theory and Social Structure,* The Free Press, 1949.

Mills, C. Wright, "Are We Losing Our Sense of Belonging?" Paper delivered at Couchiching Conference (Canada), August 10, 1954.

Moore, Barrington, "Strategy in Social Science," in Maurice Stein, and Arthur Vidich (eds.), *Sociology on Trial,* Prentice-Hall, 1963.

Morris, Robert, "Community Organization and Community Conflict," *Journal of Jewish Communal Service,* XXXIX (Fall 1962).

Morris, Robert, "Social Work Preparation for Effectiveness in Planned Change," in *Education for Social Work, 1963.* Proceedings of Annual Program Meeting, Council on Social Work Education, Boston, Mass., January 23–26, 1963, Council on Social Work Education, New York, 1963.

Morris, Robert, "Basic Factors in Planning for the Coordination of Health Services," *American Journal of Public Health,* LIII (March 1963).

Morris, Robert (ed.), *Centrally Planned Change: Prospects and Concepts,* National Association of Social Workers, New York, 1964.

Morris, Robert, and Martin Rein, "Emerging Patterns in Community Planning," in *Social Work Practice, 1963.* Selected papers, 90th Annual Forum, National Conference on Social Welfare, Cleveland, Ohio, May 19–24, 1963, Columbia University Press, 1963.

Murphy, Campbell G., *Community Organization Practice,* Houghton Mifflin, 1954.

Murphy, Gardner, *Personality, A Biosocial Approach to Origins and Structure,* Harper & Row, 1947.

Mussen, Paul H., and Anne B. Wysznski, "Personality and Political Participation," *Human Relations,* V (1952).

Myrdal, Gunnar, "Psychological Impediments to Effective International Cooperation," *The Journal of Social Issues,* Supplement Series No. 6 (1952).

National Association of Social Workers, *Community Development and*

Community Organization: An International Workshop. An account of a workshop held at Brandeis University, Waltham, Mass., April 10–14, 1960. National Association of Social Workers, New York, 1961.

Newcomb, T. M., and E. L. Hartley (eds.), *Readings in Social Psychology,* Holt, Rinehart & Winston, 1947.

Nisbet, R. A., *The Quest for Community,* Oxford University Press, 1953.

Norquay, M., *Milltown,* M. A. thesis, University of Toronto, Department of Sociology, 1940.

Pray, Kenneth L. M., W. I. Newstetter, and Violet M. Sieder, *Community Organization, Its Nature and Setting.* Three papers presented at the 1947 Annual Meeting, National Conference of Social Work. American Association of Social Workers, New York, 1947.

Pumphrey, Ralph E., and Muriel W. Pumphrey (eds.), *The Heritage of American Social Work,* Columbia University Press, 1961.

Read, Margaret, "Common Ground in Community Development Experiments," *Community Development Bulletin,* University of London Institute of Education, II (June 1951).

Reid, Ira De A., and Emily L. Ehle, "Leadership Selections in Urban Locality Areas," in Daniel Katz, Dorwin Cartwright, Samuel Eldersveld, and Alfred McClung Lee (eds.), *Public Opinion and Propaganda,* The Dryden Press, 1954.

Richmond, Mary Ellen, *The Long View,* papers and addresses of Mary Ellen Richmond, The Russell Sage Foundation, 1930.

Riesman, David, *The Lonely Crowd,* Yale University Press, 1952.

Riesman, David, and Nathan Glazer, "Criteria for Political Apathy," in Alvin W. Gouldner (ed.), *Studies in Leadership,* Harper & Row, 1950.

Rivlin, Benjamin, "Self-Determination and Dependent Areas," *International Conciliation,* No. 501 (January 1955), Carnegie Endowment for International Peace.

Ross, Murray G., *The Y.M.C.A. in Canada,* Ryerson Press, 1951.

Ross, Murray G., *Religious Beliefs of Youth,* Association Press, 1950.

Ross, Murray G., *Community Councils,* Canadian Council of Education for Citizenship, Ottawa, 1945.

Ross, Murray G., and Charles E. Hendry, *New Understanding of Leadership,* Association Press, 1957.

Rothman, Jack, "Goals and Roles in Community Organization," *Social Work,* IX (April 1964).

Salsman, Donald M., "Observations on the Social Dynamics of the Structure of Community Planning Groups," Research Department, Council of Social Agencies, New Orleans, La., 1959.

Sanders, Irwin T. "Professional Roles in Planned Change," in Robert

Morris (ed.), *Centrally Planned Change: Prospects and Concepts,* National Association of Social Workers, New York, 1964.

Selznick, Philip, *T.V.A. and the Grass Roots,* University of California Press, 1949.

Sherrard, Thomas D., and Richard C. Murray, "The Church and Neighborhood Community Organization," *Social Work,* X (July 1965).

Sieder, Violet M., "Current Developments and Problems in the Changing American Community," in *Community Development and Community Organization: An International Workshop,* National Association of Social Workers, New York, 1961.

Sieder, Violet M., "What is Community Organization Practice in Social Work?" in *The Social Welfare Forum, 1956.* Proceedings, 83rd Annual Forum, National Conference on Social Welfare, St. Louis, Mo., May 20–25, 1956, Columbia University Press, 1956.

Simpson, C. E. E. B., "An African Village Undertakes Community Development on its Own," *Mass Education Bulletin,* University of London Institute of Education, II (December 1950).

Smith, T. V., and Edward C. Lindeman, *The Democratic Way of Life,* Mentor Books, 1951.

Social Planning Council of Metropolitan Toronto, *A Study of the Needs and Resources for Community-Supported Welfare, Health and Recreation Services in Metropolitan Toronto: A Community Self-Study,* S. P. C. of Metropolitan Toronto, 1963.

Spicer, Edward H. (ed.), *Human Problems in Technological Change,* Russell Sage Foundation, 1952.

Sprott, W. J. H., *Human Groups,* Penguin Books, 1958.

Stein, Maurice R., *The Eclipse of Community,* Harper & Row, 1964.

Stroup, H. H., *Community Welfare Organization,* Harper & Row, 1952.

Sullivan, Dorothea (ed.), *Readings in Group Work,* Association Press, 1952.

Sullivan, Harry Stack, *Conceptions of Modern Psychiatry,* The William Alanson White Psychiatric Foundation, 1947.

Toynbee, Arnold J., *A Study of History* (abridgement of Vols. I–VI by D. C. Somerville), Oxford University Press, 1947.

United Nations Document E/CN 5/291, *Programme of Concerted Action in the Social Field of the United Nations and Specialized Agencies.*

United States Federal Security Agency, *An Approach to Community Development,* International Unit, Social Security Administration, 1952.

Vickers, Geoffrey, *The Undirected Society,* University of Toronto Press, 1959.

Vogt, Evon Z., and Thomas F. O'Dea, "A Comparative Study of the

Role of Values in Social Action in Two Southwestern Communities," *American Sociological Review*, XVIII (December 1953).

Warren, Roland L., *The Community in America*, Rand McNally, 1963.

Warren, Roland L., *Patterns of Community Action*, Brandeis University Papers in Social Welfare, No. 4, 1962.

Watson, Goodwin, *Civilian Morale*, Reynal & Hitchcock, 1942.

West, James, *Plainville, U.S.A.*, Columbia University Press, 1945.

Whyte, William H., Jr., *The Organization Man*, Doubleday, 1957.

Wilensky, Harold L., and Charles N. Lebeaux, *Industrial Society and Social Welfare*, Russell Sage Foundation, 1958.

Williams, Robin M., Jr., *American Society*, Knopf, 1952.

Williams, Robin M., Jr., *The Reduction of Inter-Group Tensions*, Social Science Research Council, New York, 1947.

Wilner, Daniel M., Rosabelle P. Walkley, and Stuart W. Cook, "Residential Proximity and Intergroup Relations in Public Housing Projects," *The Journal of Social Issues*, VIII (1952).

Wilson, A. T. M., "Some Aspects of Social Process," *The Journal of Social Issues*, Supplement Series No. 5 (November 1951).

Wolfenstein, Martha, "The Emergence of Fun Morality," *The Journal of Social Issues*, VII (1951).

Woolf, Leonard, *Principia Politica*, The Hogarth Press, 1953.

Index